EX AUDITU

An International Journal for the Theological Interpretation of Scripture

VOL. 34   **2018**

Ex Auditu is published annually by Pickwick Publications, an imprint of
Wipf and Stock Publishers, 199 West 8th Avenue, Suite 3, Eugene, Oregon 97401, USA

SUBSCRIPTIONS

Individuals:
U.S.A. and all other countries (in U.S. funds): $20.00
Students: $12.00

Institutions:
U.S.A. and all other countries (in U.S. funds): $30.00

This periodical is indexed in the ATLA Religion Database, published by the American Theological Library Association, 300 S. Wacker Dr., Suite 2100, Chicago, IL 60606, Email: atla@atla.com, www: http://www.atla.com/; *Internationale Zeitschriftenshau für Bibelwissenschaft; Religious and Theological Abstracts; and Old Testament Abstracts.*

Please address all subscription correspondence
and change of address information to Wipf and Stock Publishers.

©2019 by Wipf and Stock Publishers
ISSN: 0883-0053
PAPERBACK ISBN: 978-1-5326-7696-3
HARDBACK ISBN: 978-1-5326-7697-0

EX AUDITU

An International Journal for the Theological Interpretation of Scripture

Stephen J. Chester, Editor
D. Christopher Spinks, Associate Editor
Klyne R. Snodgrass, Editor Emeritus

North Park Theological Seminary
3225 West Foster Avenue
Chicago, Illinois 60625-4987
USA

Tel: (773) 244-6238
email: schester@northpark.edu
Web site: http://wipfandstock.com/catalog/journal/view/id/12/

EDITORIAL BOARD

Terence E. Fretheim, Luther Seminary, St. Paul, MN
Richard B. Hays, The Divinity School, Duke University, Durham, NC
Jon R. Stock, Wipf & Stock Publishers, Eugene, OR
Miroslav Volf, Yale Divinity School, New Haven, CT
John Wipf, Wipf & Stock Publishers, Eugene, OR

THE EDITORIAL BOARD MEMBERS AND CONSULTANTS represent various disciplines and denominations. Theological interpretation of Scripture is a task to be taken seriously by scholars who are committed to the Christian faith and tradition. However, as one editorial consultant stated: "Let people gradually get used to the idea that a sane hermeneutics is both oriented in advance toward agreement/consent and is simultaneously exigent, discriminating, critical."

EDITORIAL CONSULTANTS

M. Daniel Carroll R.
Wheaton College
Wheaton, Illinois

Simon Gathercole
University of Cambridge
Cambridge, England

Nijay Gupta
Portland Seminary,
George Fox University
Portland, Oregon

Robert Johnston
Fuller Theological Seminary
Pasadena, California

R. Walter L. Moberly
University of Durham
Durham, England

Sujin Pak Boyer
The Divinity School
Duke University
Durham, N. Carolina

Iain Provan
Regent College
Vancouver, B.C.

Kevin J. Vanhoozer
Trinity Evangelical Divinity School
Deerfield, Illinois

William H. Willimon
The Divinity School
Duke University
Durham, N. Carolina

N. T. Wright
St Mary's College,
University of St. Andrews, Scotland

CONTENTS

Abbreviations vi

Introduction vii
Stephen J. Chester

The Moral Problematics of Exodus as Liberative Narrative 1
Rubén Rosario Rodríguez

Response to Rosario Rodríguez 14
Armida Belmonte Stephens

Human Violence in the Imprecatory Psalms 19
Nancy L. deClaissé-Walford

Response to deClaissé-Walford 37
Meredith Faubel Nyberg

Jesus and the *Lēstai*: Competing Kingdom Visions 42
Jesse Nickel

Response to Nickel 62
Rebekah Eklund

Paul and Violence 67
Seyoon Kim

Response to Kim 90
Julien C. H. Smith

"I Will Put Enmity Between You...": Scriptural Arcana in Carl Schmitt's Political Theology 97
Kyle Gingerich Hiebert

Response to Gingerich Hiebert 117
Colby Dickinson

Blood Letters from a Mao Prison: A "Select Soldier of Christ" Confronts Revolutionary Violence 124
Xi Lian

Response to Xi Lian 137
Lida V. Nedilsky

Bearing Witness: Faith, Black Women, and Sexual Violence 140
Elizabeth O. Pierre

Response to Pierre 163
Melanie Baffes

Keeping Our Word (2 Samuel 9) 169
D. Darrell Griffin

Annotated Bibliography on Human Violence 177

Presenters and Respondents 186

ANNOUNCEMENT OF THE 2019 SYMPOSIUM

North Park Theological Seminary in Chicago, Illinois, is pleased to announce that the thirty-fifth Symposium on the Theological Interpretation of Scripture will take place September 26–28, 2019. The Symposium will start at 6 p.m. on Thursday, September 26 in Nyvall Hall with a worship service and will extend through to Saturday afternoon on September 28. The theme in 2019 will be "The Holy Land: Biblical Perspectives and Contemporary Conflicts." The following persons have agreed to make presentations:

    Philip Alexander, Post-Biblical Jewish Literature, University of Manchester
    Mae Cannon, Churches for Middle East Peace
    Munther Isaac, Biblical Studies, Bethlehem Bible College
    Yohanna Katanacho, Biblical Studies, Nazareth Evangelical College
    Rula Mansour, Theology, Nazareth Evangelical College
    Rabbi Yehiel Poupko, Jewish United Fund, Chicago
    Joel Willitts, New Testament, North Park University
    Lawson Younger, Old Testament, Trinity Evangelical Divinity School

Those interested in attending sessions should go to https://www.northpark.edu/seminary/calendar-and-events/symposium-on-the-theological-interpretation-of-scripture/ and follow the link provided to the registration page. Any queries should be addressed to the Symposium administrator, Mr. Luke Palmerlee (lrpalmerlee@northpark.edu) at North Park Theological Seminary, 3225 W. Foster Avenue, Chicago, Illinois, 60625. Meals may be taken at North Park and assistance can be provided in finding nearby lodging.

ABBREVIATIONS

Unless listed here, all abbreviations are as specified in *The SBL Handbook of Style: For Biblical Studies and Related Disciplines*, 2nd edition (Atlanta: Society of Biblical Literature, 2014).

CDC	Center for Disease Control
IPV	Intimate Partner Violence
JSJSup	Supplements to the Journal for the Study of Judaism in the Persian, Hellenistic, and Roman Periods
NCBC	New Cambridge Bible Commentary
SBW	Strong Black Woman
ZRMRB	Lin Zhao, "Zhi *Renmin Ribao* bianjibu xin" (Letters to the Editorial Board of the *People's Daily*)

INTRODUCTION

In contemporary western society we often feel, with good reason, that we are awash in violence and images of violence. This journal publishes the proceedings of an annual symposium on the theological interpretation of Scripture that takes place in Chicago, a city in which by March 31, 2019, there had been eighty-five murders in the calendar year. Horrifically, this statistic is the cause of some optimism since it is precisely thirty fewer murders than there had been in the corresponding period of 2018. We feel the deep wrong of all this killing, and all the inconsolable grief that it produces; we yearn for a more peaceful society, and we assume that our time and place is uniquely addicted to violence.

Our instincts are partly correct. The prophet Isaiah famously looks forward to a day when the relationships between nations are governed solely by the ways and the will of God: the peoples "shall beat their swords into plowshares, and their spears into pruning hooks; nation shall not lift up sword against nation, neither shall they learn war any more" (Isa 2:4). There is no place for human violence in God's final purposes. It is also true that the level of violence in human societies is impacted by all kinds of complex factors connected to poverty, economic inequality, and a host of other problems. Intelligent and just social policies can make a difference and their absence today is a legitimate cause for anger.

Nevertheless, the human propensity toward violence is universal. Scripture is nothing if not realistic about the part played by violence in the human condition. Once Eden is lost (Gen 3), the next episode in the narrative is that of Cain's murder of his brother Abel (Gen 4:1–16). In our own place and time, the #MeToo movement has reminded us powerfully of the endemic nature of sexual assault against women. Violence of various kinds is part of who we are as fallen human beings. It is therefore unsurprising that Scripture engages with human violence at a great variety of levels. How are we to think about Jesus' attitude toward violence and its implications for our ethics? What about the violence suffered by martyrs who refuse to abandon their allegiance to Jesus? What does God ask of us when we encounter those who have survived violent abuse and the easy option for churches and communities is denial of their witness? What about those times in the biblical narrative when deliverance for some seems to involve violence being suffered by others? Or those times when depth of anger against human violence, or depth of anger against the human rebellion against God, produces a rhetoric within Scripture that itself seems violent? Is

Introduction

censoring such rhetoric vital, or is it simply to deny human feelings that must be expressed if they are to be dealt with in healthy ways?

All these questions and more are explored by the contributors to this volume. Readers will find rich resources for thinking with Scripture about human violence. They will be compelled to ponder what it is to suffer violence and to want to call down divine anger upon enemies. They will be challenged about what is involved in participating in the ultimate overcoming of violence by the Kingdom of God. They will also be reminded that until the Kingdom is eschatologically fulfilled each of us remains complicit in violence. No one is truly good except God alone (Mark 10:18), and when we are tempted to deny this, or to ignore this, we simply fail to understand all that we are implicated in by the structures of the present evil age (Gal 1:4). Father, forgive us, for we know not what we do.

Stephen Chester
Professor of New Testament
North Park Theological Seminary

THE MORAL PROBLEMATICS OF EXODUS AS LIBERATIVE NARRATIVE

Rubén Rosario Rodríguez

Introduction

Two of the main proponents of liberation theology in the twentieth century, Gustavo Gutiérrez and James Cone, identify the Exodus as the central text for arguing that God makes a preferential option for the poor, marginalized, and politically disenfranchised. As Gutiérrez writes in *A Theology of Liberation* (1973), "The liberation from Egypt—both a historical fact and at the same time a fertile Biblical theme—enriches this vision and is moreover its true source."[1] In much the same way, Cone views the Exodus as the example par excellence of a project of human liberation in history, arguing that liberation "is not merely a thought in my head; it is the socio-historical movement of a people from oppression to freedom—Israelites from Egypt, black people from American slavery."[2]

Therefore, that the Exodus has been embraced across numerous religious and cultural contexts as a biblical grounding for contemporary movements of social and political emancipation is not surprising. What is surprising is the lack of critical engagement concerning the prevalence of violence in the Exodus narrative, including divine acts of violence as well as divinely sanctioned violence, and the problems this causes for liberation theology's commitment to nonviolence. Native American theologian Robert Allen Warrior critiques this trend of viewing Exodus as an emancipatory text by reminding us that the God who acted as the liberator of the oppressed and powerless in Egypt is the same God who condoned the genocidal conquest of Canaan:

> Yahweh promised to go before the people and give them Canaan, with its flowing milk and honey. The land, Yahweh decided, belonged to these former slaves from Egypt and Yahweh planned on giving it to them—using the same

---

1. Gustavo Gutiérrez, *A Theology of Liberation: History, Politics, and Salvation*, rev. edition, trans. Sister Caridad Inda and John Eagleson (Maryknoll, NY: Orbis, 1988) 87.

2. James H. Cone, *God of the Oppressed*, rev. edition (Maryknoll, NY: Orbis, 1997) 139–40.

power used against the enslaving Egyptians to defeat the indigenous inhabitants of Canaan. Yahweh the deliverer became Yahweh the conqueror.³

Believers need to come to terms with the troubling fact that the liberation of Israel was facilitated by divine acts of violence. Accordingly, a hermeneutics of suspicion ought to be uniformly applied, especially toward *foundational* emancipatory narratives *like* the Exodus, since in human history one people's liberation often comes at another people's expense, as most tragically witnessed in the Israeli-Palestinian struggle today.

Naim Ateek, a Palestinian Christian Anglican priest and liberation theologian, views the traditional reading of the Exodus as a "retrogression of the Jewish community into . . . its most elementary and primitive forms of the concept of God. Zionism has succeeded in reanimating the nationalist tradition within Judaism."⁴ Its narrow fixation on *Eretz Israel* ("Land of Israel") is an imposition of a modern political reality—a besieged people establishing a new nation in the aftermath of the Holocaust by occupying an already settled land—upon a rather more complex biblical tradition that *ought not* be distilled solely to the conquest and occupation of the land of Canaan. Marc Ellis, in articulating a Jewish theology of liberation, concurs with Ateek's assessment: "Often Jews, in their desire to support the state of Israel, conflate Judaism and Zionism into one entity, as if they could not be understood apart."⁵ Like Ateek, Ellis also highlights the need to critique and evaluate the various competing—even contradictory—conceptions of God found within the sacred Scriptures: "The God of the Exodus and Jesus is a God who is the grounding for the journey of a covenanted people, a God who journeys with that people through historical epochs. Especially in formative events, God is found, *but also questioned.*"⁶

This paper engages in faithful questioning in order to address the fundamental conflict between a Christian commitment to nonviolence and the biblical God who is not averse to employing violence in the unfolding of divine providence. The ambiguity of a text like the Exodus, containing both emancipatory potential and inherent moral problematics, demands deeper theological reflection on the nature of Scripture and its role in shaping communal beliefs and normative moral praxis and, more fundamentally, reflection on the conceptions of God underlying various interpretive traditions. This in turn yields a more nuanced reading of the multiplicity

---

3. Robert Allen Warrior, "Canaanites, Cowboys, and Indians: Deliverance, Conquest, and Liberation Theology Today," *Christianity and Crisis* 49.12 (September 11, 1989) 261.

4. Naim Stifan Ateek, *Justice, and only Justice: A Palestinian Theology of Liberation* (Maryknoll, NY: Orbis, 1989) 101.

5. Marc H. Ellis, *Revolutionary Forgiveness: Essays on Judaism, Christianity, and the Future of Religious Life* (Waco, TX: Baylor University Press, 2000) 101.

6. Ibid., 144 (emphasis added).

of competing traditions within the canon of scripture—what Walter Brueggemann calls the narratives and counternarratives of the Hebrew Bible.

Reframing and Reclaiming the Exodus Narrative

The Hebrew Bible contains a wide range of different, even contradictory, conceptions of God, from the most tribal and insular to the most welcoming and inclusive, which, according to Ateek, culminate in a prophetic vision "that God is the God of the whole world—not simply the greatest God among other gods, and not exclusively their God, but the only true God."[7] Ateek responds to the more nationalistic and warmongering texts in the Old Testament with a layered and nuanced argument that avoids the easy path of Christian supersessionism,[8] which juxtaposes the nonviolent Christ to the tribal warrior-God of the Hebrew Bible and often leads to Christian anti-Semitism by justifying marginalization and persecution of Jews. By viewing the whole of the Christian canon—Old and New Testaments—as *consistently* nonviolent, Ateek concludes that as Christians we ought to embrace the path of nonviolence. Why? Not because the Christian conception of God is superior to or supersedes the Old Testament conception of God, but because God *is* and has *always been* constant in his interactions with humanity:

> Humans, depending on what they are discussing about God, tend to emphasize one attribute over another to prove a point. God's attributes, however, do not exist as separate components that are only loosely joined together. They are inextricably united and harmonized within the One Being of God. God's justice cannot be separated from God's peace and love and mercy. There are no dichotomies in the person of God; the dichotomies lie in humans.[9]

In Ateek's analysis, two major issues characterize the contemporary Israeli-Palestinian situation:

1. the conflicting claims of Israelis and Palestinians to the same land, rooted in complex political, religious, and ethnic histories that became intensely magnified after the Holocaust and the establishment of the State of Israel; and

---

7. Ateek, *Justice, and only Justice*, 110.

8. Supersessionism, also known as replacement theology, is the (arguably heretical) doctrine that the new covenant in Christ (Gospel) replaces the Mosaic covenant (Law). Particularly troubling is that for many Christians who hold that the Gospel has superseded the Law, Jews who continue to live outside the church remain outside the covenant with God, giving rise and justification to Christian anti-Semitism. In the aftermath of the Holocaust many Christian theologians and denominations have explicitly rejected the doctrine of supersessionism. For a critique of Christian supersessionism in light of Christianity's complicity in Hitler's Final Solution, see R. Kendall Soulen, *The God of Israel and Christian Theology* (Minneapolis: Fortress, 1996).

9. Ateek, *Justice, and only Justice*, 139.

2. the political abuse of the Bible, especially the Hebrew Bible/Old Testament, for the sake of a Zionist political agenda.

Marc Ellis acknowledges the role of the Exodus in liberative Christian narratives while problematizing its role for the Israeli-Palestinian context: "It is perhaps an oddity of history that the Exodus and the prophetic stories the Jewish people formed and bequeathed to the world are being taken seriously by contemporary Christians in a way that is increasingly difficult for the Jewish community to understand."[10] By elevating the Jewish prophetic tradition as the privileged narrative lens through which one ought to read the entire biblical tradition, Ellis provides one potential avenue for reclaiming the Exodus as the core of the Torah despite the text being used to provide justification for genocidal and xenophobic theologies. By reading the Exodus narrative as a *prophetic* text, it becomes evident that the narrative is first and foremost an affirmation of human dignity and second that the God of the Exodus does not act in human history independently of human moral agency. Accordingly, the emancipatory potential of the Exodus narrative rests on a prophetic understanding of human moral agency as the existential appropriation and historical embodiment of the divine will by believers engaged in struggles for dignity and justice.

The troubling "double existence" of the Exodus narrative, as both liberative of the Israelites and oppressive of the Canaanites, demands exegetical and theological reflection in light of Naim Ateek's and Marc Ellis's challenge that we should embody a dissenting voice of prophecy in solidarity with the victims of unchecked state power. The argument could be made, therefore, that the theological core of the Exodus narrative is contained in the ethical demand identified by Marc Ellis's prophetic reading *as resistance to tyranny*, and that post-Exodus narratives about the conquest of Canaan reflect a later, nationalist and imperialist agenda that deviates from YHWH's core narrative.

Contextualizing Violence in the Hebrew Bible

In order to engage religiously motivated political violence in the world today *without* positing a Christian supersession of the Hebrew Scriptures, it becomes necessary to identify a consistent biblical narrative about God and violence—especially the place of liberating violence—in God's covenantal relationship with humanity. For it cannot be denied that God uses violence in delivering the Hebrews out of slavery in Egypt by means of plagues, including a pestilence that destroyed the livestock of Egypt while sparing that of the Israelites (Exod 9:3–4), another that caused festering

---

10. Marc H. Ellis, *Toward a Jewish Theology of Liberation*, 3rd expanded edition (Waco: Baylor University Press, 2004) 145.

boils on the flesh of humans and animals (Exod 9:9-11), and ultimately, by causing the death of all the firstborn sons of Egypt (Exod 11-12). Later, when Pharaoh changed his mind about freeing the Israelites and sent his army in pursuit, God intervened on behalf of the Israelites against Pharaoh's army so that "not one of them remained" (Exod 14:28, NRSV). This is a God who not only condones but also *actively participates* in political violence.

More troubling is that after wandering in the wilderness for forty years, the people of Israel are allowed to enter the Promised Land—a land already occupied by the Canaanites—and under the leadership of Joshua undertake a genocidal holy war with YHWH's explicit approval.[11] Joshua is described as conducting a swift war of conquest that put city after city to the sword, executing all the citizenry, and then claiming for Israel the great fortified walled cities of the Canaanites. With YHWH's help, under the confederacy of the twelve tribes, Israel quickly established itself as a hegemonic regional power with the understanding that in return for this gift of the land, Israel would set aside all other gods and worship YHWH exclusively (Josh 24:16-18). Without question, Zion theology irrevocably linked the covenant between God and the people of Israel to the land,[12] and it was this golden era of Israelite imperial expansion that many of those holding messianic expectations during Jesus' lifetime aspired to see restored (Matt 21; Mark 11).

The phrase "land of Israel" (*Eretz Israel*) is first found in the history of the Davidic monarchy preserved in 2 Kings and the Chronicles, written after the height of Israel's imperial expansion, during a time of renewed tribal tensions as the northern tribes revolted against the Davidic monarchy, *suggesting* that Zion theology developed *in response* to the breakdown of Israel's short-lived regional hegemony. Regardless, the period between the death of Solomon (c. 931 BCE) and the Babylonian exile (586 BCE) is marked by a pattern of Israelite infidelity to the covenant with YHWH

---

11. See Maxwell J. Miller and Gene M. Tucker, *The Book of Joshua*, CBC (Cambridge: Cambridge University Press, 1974) 49-50. The commentators argue that the call of Joshua (Josh 5:13-15) echoes the call of Moses (Exod 3:1ff) in order to affirm YHWH's approval and participation in this holy war.

12. See Walter Brueggemann, *Old Testament Theology: An Introduction* (Nashville: Abingdon, 2008) 265-82. The author explores the role of the land in YHWH's covenantal promises to Israel, concluding that despite Christian tendencies to spiritualize God's promises, the "Old Testament is very much preoccupied with the gift of the land, the loss of the land, and the prospect of restoration to the land" as a material reality (276). See Max. E. Polley, *Amos and the Davidic Empire: A Socio-Historical Approach* (Oxford: Oxford University Press, 1989) 83-111. Polley posits that the prophet Amos is a defender of a united kingdom under Davidic rule and prophesies the northern kingdom's destruction as a result of its religious apostasy against the temple in Jerusalem. Also see Jon D. Levenson, *Sinai and Zion: An Entry into the Jewish Bible*, reprint (San Francisco: HarperSanFrancisco, 1987) 187-218, in which he interprets the Sinaitic and Davidic covenants as distinct yet interrelated national theologies, with the latter emphasizing "the constancy of God rather than the changeability of man, it brings to light what is secure and inviolable, whereas the Sinaitic texts tend to emphasize the precariousness of life and the consequent need for a continuously reinvigorated obedience" (101).

giving rise to a series of prophetic warnings in which God threatens to devastate the land and send the people into exile. However, these same warnings also promise that if they repent, God will restore the land to them. Throughout the prophetic literature sovereignty over the land belongs *only* to God, with God granting or withdrawing this blessing in accord with Israel's obedience or disobedience.

In the preaching of the Hebrew prophets, possession of the land is part of YHWH's eschatological redemption of Israel, but YHWH's judgment is held in reserve, with exile hanging over Israel like the sword of Damocles—always a possibility as a judgment against future sins. Thus, while YHWH condoned political violence in establishing Israel as a nation (by taking lands formerly held by the Canaanites), YHWH also allowed political violence *to be done to Israel* as punishment for breaking the covenant, demonstrating that the land belongs exclusively to YHWH and that God's sovereignty extends to all nations (Isa 2:2-4). According to Gustavo Gutiérrez, Israel's national identity as God's chosen people "is rooted in the relation between the poor and the nation: the chosen people lose their dignity if they do not establish justice in their midst."[13] This is a reality echoed in the Deuteronomic tradition: "You must not distort justice; you must not show partiality; and you must not accept bribes, for a bribe blinds the eyes of the wise and subverts the cause of those who are in the right. Justice, and only justice, you shall pursue, so that you may live and occupy the land that the Lord your God is giving you" (Deut 20:19-20, NRSV). Consequently, the Hebrew Bible underscores the *conditional* nature of Israel's covenant with YHWH by linking it to the people's obedient moral action and *not*—as some modern-day Jewish and Christian Zionists would argue—Israel's *unconditional* birthright. Under the covenant, YHWH has promised Israel the land of Canaan, but should Israel prove unfaithful—by subverting God's justice and righteousness—they will lose the land. Accordingly, in the preaching of prophets like Jeremiah, Amos, and Hosea, the destruction of Israel by the Assyrians (721 BCE), and Judah by the Babylonians (586 BCE), is understood as punishment for Israel's continuing sinfulness and disobedience, sins which, according to a liberationist reading, are most often manifest as social injustice.

Though these violent depictions of Israel's God stand out, they do so in great part because they run against the grain of the core biblical testimony concerning YHWH's character. The overwhelming witness in the Hebrew Scriptures is that of a sovereign God who is "steadfast" and "faithful" (Deut 7:9; Ps 85), who is a "lover of justice" (Ps 37:28), who is "compassionate" and "slow to anger" (Exod 34:6; 2 Kings 13:23), and who has chosen Israel from all the nations of the world (Deut 7:6).

---

13. Gustavo Gutiérrez, *The God of Life*, trans. Matthew J. O'Connell (Maryknoll, NY: Orbis, 1991) 22-23.

However, the Bible's core message also speaks of God as mystery, remaining hidden even in God's own self-revelation. There is a strong tradition of divine hiddenness in the Hebrew Bible, most notably in the psalmists' lamentations: "O Lord, why do you cast me off? Why do you hide your face from me?" (Ps 88:14). Psalm 10 goes so far as to accuse YHWH of intentionally hiding from humanity: "Why, O Lord, do you stand far off? Why do you hide yourself in times of trouble?" (Ps 10:1), and this theme is also found within the prophetic tradition: "Truly you are a God who hides himself, O God of Israel, the Savior" (Isa 45:15). However, no Jewish narrative captures the frustration and inscrutability caused by divine hiddenness better than Job's complaint to the Creator: "Why do you hide your face and count me as your enemy?" (Job 13:24).

Consequently, this testimony of a just and loving God is counterbalanced with protests and lamentations that God has disavowed the covenant (Lev 26:14–33; Deut 28:15–68; Amos 4:6–11), allows evil to reign in the world (Isa 45:7), and abandons Israel to her enemies (Mic 3:12; Isa 5:13). Since God cannot be contained and limited by human thought, human discourse about God is constrained by these apparently contradictory testimonies and must accept in faith the mystery of a God who is both the God of life *and* of death (1 Sam 2:6). According to Brueggemann, this biblical "counter-testimony" to Israel's core testimony concerning YHWH arises "because Israel experiences the negativity of Yahweh in seemingly great disproportion to disobedience, affront, or mocking."[14] In other words, such passages are not a rejection of the covenant on Israel's part, or a denial of God's sovereignty in administering the covenant, but *a protest in faith* against what Israel views as punishment incommensurate with Israel's sins or, in some cases, as a protest "against Yahweh's silence and neglect when Israel is in need."[15] This canonical voice of protest, indicting God for violating God's very steadfastness, justice, and mercy, provides further attestation of Israel's core witness concerning YHWH's character insofar as it appeals to YHWH's character in demanding—and ultimately receiving—justice. As Brueggemann notes, "The odd thing is that Israel's rhetorical urging of Yahweh and Israel's occasional assault against Yahweh do move Yahweh to new, rescuing activity."[16] Thus, rather than resolving the tension between these competing witnesses within sacred scripture concerning the nature of the one true God, Brueggemann opts to preserve the mystery of the hidden God by insisting that *both* testimonies coexist within the biblical narrative.

---

14. Walter Brueggemann, *Theology of the Old Testament: Testimony, Dispute, Advocacy* (Minneapolis: Fortress, 1997) 373.

15. Ibid.

16. Ibid., 380.

As Brueggemann, Ateek, and Ellis have argued, each in their own way, *the prophetic tradition stands as the ultimate counter-testimony* to the various competing nationalist and imperialist narratives within the biblical canon. Despite this strong voice advocating mercy toward Israel, there is no canonical counter-testimony questioning God's use of political violence against the Canaanites and other non-Jews, with one glaring exception: the book of the prophet Jonah. This unique text becomes the focus of a creative rereading of the canon in Naim Ateek's Christian Palestinian liberation theology through which God's sovereignty over all nations, peoples, and religions is established *in rejection of* theologically justified partisan political violence. This inquiry argues that Jonah's revered place within the canon of the Hebrew Scriptures represents Israel's *ultimate* counter-testimony and provides a useful paradigm within Judaism, Christianity, and Islam for resisting political violence.

Jonah, Reluctant Prophet of Liberation

The book of the prophet Jonah stands as a paradigmatic narrative for addressing religious pluralism and political violence.[17] Jonah, a canonical text for both Judaism and Christianity, is also important in Islam: it is the only one of the twelve Minor Prophets of the Hebrew Scriptures/Old Testament to be named in the Qur'an. This brief but revered narrative is a prophetic text whose central protagonist is a Jewish nationalist who reluctantly delivers a warning from YHWH to the imperial occupiers of Israel, the Assyrians, and then becomes angry with God for showing mercy toward Jonah's enemies. The presence of this surprisingly subversive text within the canon destabilizes the pervasive nationalism of the Hebrew Scriptures and provides a paradigm for resisting the violence that often typifies interactions between competing religious traditions.

The book of Jonah is unique within the prophetic writings of the Hebrew Bible.[18] First, unlike the other books of the prophets, this book is not a collection of

17. I first suggested using the book of the prophet Jonah as a model for tolerance and nonviolence between competing religions in "De orilla a orilla: The Ecumenical Theology of Luis Rivera Pagán," *Journal of Hispanic/Latino Theology* 18.1 (2012) 26–34. I want to say a word of thanks to Dr. Rivera Pagán who, in responding to my paper, introduced me to the work of Naim Stifan Ateek. Ateek describes Jonah as the first Palestinian liberation theologian in *A Palestinian Cry for Reconciliation* (Maryknoll, NY: Orbis, 2008) 67–77. Though differing from Ateek on several key points, this paper benefits greatly from his analysis of Jonah as a canonical witness that "condemns all narrow, restrictive, or exclusive theologies" (77). For a fuller treatment of the book of Jonah as a paradigm for nonviolent resistance, see Rubén Rosario Rodríguez, *Christian Martyrdom and Political Violence: A Comparative Theology with Judaism and Islam* (Cambridge: Cambridge University Press, 2017) 71–82.

18. For an introduction to the issues surrounding Jonah's placement in the Hebrew canon, its categorization as a prophetic book over other genres, and related issues of authorship, dating, and canonical status, see James Limburg, *Jonah: A Commentary* (Louisville: Westminster John Knox, 1993) 19–36; Jack M. Sasson, *Jonah*, AB 24B (New York: Doubleday, 1990) 9–29; and Uriel Simon, *Jonah*,

the prophet's preaching but a collection of narrative vignettes about Jonah. Tradition has located Jonah among the Twelve Prophets on the assumption that Jonah is the son of Amittai mentioned in the book of Kings and therefore a contemporary of Jeroboam II (c. 786–746 BCE), explaining its place in the canon alongside the prophets Hosea and Amos. However, as a prophetic text, Jonah is unlike any other in the Hebrew canon. Prophetic books typically consist of the word of God to the people of Israel as mediated by the preaching of the prophet (marked off by the phrases "Thus says the Lord" and "the word of the Lord"), the prophet's response—often a word of protest in the form of a prayer or lamentation—to God, as well as a brief biographical or autobiographical segment locating the prophet at a specific moment in Israel's history.[19] The book of the prophet Jonah includes only one biographical tidbit (Jonah 1:1), contains a lengthy prayer tenuously connected to the rest of the narrative (Jonah 2:2–9), and presents only the briefest message from God—and that message not directed to the people of Israel. Instead, the prophet Jonah is commissioned to speak the word of God to gentiles—and not just any gentile nation, but the people of Nineveh, the capital of the Assyrian Empire responsible for the conquest and exile of the northern kingdom of Israel in 721 BCE. Not surprisingly, Jonah is reluctant to travel to the land of his political enemies to deliver a prophetic warning from God and flees to the west by boarding a boat to Tarshish "away from the presence of the Lord" (Jonah 1:3, NRSV). Eventually, Jonah accepts God's call and delivers YHWH's prophetic warning. Jonah's sermon is similar in form to other prophetic preaching in the Hebrew Bible, communicating YHWH's judgment against the people of Nineveh, but it is distinguished by its brevity (five words in Hebrew, eight in English): "Forty days more, and Nineveh shall be overthrown!" (Jonah 3:4, NRSV). Reinforcing the core testimony of Israel concerning YHWH's sovereignty over all nations and compassion toward all people, the story of Jonah bears witness to the power of the word of God as the entire populace, from the king to the animals, responds to God's prophetic word with same sincere piety. By sparing the city of Nineveh, the author of the book of Jonah emphasizes and makes central a theme also present in other prophetic texts: YHWH's sovereignty and compassion is not limited to Israel but extends to all the nations.

The main character in the book of Jonah is an adherent of ethnic nationalism, claiming YHWH and YHWH's blessings *exclusively* for the people of Israel. The author of the narrative—the truly prophetic voice in this story—uses humor to portray

JPS Bible Commentary (Philadelphia: Jewish Publication Society, 1999) vii–xliii.

19. For an introduction to Hebrew prophetic literature, see James M. Ward, *Thus Says the Lord: The Message of the Prophets* (Nashville: Abingdon, 1991) 13–33; also see Abraham Joshua Heschel, *The Prophets* (New York: Harper Perennial Classics, 2001) 3–31; and Walter Brueggemann, *The Prophetic Imagination* (Minneapolis: Fortress, 1978) 44–61.

one of the prophets of Israel as a narrow-minded xenophobe who is blinded to the word of God by his hatred of the people of Nineveh. YHWH, being merciful and slow to anger, refrains from punishing Jonah in the hopes that Jonah, like the people of Nineveh, will repent of his evil ways and embrace the word of God. Therefore, the prophetic counter-testimony preserved in this narrative—an authoritative narrative for all three Abrahamic religions—speaks directly to the twenty-first-century context. Despite the fact that the sailors and the people of Nineveh worship other gods—and so are technically guilty of idolatry—YHWH receives their prayers, vows, and sacrifices because they are offered sincerely. YHWH is portrayed as the one true God who is the God of all humankind, regardless of national origin or religious affiliation, and who demands mercy and compassion in situations where the human inclination is toward intolerance and violence.

These theological themes mark Jonah as an exemplary text for developing a comparative theology that brings Judaism, Christianity, and Islam into conversation over the question of religious tolerance and cooperation by nurturing those shared values and beliefs that contribute to nonviolent solutions for religious conflicts. Having articulated an exegetical strategy for reconciling divinely orchestrated political violence in the Abrahamic sacred Scriptures with the divine imperative to love God and neighbor—including one's enemy—it is possible to return to the Exodus narrative keenly aware of Warrior's and Ateek's warnings about the historical use of the Exodus in justifying genocidal and imperialistic political violence.

Conclusion

How do we evaluate the success or failure of liberation struggles? What criteria do we employ to judge whether or not a historical movement has attained its political goals? More importantly, is political "success" possible without compromising a movement's core beliefs? I come at this question at a moment in history when dystopia no longer refers to a *future* potentiality but more aptly describes the political *status quo*. Given the persistence of political regimes that perpetuate unjust social structures, liberation theologians have begun to question the utopian vision underlying historical struggles for liberation. None have done so more vocally than Miguel A. De La Torre, whose most recent monograph, *Embracing Hopelessness* (2017), argues that the "*first step toward liberation requires the crucifixion of hope*—for as long as hope exists, the world's wretched have something to lose, and thus will not risk all to change the social structure."[20] In other words, De La Torre suggests that by "embracing hopelessness" we are not surrendering to despair. Rather, the "realization

---

20. Miguel A. De La Torre, *Embracing Hopelessness* (Minneapolis: Fortress Press, 2017) 5–6.

that there is nothing to lose becomes a catalyst for praxis" shifting the focus away from a transcendent future hope unto a present radical praxis.[21] Accordingly, genuine liberation "requires a rejection of the official history of the dominant culture,"[22] which includes rejecting those *religious* understandings of hope that are easily manipulated into an opiate that allows oppressive structures to persist unchallenged.

This investigation contends that within the canons of Jewish and Christian thought, the prophetic serves as a counterweight to the utopian anesthetic of religious hope, providing a paradigm for radical liberative praxis that is at once deeply theological and historically immanent. At the heart of liberation theology's emancipatory discourse, we find the foundational text of ancient Israel and modern-day Judaism—the Exodus narrative—a text fraught with moral ambiguity. Religious communities, especially those committed to universal human liberation, might have to abandon the Exodus as a foundational text. Or, at the very least, reclaim the emancipatory potential of Exodus by severing it from the Zionist narrative of *Eretz Israel* as only for Jews by appealing to the rich prophetic counter-testimony that runs through the whole of the Hebrew Bible, thus challenging the nation of Israel to commit itself to struggles for dignity and justice that run against the grain of political expediency, pragmatic considerations, and exclusionary nationalisms.

Consequently, the prophetic is not something that can be understood in the abstract but must be confronted in its concrete historicity. For Marc Ellis, the Holocaust as the nadir of Jewish powerlessness has led to the elevation of the modern state of Israel as the embodiment of Jewish political power, which in turn has created a spiritual crisis for Jews of conscience who must confront "Constantinian Judaism" in order to stand in solidarity with the Palestinian people. The consequence of embracing a prophetic Jewish theology—a Jewish theology of liberation—is a life in exile as dissenting Jews in what Marc Ellis calls the new diaspora. The vision Ellis has called forth from amidst the never-ending dystopia that is the Israeli-Palestinian conflict is not offered as a utopian distraction, but as a praxis of radical forgiveness "where people of different faiths and worldviews come together"[23] and let themselves be guided by the "voices of the Exodus movement and of the prophets, of the martyrs who went to their death with a prayer to god, and of those who refused prayer, of those who resisted with arms, and of those who resisted with the written word."[24] What is needed is a biblical paradigm for those who seek to be part of the new diaspora, rejecting the addictive power of the state and its accompanying violence in

21. Ibid., 6.
22. Ibid., 32.
23. Ellis, *Toward a Jewish Theology of Liberation*, 206.
24. Ibid., 207.

order to become prophetic witnesses for truth, justice, and compassion as dissenting exiles.

Moral reasoning is *least* effective when involved parties lack a common moral discourse. Yet that is precisely when we *most need* moral reasoning. How do we employ the Exodus narrative when our interlocutor refuses to dialogue? In other words, Pharaoh was not convinced by moral persuasion to free the Israelite slaves. In fact, it took an act of divine violence (drowning Pharaoh's army) ultimately to guarantee Israel's safe passage across the Red Sea. When we start talking about divinely sanctioned violence we are truly mired in moral ambiguity. Recalling Robert Warrior's critique that the liberator of slaves becomes the conqueror of the Canaanites, how do we navigate these moral ambiguities without creating our own false idols? How do we avoid the temptation of claiming "God on our side" as a justification for whatever we want? Does not that path inevitably lead to empire and domination? Can the Exodus narrative *alone* help us navigate these moral problematics, or do we need to appeal to other parts of the canon to articulate a more holistic emancipatory ethic?

Taking Marc Ellis's challenge seriously—that the new diaspora is characterized as a life of exile in which people of different faiths come together in resisting the Constantinian state and religion—this condition in which "exiles begin to recognize one another . . . gives way to the possibility of solidarity. The present situation opens toward a future where exiles form a diaspora community."[25] This new exile community needs to move beyond the Judeo-Christian binary and begin to engage Islamic efforts to read the Exodus as an emancipatory text, which is an authoritative narrative that appears in the sacred Scriptures of all three Abrahamic religions. The Qur'anic retelling of the Exodus not only reveals that God is a liberator but also demonstrates God's patience and compassion toward God's people even when they lose faith and reject God. Like the Hebrew Bible, the Qur'an tells the story of God's liberation of Israel under the leadership of Moses and his struggle with Pharaoh in several chapters scattered throughout the text (Q Baqarah 2:47–73; Q A`raf 7:103–62; Q Yunus 10:74–92; Q Ta-Ha 20:9–98; Q Shu`ara' 26:10–69; Q Nami 27:7–14; Q Qasas 28:1–42), covering the early years of Moses' life, his exile, the manifestation of God in the burning bush, the confrontation with Pharaoh's magicians, and Moses' demand that Pharaoh free the Israelites. The Qur'an also describes their eventual liberation, including the drowning of Pharaoh's army in the Red Sea, before recounting Israel's forty years of wandering in the wilderness, its rebelliousness and apostasy with the golden calf, God's revelation to Moses on Mt. Sinai, and even Moses' death before Israel was allowed to enter the promised land, paralleling the same major narrative arc found in the Hebrew Scriptures. A way forward past strife and division

---

25. Ibid., 199.

in the midst of religious pluralism can be found in a critical retrieval of the Exodus as an emancipatory text, but only when we strip away the traditions of exclusion and nationalism that have accumulated across multiple layers of redaction to undermine God's prophetic call to universal liberation. Solidarity begins with the rejection of idolatrous theologies grounded in the all-too-human need to find safety in ethnic and political unity at the expense of the religiously, ethnically, and politically other.

The emphasis on prophetic solidarity is what makes Marc Ellis's work so important and so relevant, not just for confronting the Israeli-Palestinian struggle, but for anyone navigating the treacherous path of the political and religious exile living in a world where established religious institutions continue to grasp the specters of a now-dead but still longed-for Constantinian state religion. *How do we evaluate the success or failure of liberation struggles?* Marc Ellis provides clarity of vision in which success is not measured by quantitative gains but by more qualitative criteria in which *how* one walks the path is just as important as the path one chooses. Crucial to remaining faithful to prophetic Judaism is the need to acknowledge our social location as exiles removed from the centers of political power. In Ellis's words, "If we throw strategy to the wind and end our hope for victory, then we are free to be faithful."[26]

---

26. Ibid., 233.

RESPONSE TO ROSARIO RODRÍGUEZ

Armida Belmonte Stephens

In his paper, "The Moral Problematics of Exodus as Liberative Narrative," Dr. Rosario argues that despite the troubling features of divine and human violence in the conquest of Canaan, liberation theology has often centered on the exodus narrative as foundational and normative, much to its detriment. This unexamined acceptance of violence leaves little, if any, room for the exodus narrative to speak into contexts fraught with violence and questions surrounding settlement, such as those of First Peoples in North America and the Israeli-Palestinian situation. Engaging the Jewish liberation theology of Marc Ellis, as well as liberation theologian and Palestinian Christian Naim Ateek, he echoes their concerns about "the distortion and manipulation of biblical texts for the sake of contemporary political agendas in providing theological rationalization for contemporary political violence." He follows with an exploration of the tensions and conflicts inherent in various approaches to liberation theology between the nonviolence to which they aspire and the biblical portrayal of a God who uses political violence to achieve his purposes—what Rosario calls "liberative violence." Reflecting on the work of Walter Brueggemann, Ateek, and Ellis, he proposes that the way forward is found in the Bible's prophetic literature as a counter-testimony to what he describes as "nationalist and imperial narratives" in the texts of the Old Testament. Further, he claims that the Book of Jonah stands as "Israel's *ultimate* counter-testimony" having the moral authority to address political violence in the context of religious pluralism. For this reason, Jonah serves as a model text for comparative theology's discourse among Judaism, Christianity, and Islam regarding questions of collaboration and working toward nonviolence.

There is much to be commended in Dr. Rosario's proposal and, overall, I find his argument persuasive and his proposal helpful for furthering conversation within liberation theology. His critique that the conquest of Canaan raises significant questions regarding divine and human violence is important not only ethically, but also rhetorically. Not only is conquest a questionable metaphor for a liberative ethic, it is also problematic for diaspora and refugee communities that may have left their respective Egypts—not by choice, but through forced migration—to think of their new countries of residence as the promised land, particularly when they are not well-received. Sadly, the use of the promised land rhetoric is part of what informs the pervasive Christian nationalism we see in our country today.

Additionally, Dr. Rosario's assertion that prophetic discourse may prove more fruitful for the goals and ethics of liberation is worth consideration, as is his call to accommodate new paradigms that are sensitive, functionally liberative to other contexts and particularities that would otherwise be excluded by one dominant textual paradigm, and helpful in creating opportunities for common spaces of reflection and collaboration. To quote James Cone:

> While we must begin our theological reflection with the particularity of our own struggle for justice, we should never stop there. The truth of our particular struggle pushes us beyond ourselves to the truth of other struggles. The Bible and the struggles of the oppressed throughout history broaden our vision of the truth and thereby impel us to make real the beloved community that Martin Luther King, Jr., spoke so eloquently about. Human beings are made for each other and no people can realize their full humanity except as they participate in its realization for others.[1]

The proposal also raises some questions for further discussion. While I find Dr. Rosario's argument compelling, my comments have to do more with nuance, and the nature of areas where I find certain of his assertions to be overstated or that he over-problematizes past approaches. The first regards the characterization of Latin American and black theology as centering on the exodus narrative to the exclusion of other paradigms. While it cannot be denied that the exodus narrative plays a significant role in these liberation theologies, it is not clear or to be taken for granted that it is the *only* or even the main paradigm—not only because Latin American and black theologies are not monolithic, but also because this is not evident in the work of the theologians chosen as representative. In his *The Truth Shall Make You Free*, Gustavo Gutiérrez—mentioned early in Dr. Rosario's paper—makes a point of stating that other themes such as covenant and communion take up more space in his writing than that of exodus.[2] Moreover, as far as I am aware, *when* paradigmatic, the exodus narrative used in Latin American liberation theology—and perhaps the same is true for black theology as well—does not include the conquest.[3] The

---

1. James H. Cone, *God of the Oppressed* (Maryknoll, NY: Orbis, 1997) xii-xiii.

2. See Gustavo Gutiérrez, *The Truth Shall Make You Free: Confrontations* (Maryknoll, NY: Orbis, 1990) 119, nn. 77-79. Also, "The theme of the exodus has been and is still an important one for us, but I think it an overstatement to say that it was the major theme in our theology of liberation. It is important to us because the exodus has been the basic historical experience of the Jewish people and has set its mark on the entire Bible. But I think that we have also treated other themes as important. From the outset, other aspects have been central in our view—for example, poverty according to the Bible" (29).

3. Additionally, from an organizational and literary standpoint of the Hebrew Bible, there is no

key theological aspects drawn from the exodus narrative are the themes of God as liberator and new creation. James Cone, for his part, affirms the centrality of the exodus for black liberation theology, but also describes the liberation motif as being based on "Exodus, prophets and the Gospels' portrayal of Jesus in solidarity with the poor."[4] Other liberation theologians have called for a paradigm of exile instead. *Subversive Scriptures: Revolutionary Readings of the Christian Bible in Latin America*,[5] is a volume of essays written in order to overcome this very mischaracterization and deals with texts in Genesis, 2 Samuel, Psalms, Nehemiah, 2 Peter, and Revelation among others. The theme of exile is also appropriated to give expression to painful Latina realities of marginality—exile in both literal and cultural terms: "By the waters of Babylon we shall live and die."[6]

Another point of discussion has to do with the move away from the hermeneutics of classical liberation theology[7] to a revised liberation theology informed both by post-colonial sensitivities and by contexts increasingly marked by religious pluralism. Although this is a welcome approach, a potential problem is that this shift could replace existing theologies of liberation rather than complement them. In other words, while it should certainly be acknowledged that some paradigms have limited use and cannot have universal liberative function, there should not be a corresponding expectation that the aims and purposes of this more inclusive or identity-specific hermeneutic will be universalized. To do so would, ironically, work against the particularities of those marginalized communities that liberation theology sought to address in the first place. This caution stems from a desire to avoid the impulse of academic discourse to minimize or trivialize marginalized peoples' readings, an impulse that can easily be unconscious for those who enjoy the privileges of

---

reason to include the conquest as a part of the exodus narrative. The exodus narrative marks the end of the Torah and the conquest is picked up in the Former Prophets of the Nevi'im. Or, for a literary and rhetorical perspective arguing against a literal interpretation of the Book of Joshua, see Hélène M. Dallaire, "Taking the Land by Force: Divine Violence in Joshua," in *Wrestling with the Violence of God: Soundings in the Old Testament*, BBRSup 10, ed. M. Daniel Carroll R. and J. Blair Wilgus (Winona Lake: Eisenbrauns, 2015).

4. Cone, *God of the Oppressed*, xii.

5. Leif E. Vaage, ed., *Subversive Scriptures: Revolutionary Readings of the Christian Bible in Latin America* (Valley Forge, PA: Trinity Press International, 1997). Cited in "Engaging Liberation: Texts as a Vehicle of Emancipation," in R. S. Sugirtharajah, *The Bible and the Third World: Precolonial, Colonial, and Postcolonial Encounters* (Cambridge: University Press, 2001) 209.

6. See Justo L. González, *Mañana: Christian Theology from a Hispanic Perspective* (Nashville: Abingdon, 1990) 41–42. The theme of exile here is also appropriated to describe the realities affecting the Latina community and the ambiguous nature of living in liminal spaces.

7. For a brief typology of liberation theologies see Sugirtharajah, *Bible and the Third World*, 203–43. Sugirtharajah compares classical liberation hermeneutics (e.g., Gustavo Gutiérrez and Elsa Tamez), with that of Christian base communities, as well as identity-specific readings (e.g., Robert Allen Warrior and Naim Ateek).

education, access, and successful navigation of a globalized world. These conversations—often resulting in calls for unity, inclusion, and collaboration—have tended toward solutions in the abstract that have historically given way to the abdication of justice.[8]

More concretely, a both/and approach is needed. When speaking of particularities, there may be some paradigms that are more helpful than others to a community depending on its time and place in its historical trajectory. For example, speaking from a Latina perspective, it may now be that when speaking of an ecclesial immigrant community's realities, the exodus motif remains an incredibly rich resource. Those who find themselves under the weight of exploitation, racial profiling, and family separations may need the comfort and healing that comes, for example, from the expectation that the strong arm of God is heavier than the arm of the pharaohs in their lives. Not only is there a benefit from such an approach, it may also be a necessary stepping stone before a community can properly engage in more cosmopolitan or globalized realities outside of their own situations. Describing the difficulties the Israelites faced in the desert as they began to complain against God and their memories of what they thought were better times, Gutiérrez explains that "A gradual pedagogy of successes and failures would be necessary for the Jewish people to become aware of the roots of their oppression, to struggle against it, and to perceive the profound sense of the liberation to which they were called. The Creator of the world is the Creator and Liberator of Israel, to whom is entrusted the mission of establishing justice."[9] At the same time, Latinos who are more acculturated, privileged, and comfortable in this society would perhaps benefit more from a paradigm centered upon exile or Jonah.[10] It is not altogether clear to me how Dr. Rosario would view the continuing use of the exodus narrative alongside newer postcolonial approaches.

---

8. Referencing the work of Juan Luis Segundo, Sugirtharajah describes the differences of context and approach by professional theologians and ordinary readers in the early stages of liberation theology: "Segundo opined that one could not conceal the fact that 'we are faced here with two different theologies under the same name: different in scope, different in method, different in presuppositions, and different in pastoral consequences'" (Sugirtharajah, *Bible and the Third World*, 204).

9. Gustavo Gutiérrez, *Theology of Liberation* (Maryknoll, NY: Orbis, 1988) 88. He is here referencing Isa 42:5–7.

10. One cannot assume, however, such clear-cut distinctions or defined boundaries for the many American Latinos whose lives are marked by transnational and polycentric realities. Although his book deals mainly with Latino Protestants, Juan F. Martínez summarizes American Latino realities irrespective of traditional ties: "It is the Latinos who have a polycentric identity who do not easily fit in churches that seem monocultural. The bicultural, marginal, fleeing, and returning are people who have a fluid ethnic and cultural identity, or who compartmentalize their lives, expressing certain cultural traits in one environment and claiming strong ethnic identity in another." See Juan F. Martínez, *An Introduction to Latino Protestantism in the United States* (Santa Barbara: Praeger, 2011) 123–25. On the other hand, for the same reasons, he also raises the question of evolving needs as lived experiences lead to changing identities. "Is 'exile' still a term that helps them understand how they experience God

Finally, while Dr. Rosario concedes that liberative violence is a divine accommodation to human failure, the portrayal of the Jonah narrative as Israel's *ultimate* counter-testimony having the moral authority to address political violence raises the question of whether this is an explicit creation of a canon within a canon.[11] If so, as it is not simply God's nonviolence that is in view in Jonah, but also God's *grace and mercy* to Nineveh, clarification about the basis of such a hermeneutic would be helpful. Because the very definitions of grace and mercy stand in stark opposition to human presumption or expectation, one wonders whether the justification for the acknowledgement of the moral authority of the Bible can be reduced to a litmus test in which divine mercy and grace can be *assumed*.

These are a few of the questions that came to mind as I read this thought-provoking and compelling proposal.

---

in the world, or are there new terms that need to be brought into the conversation?" (113).

11. This is the case for Naim Ateek who views Jonah as the theological climax of the Old Testament as it depicts a gracious God, an inclusive people of God, and God's concern for all land. See *A Palestinian Theology of Liberation: The Bible, Justice, and the Palestine-Israel Conflict* (Maryknoll, NY: Orbis, 2017) 76–80. He advocates a christological hermeneutic to aid the reader "discern the authentic word of God. . . . [W]e can no longer say simply that the Bible is the word of God. We can no longer make such a blanket statement. God can still speak to us through some biblical texts, but Jesus Christ must be the determining hermeneutic" (141).

HUMAN VIOLENCE IN THE IMPRECATORY PSALMS

Nancy L. deClaissé-Walford

Introduction

A number of psalms in the Psalter are classified as "Imprecatory Psalms": Pss 12, 58, 69, 83, 94, 109, 129, and 137.[1] Many others contain imprecatory language, including 17:13; 31:17; 35:4; 59:11–13; 69:22–28; 70:2–3; and 139:19–22. John Day maintains, in fact, that over one hundred verses in the book of Psalms contain imprecatory words.[2] J. Carl Laney, in "A Fresh Look at the Imprecatory Psalms," defines "imprecation" in the Bible as "an invocation of judgment, calamity, or curse uttered against one's enemies, or the enemies of God."[3] The words of imprecatory psalms are harsh and shrill as the singers invoke God's wrath upon their foes:

> Do not grant, O LORD, the desires of the wicked;
>> do not further their evil plot.
> Those who surround me are uplifted in head;
>> let the mischief of their lips overwhelm them!
> Let burning coals fall on them!
>> Let them be flung into pits, no more to rise!
> Do not let the slanderer be established in the land;
>> let evil speedily hunt down the violent! (Ps 140:8–11)

> Let his days be few;
>> let another take his position.
> Let his children become orphans,
>> and his wives widows.
> Let his children continuously roam about and beg;
>> let them offer entreaties from their desolate ruins.

---

1. See Erich Zenger, *A God of Vengeance? Understanding the Psalms of Divine Wrath*, trans. Linda M. Maloney (Louisville: Westminster John Knox, 1996). He states that Pss 12, 58, 83, 109, and 137 are imprecatory. I add Pss 94 and 129 to Zenger's list.

2. See also Pss 7, 52, 55, 79, 97, and 140. John N. Day, in "The Imprecatory Psalms and Christian Ethics," *BSac* 159 (2002) 169.

3. J. Carl Laney, "A Fresh Look at the Imprecatory Psalms," *BSac* 1 (1981) 35.

> Let a lender lay a snare for all that belongs to him,
>> and let strangers treat his possessions with contempt. (Ps 109:8–11, author's translation)
>
> Let their eyes be darkened so that they cannot see,
>> and make their loins tremble continually.
>
> Pour out your indignation upon them,
>> and let your burning anger overtake them.
>
> May their camp be a desolation;
>> let no one live in their tents. (69:23–25 [Heb 24–26])[4]

C. S. Lewis said of the imprecatory psalms, "In some of the Psalms, the spirit of hatred is like the heat from a furnace mouth."[5]

How are we to read and interpret these harsh and vindictive words? How do they inform our understanding of God and God's relationship with humanity? Should we read, study, pray, and preach the imprecatory psalms and the vengeance-filled words of so many of the psalms? For, and this is perhaps the hardest part of these psalms and psalmic words to reconcile—they are outcries against violence that demand just such violence by God on behalf of the psalm-singers.[6] They ask for, indeed they demand, violence as an answer to violence.

Phyllis Trible offers, I believe, some insight into coming to grips with these troubling words in the Psalter. In an article titled "Take Back the Bible," she recounted that during her academic journey through college and graduate school, she came to embrace feminism as an interpretive tool for studying the Bible, something that was very foreign to her conservative Baptist upbringing. But she was also disturbed that, as she states, "feminists were faulting the Bible for patriarchy, faulting it for promoting the pernicious paradigm of male dominance and female subordination," but yet she could not let go of her love of the Bible. She reflects, "I was of all women most wretched—or whatever adjective seems fitting: schizophrenic, misguided, conservative, or just plain wrong. So my predicament grew as I heard the challenge of feminism."

And then Trible read anew the story of Jacob at the Jabbok. Jacob struggled with an uncertain future and demanded a blessing, saying in Gen 32:36, "I will not let you go, unless you bless me." Trible writes, "That declaration became my challenge to the Bible from the perspective of feminism. I will not let go this book of words unless and until it blesses me. I will struggle with it. . ... I shall hold fast for a blessing." But,

---

4. All biblical quotations are from the NRSV, unless otherwise stated.
5. C. S. Lewis, *Reflections on the Psalms* (San Diego: Harcourt, 1958) 20.
6. Zenger, *God of Vengeance?*, 11.

she adds, "I am under no illusion that the blessing will come on my terms—that I will not be changed in the process. After all, Jacob, the blessed man, limped away."[7] The imprecatory words of the book of Psalms require wrestling on our part. And we are justified in demanding a blessing from them.

This article will first discuss the scriptural "status" of the imprecatory psalms and psalmic words; second, it will examine the poetic literary style of these psalms; third, it will present various scholarly and ecclesial interpretations of the imprecatory language in the Psalter; fourth, it will consider the ethical dimensions of such language; and finally it will suggest options for reading and appropriating the imprecatory language of the Psalter into the life of believing communities today.

The Scriptural Status of the Words of Imprecation

The imprecatory psalms and psalmic words, with all of the difficulties they present to many readers, are part of the canon of Jewish and Christian Scripture. The communities of faith who shaped texts into what became known as the Hebrew Bible and the Christian Old Testament incorporated the whole of the book of Psalms, with its imprecatory words, into their canon.[8] In addition, the Septuagint includes the imprecatory psalms (all of them) as do the various Psalters discovered among the Dead Sea Scrolls.[9]

While many, perhaps all, of the imprecatory psalms were originally oral in nature, composed by individuals or the community as addresses *to* God, they were transformed by their inclusion in the canon from words from the faithful to God to words *from* and *about* God *to* the faithful. They are no longer the utterances of a particular individual or community to God; they have become words about God for all communities of faith across all times and places.

In the act of accepting the imprecatory psalms as a part of their canons of "Scripture," the Jewish rabbis and Christian church leaders acknowledged the importance and value of these psalms for their overall understanding of the relationship between the God of the biblical text and the people who choose to worship that God. That is, communities of faith must have found value and insight into the character of their God in these texts or they would not have preserved the texts for subsequent

---

7. Phyllis Trible, "Take Back the Bible," *RevExp* 97 (2000) 425–31.

8. "Canon" is, of course, a word first applied to Scripture by the Christian Council of Carthage in 397. When speaking of the Hebrew Bible as a corpus of literature, it is better to use the term "authoritative literature."

9. All of the imprecatory psalms are attested in the Dead Sea Scrolls except Ps 58. Psalm 12 is included in 11QPs[c] and 5/6 HevPs; Ps 83 in MasPs[a]; Ps 94 in 4QPs[b] and 1PPs[a]; Ps 109 in 4QPs[e], 4QPs[f], and 11QPs[a]; Ps 129 in 11QPs[a] and 4QPs[e]; and Ps 137 in 11QPs[a]. See James Vanderkam and Peter Flint, *The Meaning of the Dead Sea Scrolls* (San Francisco: HarperSanFrancisco, 2002) 419–22.

communities of faith. James A. Sanders, in his 1980 essay, "Canonical Context and Canonical Criticism," writes:

> There has been a relationship between tradition, written and oral, and community, a constant, ongoing dialogue, a historical memory passed on from generation to generation, in which the specific relationship between canon and community resided.[10]

Sanders goes on to say that communities find value in stories and texts when those texts provide answers to two basic existential questions: "Who are we?" and "What are we to do?"[11] The ancient Israelites repeatedly asked these questions of, and found answers to them in, their traditions—the stories and texts that they passed on from generation to generation. The stories and texts, including the psalmic words of imprecation, became authoritative for the life of the people.

Thus, we cannot summarily banish the imprecatory psalms and psalmic words to the periphery of the canon. They are an integral part of the words of the psalmists, rendered by their inclusion in the book of Psalms as the words of God and embraced by millennia of the faithful as part of Scripture. To pick and choose which biblical texts one will read and appropriate into one's life of faith and which texts one will choose not read and appropriate is creating, in effect, "a canon within a canon," a common phenomenon in faith communities.[12]

In addition, imprecatory words are not confined to the book of Psalms; they occur in various places in the text of the Hebrew Bible/Old Testament. In Num 10:35 Moses speaks words of imprecation each time the ark of the covenant sets out during the wilderness journey:

> Arise, O LORD, let your enemies be scattered,
>> and your foes flee before you.

Deborah sings in Judges 5:

> So perish all your enemies, O LORD,
> But may your friends be like the sun as it rises in its might. (v. 31)

In Jer 18:21, the prophet implores God to take vengeance on his oppressors:

> Give their children over to famine;
>> hurl them out to the power of the sword,

---

10. James A. Sanders, "Canonical Context and Canonical Criticism," in *From Sacred Story to Sacred Text* (Philadelphia: Fortress, 1987) 166.

11. James A. Sanders, *Torah and Canon* (Philadelphia: Fortress, 1972) xv.

12. For an excellent discussion of the concept of canon, see Lee Martin McDonald and James A. Sanders, eds., *The Canon Debate* (Peabody, MA: Hendrickson, 2002).

> let their wives become childless and widowed.
>> May their men meet death by pestilence,
> their youths be slain by the sword in battle.

The author of Lamentations writes of those who participated in the destruction of Jerusalem:

> Pay them back for their deeds, O LORD,
>> according to the work of their hands!
>
> Give them anguish of heart;
>> your curse be on them!
>
> Pursue them in anger and destroy them
>> from under the LORD's heavens. (3:64–66)

The writers of the New Testament both quote from the imprecatory psalms and provide their own words of imprecation against enemies. In Acts 1, Peter quotes from Pss 69:25 and 109:8:

> For it is written in the book of Psalms,
> "Let his homestead become desolate,
>> and let there be no one to live in it";

and

> "Let another take his position of overseer." (v. 20)

Matthew 10 tells us that Jesus sent out the disciples with specific instructions:

> If anyone will not welcome you or listen to your words, shake off the dust from your feet as you leave that house or town. Truly I tell you, it will be more tolerable for the land of Sodom and Gomorrah on the day of judgment than for that town. (vv. 14–15)

Paul says in 1 Corinthians:

> Let anyone be accursed who has no love for the Lord. (16:22)

and in Galatians:

> But even if we or an angel from heaven should proclaim to you a gospel contrary to what we proclaimed to you, let that one be accursed! (1:8)

Imprecatory words, words that invoke the wrath of God upon others, are found throughout the biblical text, not just in the words of the psalmists. They must be wrestled with and appropriated into our understanding of God and humanity's relationship with God.

The Poetic and Literary Style of the Imprecatory Psalms

The book of Psalms is a book of poetry and, thus, an understanding of the nature of poetry in general and Hebrew poetry in particular is essential to reading and interpreting its words. Barbara Herrnstein Smith, an American literary critic and theorist, defines poetic form as "the kind of structure produced by a patterning of the formal properties of language according to some principle of organization and/or representation."[13]

She describes one of the principles in this way, "As soon as we perceive that a verbal sequence has a sustained rhythm, that it is formally structured according to a continuously operating principle of organization, we know that we are in the presence of poetry and we respond to it accordingly ... granting certain conventions to it and not others."[14] While we read the psalms that were originally composed in Hebrew in English translation, an exercise in transliteration can demonstrate the "sustained rhythm" of Hebrew poetry. The introduction to this article quoted vv. 23–25 of Ps 69:

> Let their eyes be darkened so that they cannot see,
>> and make their loins tremble continually.
>
> Pour out your indignation upon them,
>> and let your burning anger overtake them.
>
> May their camp be a desolation;
>> let no one live in their tents. (69:23–25 [Heb 24–26])

While the "rhythm" is somewhat hidden in any translated rendering, it is far more evident in a transliterated rendering, as follows with the accented syllables in bold type and underlined.

> tekh-**_shak_**-nah 'ey-ney-hem mer-'**_oth_**
>> u-math-**_ney_**-hem ta-**_miyd_** ham-'**_ad_**
>
> she-**_phak_**-'a-ley-**_hem_** za '-**_me_**-ka
>> va-kha-**_ron_** 'ap-pe-**_ka_** yis-siy-**_gem_**
>
> te-hiy-**_tiy_**-ra-**_tam_** ne-sham-**_mah_**
>> be-'a-ha-ley-**_hem_** 'al-ye-**_hiy_** yo-**_shev_**

Psalm scholars describe the "rhythm" of the above verses as 3 + 3, with the two lines of each verse having three accented syllables each.[15]

---

13. Barbara Herrnstein Smith, *Poetic Closure: A Study of How Poems End* (Chicago: University of Chicago Press, 1968) 21.

14. Herrnstein Smith, *Poetic Closure*, 21.

15. See Hans-Joachim Kraus, *Psalms 60–150*, A Continental Commentary, trans. Hilton C. Oswald

Another major organizing principle of Hebrew poetry is its two- and sometimes three-line parallel structure. The first line of a verse makes a statement, and the second (and sometimes third) line adds to the sentiment of the first line in some way or another. In the example from Ps 69 above, the first line of v. 23 says, "Let their eyes be darkened so that they cannot see." The second line adds more information concerning what the psalmist wishes: "and make their loins tremble continually." In v. 24, we find first, "Pour out your indignation upon them," and then a nearly synonymous statement, "and let your burning anger overtake them." In v. 25, "May their camp be a desolation" is followed by the synonymous "let no one live in their tents."[16]

In addition to its somewhat unique qualities of meter and parallelism,[17] Hebrew poetry shares some of the universal characteristics of poetry in general. The first is its extensive use of metaphors and similes. In vv. 14 and 15 of Ps 69, the psalm singer pleads with God "rescue me from the sinking mire . . . and from the deep waters. Do not let the flood sweep over me, or the deep swallow me up, or the Pit close its mouth over me." And in v. 25, the psalmist refers figuratively to the "camp" and "tents" of the persecutors. The metaphors in poetry convey a depth of meaning that simple prose cannot. The singer of Ps 69 is not speaking literally of floods, the deep, the Pit, or camps and tents, but of what those images convey to the reader/hearer. Robert Alter, in *The Art of Biblical Poetry* maintains, "Poetry is not just a set of techniques for saying impressively what could be said otherwise. Rather, it is a particular way of imagining the world . . . [it has] its own ways of making connections and engendering implications."[18] Literary theorists use the terms "target" and "tenor" to describe the two elements of metaphoric imagery. "Target" is the image that is used to convey the comparison—in our example, "floods," "the deep," "the Pit," and "camps and tents." The "tenor" is the concept, object, or person meant to be identified in the "target" language. Thus, "floods" and "the deep" identify the overwhelming feeling of helplessness of the psalm singer, while "camps and tents" refer to the comfortable, secure spaces of the psalmist's persecutors.

The second characteristic that Hebrew poetry shares with poetry in general is its pithy, terse mode of communication. With its image-filled words, poetry conveys in a few words what prose would take scores to communicate. The words of Ps 69:15, "Do not let the floods sweep over me," and those of v. 25, "let no one live in their tents," employ a great economy of words (only eight words in Hebrew) to paint vivid

---

(Minneapolis: Fortress, 1993) 59–60.

16. For a detailed treatment of Hebrew poetic parallelism, see J. P. Fokkelman, "Parallelism: Cola and Verses," in *Reading Biblical Poetry: An Introductory Guide,* trans. Ineke Smit (Louisville: Westminster John Knox, 2001) 61–86.

17. There are, of course, many examples of English poetry that are metrical and parallel in structure.

18. Robert Alter, *The Art of Biblical Poetry* (New York: Basic Books, 1985) 151.

pictures of the sentiments of the psalm singer. To present the same sentiments in prose would require far more rhetoric, since "floods" and "tents" are not the true subjects of the singer's words, but are, as stated above, metaphoric images of real-world situations (i.e., the "target" and the "tenor").

Thus, the rhythmic speech, the poetic parallelism, the metaphoric imagery, and the terseness of the imprecatory psalms must be taken into account as we attempt to understand their role in the book of Psalms and the Hebrew Bible/Old Testament.

Ecclesial and Scholarly Interpretations of the Imprecatory Psalms

Erich Zenger, in *A God of Vengeance? Understanding the Psalms of Divine Wrath*, tells the story of Gemma Hinricher, the prioress of a Carmelite convent in Dachau, Germany—an important stop for pilgrims who travel the paths of the Nazi annihilation of the Jewish people. In 1965, the nuns were given permission to "pray the Office" (the daily prayers of the church) in German rather than in Latin. After a trial period of reciting the psalms in German, the prioress wrote:

> However, this vernacular prayer, which had become necessary and requisite for the sake of the tourists, also brought with it serious problems with our recitation of prayer in choir, because of the so-called imprecatory or vengeance psalms, and the cursing passages in a number of the psalms. We were soon tempted to return to Latin, for no matter how much the vernacular brought home to us the riches of the psalms, the Latin had at least covered up the weaknesses of the psalms as prayer. In the immediate vicinity of the concentration camp, we felt ourselves unable to say out loud psalms that spoke of a punishing, angry God and of the destruction of enemies, often in hideous images, and whose content was the desire for destruction and vengeance, in the presence of people who came into our church agitated and mentally distressed by their visit to the camp.... Our church is the only calming influence in the camp compound.... Our prayer should be such that it can encourage people to reconciliation, forgiveness, and love.... Calls for vengeance and destruction, and similar utterances, are unbearable in public utterance, and for those who pray the psalms together out loud ... the texts of cursing and calls for vengeance also introduce special psychological difficulties when there is prayer in common.

In the end, the prioress chose to eliminate the imprecatory psalms from the public observance of the Liturgy of the Hours at the convent in Dachau.[19]

---

19. Zenger, *God of Vengeance?*, 20–22. Taken from G. Hinricher, "Die Fluch- und Vergeltungspsalmen im Stundengebet," *BK* (1980) 55.

Scholars have presented, throughout the years, mixed assessments of the imprecatory psalms. Some choose to contrast the violent and vengeful God of the Old Testament with the loving and forgiving God of the New Testament, thus rendering a discontinuity between Judaism and Christianity. Artur Weiser, in his Old Testament Library commentary, states in regard to Ps 58, which contains the following words in vv. 6–8:

> O God, break the teeth in their mouths;
>> tear out the fangs of the young lions, O LORD!
> Let them vanish like water that runs away;
>> like grass let them be trodden down and wither.
> Let them be like the snail that dissolves into slime;
>> like the untimely birth that never sees the sun.

> "The psalm . . . shows the undisguised gloating and the cruel vindictiveness of an intolerant religious fanaticism; it is one of those dangerous poisonous blossoms which are liable to grow even on the tree of religious knowledge and clearly shows the limits set to the Old Testament religion."[20]

Edwin Poteat, in the 1955 edition of *The Interpreter's Bible* says of Ps 83:

> This psalm is an unedifying and tedious catalogue of bloody violence . . . these factors are largely responsible for the consensus that regards this psalm as one of the least religious of all the poems in the Psalter.[21]

Perhaps one of the most heartfelt and well-known imprecatory psalm is Ps 137, where the psalm singers cry out in vv. 8 and 9:

> O daughter Babylon, you devastator!
>> Happy shall they be who pay you back
>> what you have done to us!
> Happy shall they be who take your little ones
>> and dash them against the rock!

Hans-Joachim Kraus, in the Continental Commentary, writes of Ps 137:

> The Christian community—in situations of oppression and sadness—will take up the lament of Israel; but only with reservations and critical deliberation will

---

20. Artur Weiser, *The Psalms: A Commentary*, Old Testament Library, trans. Herbert Hartwell (Philadelphia: Westminster, 1962) 432.

21. Edwin McNeill Poteat, "Exposition on Psalms 42–89," in *The Interpreter's Bible*, vol. 4, ed. George Arthur Buttrick (Nashville: Abingdon, 1955) 450–51.

it be able to agree with the tenor of vv. 7–9 (Happy shall they be who pay you back what you have done to us!).²²

In 1962, W.O.E. Oesterley wrote that the author of Ps 137 was "a man of passionate feelings" and maintained that "among the best of those with a temperament like that, evil will at times predominate."²³ And, Howard Goodall, a renowned English composer of musicals, choral works, and television music in 2010 produced an album of psalmic choral pieces, which included Ps 137, called *The Pelican in the Wilderness*. Interestingly, the composition includes only vv. 1–7 of the psalm, omitting the imprecatory words of vv. 8 and 9.²⁴

Charles Spurgeon, though, wrote this about Ps 137:

> Let those find fault with it who have never seen their temple burned, their city ruined, their wives ravished, and their children slain; they might not, perhaps, be so velvet-mouthed if they had suffered after this fashion.²⁵

J. Clinton McCann, Jr., writes this of Ps 137 in his 1993 work *A Theological Introduction to the Book of Psalms*:

> In the face of monstrous evil, the worst possible response is to feel *nothing*. What *must* be felt is grief, rage, and outrage. In their absence, evil becomes an acceptable commonplace. To forget is to submit to evil, to wither and die; to remember is to resist, be faithful, and live again.... The psalmist in Ps 137 submits the anger to God. This submission of anger to God obviates the need for actual revenge on the enemy. For survivors of victimization, to express grief and rage and outrage is to live—to remember is to bear the pain of reliving an unutterable horror—a cross. But to remember is also to resist the forces of evil in the hope of living again—resurrection.²⁶

Walter Brueggemann maintains that the community lament psalms (and, this author adds, especially the imprecatory psalms) are a complaint that makes the shrill insistence to God that:

1. Things are not right in the present arrangement.
2. They need not stay this way and can be changed.
3. The psalm singer will not accept them in this way, for the present arrangement is intolerable.

---

22. Kraus, *Psalms 60–150*, 504.

23. W. O. E. Oesterley, *The Psalms* (London: SPCK, 1962) 549.

24. Howard Goodall, *Pelican in the Wilderness: Songs from the Psalms*, CFM, May 2010, compact disc. https://www.prestoclassical.co.uk/classical/products/7986428--goodall-pelican-in-the-wilderness.

25. Charles H. Spurgeon, *The Treasury of David: Spurgeon's Classic Work on the Psalms* (Grand Rapids: Kregel, 2004) 627.

26. J. Clinton McCann, Jr., *A Theological Introduction to the Book of Psalms: The Psalms as Torah* (Nashville: Abingdon, 1993) 119–20.

4. It is God's obligation to change things.[27]

Ethical Dimensions of Psalmic Imprecatory Language

The imprecatory words of the Psalter call upon God to take vengeance on other nations (Ps 137) and other individuals (Ps 109) who have harmed the psalmists in some way, those who have deprived the psalmists of freedom or have sought to destroy them physically, mentally, or spiritually. The words are spoken to God:

> Let them vanish like water that runs away;
>> like grass let them be trodden down and wither.
> Let them be like the snail that dissolves into slime;
>> like the untimely birth that never sees the sun. (58:7–8)

And the words are spoken to the oppressors:

> O daughter of Babylon, the one destroyed,
>> content will be the one who repays you
>>> for your doings, that which you have done to us.
> Content will be the one who seizes and dashes
>> your suckling children against the rock. (137:8–9, author's translation)

There is no way to soften the words or alter the sentiments expressed in these psalms. Each is a heartfelt cry to God, asking for God's justice to be meted out in the face of absolute despair and hopelessness. Each is a song of revenge sung on behalf of the victims of cruelty, despair, and destruction. Erich Zenger maintains:

> The cries for help or vengeance in the psalms are not about lesser or greater conflicts that could be resolved by wise generosity on the part of the one praying, or through "love of neighbor." Instead, those who pray these psalms are shouting out their suffering because of injustice and the hubris of the violent. They confront their own God with the mystery of evil and the contradiction represented by evil persons in a world that is in the care of God.[28]

Asking God to act in vengeance on behalf of a community or an individual is not an easy thing, though, to appropriate into twenty-first-century Christianity. We think of church, and most especially the worship experience, as a place and time where we are uplifted and where we praise God for God's goodness to us.

---

27. Walter Brueggemann, "The Costly Loss of Lament," in *The Psalms and the Life of Faith*, ed. Patrick D. Miller (Minneapolis: Fortress, 1995) 105.
28. Zenger, *God of Vengeance?*, 66.

The ethical questions surrounding imprecatory language are immense. J. Clinton McCann defends the importance of imprecatory words. As stated in the previous section, he sees the imprecatory cries of the psalmist as a form of release, of letting go and giving the grief, anger, and despair to God. He maintains that Ps 109, for example, "teaches us a basic principle of pastoral care: Anger is the legitimate response to victimization, and appropriate anger must be expressed. Such catharsis is healing. . . . This angry, honest prayer obviates the need for the psalmist to take actual revenge on the enemy."[29] Walter Brueggemann, again as stated in the previous section, maintains that words of lament (and imprecation) are a call to action to God from those who have been grievously wronged. He challenges the reluctance of faith communities to embrace such words in an essay titled "The Costly Loss of Lament":

> A community of faith that negates laments soon concludes that the hard issues of justice are improper questions to pose at the throne, because the throne seems to be only a place of praise. . . . If justice questions are improper questions at the throne . . . they soon appear to be improper questions in public places, in schools, in hospitals, with the government, and eventually even in the courts. Justice questions disappear into civility and docility.[30]

Joel LeMon, though, in "Saying Amen to Violent Psalms: Patterns of Prayer, Belief, and Action in the Psalter," cites a dictum in the Christian theological tradition that states *lex orandi lex credendi*—"the pattern (or rule) of prayer is the pattern of belief."[31] The violence against which the psalm singers are protesting is precisely the kind of violence they are asking God to carry out on their behalves. And thus, if one prays in this way, what effect does it have on one's moral imagination? In other words, as Joel LeMon asks, "What is the relationship between *lex orandi* and *lex agendi* when it comes to violent prayer?"[32] The imprecatory words in the Psalter are spoken to God, but the revenge sought by the psalm singer would come, in many instances, at the hands of other human beings:

> Do to them as you did to Midian,
>> as to Sisera and Jabin at the Wadi Kishon. (Ps 83:9)

> May his children wander about and beg;
>> may they be driven out of the ruins they inhabit.

---

29. McCann, *Theological Introduction to the Book of Psalms*, 115.
30. Brueggemann, "Costly Loss of Lament," 107.
31. Joel M. LeMon, "Saying Amen to Violent Psalms: Patterns of Prayer, Belief, and Action in the Psalter," in *Soundings in the Theology of Psalms: Perspectives and Methods in Contemporary Scholarship*, ed. Rolf A. Jacobson (Minneapolis: Fortress, 2011) 93.
32. LeMon, "Saying Amen to Violent Psalms," 98.

> May the creditor seize all that he has;
>> may strangers plunder the fruits of his toil. (Ps 109:10–11)

> O daughter Babylon, you devastator!
>> Happy shall they be who pay you back what you have done to us!
>
> Happy shall they be who take your little ones
>> and dash them against the rock! (Ps 137:8–9)

Brent Strawn reminds us, though, that the *lex orandi lex credendi*—"the pattern (or rule) of prayer is the pattern of belief" presented by the words of the imprecatory psalms must always be read in the context of the Psalter as a whole. He states:

> Even the harshest imprecatory psalm is housed within the larger liturgical and literary context of prayer [the Psalter], which helps to hold the violence back from one's enemies, even as it lets the violence go to God.[33]

Further, Ellen Davis and Erhard Gerstenberger ask the question, "Might the imprecatory words of the Psalter help faith communities identify *themselves* as perpetuators of violence?" Can they act as something of a mirror for readers to bring about introspection regarding the nature of vindictiveness and readers' involvement in such sentiments? Roland Murphy suggests that when violent wishes are "heard in prayer, they illumine our own feelings, and even . . . accuse us of our own acts of vengeance."[34]

And so we return to the question. Ought we to dismiss such language to the periphery of the Psalter, to a few compositions in this otherwise praise-filled book? Ought we, along with the prioress of Dachau, to eliminate these psalms from our "liturgy"? An examination of the *Revised Common Lectionary* reveals some interesting insights. While most of the so-called "psalms of vengeance" are not included in the Lectionary (Pss 12, 58, 83, 94, 109, and 129 are not), a few are, such as Ps 79:1–9. And included in the reading from Ps 79 are the words:

> Pour out your anger on the nations that do not know you,
> and on the kingdoms that do not call on your name.
> For they have devoured Jacob
> and laid waste his habitation. (v. 6)

Psalm 137—all of it—is also included, as are a number of passages that the Prioress of Dachau labeled "cursing passages." Thus, we cannot summarily eliminate these psalms from our "liturgy." We must find a way to include them in our own "canons

---

33. Brent A. Strawn, "Sanctified and Commercially Successful Curses: On Gangsta Rap and the Canonization of the Imprecatory Psalms," *ThTo* 69/4 (2013) 414.

34. Roland E. Murphy, *The Psalms, Job* (Philadelphia: Fortress, 1977) 29.

within canons" and to find within them insight into the nature of God. A look at four characteristics of the imprecatory psalms may be helpful in this endeavor:

1.   The book of Psalms, not just the imprecatory psalms, is filled with references to "the enemy" and "the oppressor." Erich Zenger maintains, "The life of the people of Israel appears overwhelmingly to be a daily struggle, an ongoing battle against enemies."[35] The people who pray the psalms feel themselves surrounded, threatened, and engaged in battle by a gigantic army of oppressors; they feel like animals pursued by hunters and trappers; or they see themselves surrounded and attacked by rapacious wild beasts, trampling bulls, or poisonous snakes. Othmar Keel, in his 1969 work, *Feinde und Gottesluegner*, lists ninety-four words used in the Psalter to describe the psalmists' enemies.[36]

But, the "enemies," "foes," and "oppressors" in the Psalter are rarely named specifically. The references are general, leaving the readers or hearers to "fill in the gap" of identity, so to speak:

> Ps 7: "Oh Lord, lift yourself up against the fury of my enemies."
>
> Ps 58: "O God, break the teeth in their mouths; tear out the fangs of the young lions, O LORD!"
>
> Ps 129: "May all who hate Zion be put to shame "

2.   The majority of the psalms that are identified as "imprecatory" are community psalms—expressing the voice of the gathered community of faith—not individual psalms expressing the voice of an individual. Psalms 12, 58, 83, 129 and 137 all express the voice of the community.[37]

3.   As we seek ways to answer the question, "Why the imprecatory psalms?" and "Why and how should we incorporate them into our worship events?" we must keep in mind that the cries for vengeance in the psalms are not about lesser or greater conflicts that could be resolved by generosity on the part of the ones praying, or through "turning the other cheek." Those who pray these psalms are shouting out their suffering because of the overwhelming injustices and abject indifferences of their foes, their enemies. Erich Zenger writes, "The psalmists confront their God with the mystery of evil and the contradiction represented by evil persons in a world

---

35. LeMon, "Saying Amen to Violent Psalms," 9.

36. Othmar Keel, *Feinde und Gottesleugner. Studien zum Image der Widersacher in den Individualpsalmen*, SBM 7 (Stuttgart: Katholisches Bibelwerk, 1969) 93–131.

37. Psalms 69, 94, and 109 are categorized as Individual Laments.

that is in the care of God."[38] The psalm singers cry out to God in the midst of an unjust world—a world in which poverty, oppression, violence, and frightful indifference seem to be ever with them.

The Imprecatory Psalms in Twenty-first-century Faith Communities

In *Performing the Psalms*, John Mark Hicks writes this about Ps 58,

> The reality of a victimized world must be taken seriously, especially when structures of power oppress the poor. Ps 58 evokes a vision of God's justice that takes the side of the oppressed over against those who abuse their power. It challenges us to enter into their experience and cry to the Lord with them. It challenges us to seek God's kingdom and God's righteousness . . . it expresses righteous indignation against structural injustice within society.[39]

The imprecatory words in the Psalter and in other books in the Hebrew Bible/Old Testament and the New Testament bespeak an aspect of reality with which humanity has grappled since the beginning of time. At each stage of the creation story in Gen 1, God declares creation "good" (vv. 4, 10, 12, 18, 21, 25). And at the completion of that creation story, God declares creation "very good" (v. 31). In the more "earthy" story of creation in Gen 2, however, God declares that it is "not good" for the human to be alone in the garden (v. 18). God creates a partner for the human as the solution for the "not good" dilemma. Humanity was created to live in community, and we are to be "strong helpers as partners"—*'e-zer ke-neg-do* (Gen 2:18–19, author's translation) to one another.

Thus the questions arise. If God created the world as "good" and "very good," and humanity was meant to live in partnership with one another, then how do we understand the violence, hatred, exploitation, and base greed in our world and how ought we to react? Walter Brueggemann reminds us that "The real theological problem . . . is not that vengeance is there in the Psalms, but that it is here in our midst. . . . The capacity for hatred belongs to the mystery of personhood."[40] As so the imprecatory words of the psalms have to do with questions of theodicy—questions of the source of, and solution for, evil in the world.

How do we appropriate the imprecatory psalms into our life of faith, into our theology, into the fabric of our communal being as the people of God?

---

38. Zenger, *God of Vengeance?*, 66.

39. John Mark Hicks, "Preaching Community Laments: Responding to Disillusionment with God and Injustice in the World," in *Performing the Psalms*, ed. David Fleer and David Bland (St. Louis: Chalice, 2005) 75–76.

40. Walter Brueggemann, *Praying the Psalms: Engaging Scripture and the Life of the Spirit*, 2nd ed. (Eugene, OR: Cascade, 2007) 64–65.

1. First, Patrick Miller writes in an essay titled "The Hermeneutics of Imprecation" that a congregation who regularly hears sermons and lessons on psalms will find the imprecatory psalms easier to appropriate into their life of faith. In that way, says Miller, the imprecatory psalms and verses are:

> placed in a larger context . . . they are abrasive pieces of a larger whole and not lifted up to a special place or made a point of focus by reading them by themselves. The rage is clear, but it is set in the context of all the psalms and in the constant listening of the congregation to the images, the deep emotions, the hyperbole—to all the strong and intense language of the Psalms.[41]

Brent Strawn echoes Miller's sentiment. He maintains:

> The continued and simultaneous praying of the Psalms and the praying of many different psalms means . . . the pray-er is given a full grammar of prayer, one that is as brutally honest as it is heart-wrenchingly beautiful.[42]

and:

> The larger Psalter exhibits that there are more ways to deal with one's enemies than just cursing them or making war against them (see, e.g., Ps 35:13–14) . . . [thus] the harshest of psalms . . . will be balanced by [in the words of C. S. Lewis] "the most exquisite things."[43]

2. Second, congregations must understand the nature of poetry in general and of Hebrew poetry in particular. The Psalter is poetry. And it must be read and interpreted as such. Poetry is evocative, emotional, image-filled, and replete with hyperbole, and it cannot, indeed must not, be read literally. Thus, the words of Ps 83 must be understood in their poetic context:

> O my God, make them like whirling dust,
> > like chaff before the wind.
> As fire consumes the forest,
> > as the flame sets the mountains ablaze,
> so pursue them with your tempest
> > and terrify them with your hurricane. (vv. 13–15)

---

41. Patrick D. Miller, "The Hermeneutics of Imprecation," in *Theology in the Service of the Church: Essays in Honor of Thomas W. Gillespie*, ed. Wallace M. Alston, Jr. (Grand Rapids: Eerdmans, 2000) 162.

42. Strawn, "Sanctified and Commercially Successful Curses," 414–15.

43. Ibid., 414–15.

A recognition of the imprecatory psalms' poetic qualities are not meant to diminish their raw and heartfelt depths, but, in order to appropriate the words into our own life experiences, understanding their poetic nature is essential.

3. Third, positing or suggesting historical settings for the imprecatory words will help congregations ground them in a real-life story-world. They provide "initial hooks" for readers/hearers—a reminder that the cries for vengeance in the psalms are not about lesser or greater conflicts that could be resolved by generosity on the part of the one praying, or through "turning the other cheek." The singers of these psalms are shouting out their suffering because of the overwhelming injustices and abject indifferences of their foes, their enemies. Recall the words of Charles Spurgeon regarding Ps 137: "Let those find fault with it who have never seen their temple burned, their city ruined, their wives ravished, and their children slain."[44]

4. Fourth, the words of the imprecatory psalms are words of giving over as much as they are words of crying out. As Clint McCann reminds us, monstrous evil *does* take place in our world. It hurts. We must speak out against injustice, inequality, and acts of violence. And in that speaking out, we give the anger and rage over to God. Erich Zenger maintains that Ps 137, for example, is an attempt, in the face of the most profound humiliation and helplessness, to suppress the primitive human lust for violence in one's own heart by surrendering everything to God—a God whose word of judgment is presumed to be so universally just that even those who pray the psalm submit themselves to it.[45] Walter Brueggemann adds:

> When we sense the need for retaliation, should we say it? Because if we say it, we challenge the veneer of cultural propriety. But if we do not say what is real to us, then the rage goes unacknowledged and unanswered, and it continues its unnoticed destructive force in our lives and the lives of our neighbors.[46]

5. But fifth and most important, giving the anger and the rage over to God does not absolve humanity of responsibility for the source of the anger and rage. When and to what extent do we act ourselves and what do we commit to the safekeeping of the God of all creation? Giving the outrage over to God does not mean giving the responsibility of the community over to God. With giving over comes not, in the words of Clint McCann, acceptance, capitulation, and indifference. With giving over comes moving past the need for human vengeance and moving on to working to

---

44. Spurgeon, *Treasury of David*, 627.
45. Zenger, *God of Vengeance?*, 48.
46. Walter Brueggemann, *From Whom No Secrets Are Hid: Introducing the Psalms*, ed. Brent A. Strawn (Louisville: Westminster John Knox, 2014) 97.

make sure that the source of what brought on the imprecatory words never happens again. As long as people are angry and vengeful against the leaders of those countries who deprive their citizens of the basic human needs of food, water, and shelter, we will never have the energy to find ways to provide folk with those basic needs. As long as we are angry and feel vengeful against those who commit violent crimes, we will never have the energy to move out into our communities and work to eradicate the root causes of those violent crimes. As long as we harbor absolute and abhorrent hate for those who commit terrorist acts, we will never have the energy to attempt to build bridges across the great divide of our world views.

This article ends where it began—with the words of Phyllis Trible. The imprecatory psalms are heartfelt, raw, angry, and difficult. Do they need to be heard? Do they need to be studied and preached and taught? Do they yield an insight into the nature and character of the God we worship? The answer to all three questions is a resounding "yes." Trible writes this of the biblical text—all of it, even the stories and passages she found difficult to integrate into her feminist journey: "I will not let go this book of words unless and until it blesses me. I will struggle with it. . . . I shall hold fast for a blessing. . . . [But] I am under no illusion that the blessing will come on my terms—that I will not be changed in the process."[47] The imprecatory words of the book of Psalms require wrestling on our part. And we are justified in demanding a blessing from them.

---

47. Trible, "Take Back the Bible," 425–31.

RESPONSE TO DECLAISSÉ-WALFORD

Meredith Faubel Nyberg

In my response to Dr. deClaissé-Walford, I come from a background of research primarily in the narrative of 1 Samuel with a focus on the literary patterns of characterization used to develop the presentation of the prophet Samuel and the first two kings of Israel, Saul and David. Thus, literary patterns are of great interest to me as they help to clarify what the reader might glean from the writings of an ancient culture composed in a different language with different literary ideals and expectations. In my response I suggest that similar literary questions may be applied to the expected pattern of elements in the psalms, including the imprecatory psalms. From this perspective, I respond to Dr. deClaissé-Walford's helpful and thought-provoking paper with a few suggestions and questions.

The paper begins with a listing of the psalms described as "imprecatory" with a definition of this term immediately following. Perhaps an introductory sentence including this definition would ease the reader into the topic with a good understanding. After offering several examples of the violence of imprecatory psalms, the main questions of the paper are offered as:

- "How are we to read and interpret these harsh and vindictive words?"
- "How do they inform our understanding of God and God's relationship with humanity?"
- "Should we read, study, pray, and preach the imprecatory psalms and the vengeance-filled words of so many of the psalms?"

These three questions suggest the threefold focus of the paper to be an improved interpretation of the imprecatory psalms, a better understanding of God, and an evaluation of the usefulness and applicability of the imprecatory psalms. With these goals set, it might be helpful for the paper to clarify its expected audience—the "we" that the author hopes to reach. Are these questions addressed to a scholarly audience, to fellow people of faith, or to both groups?

An evocative example is given of the scholar Phyllis Trible determining to ask difficult questions of the biblical text through a feminist paradigm and saying with Jacob, "I will not let you go, unless you bless me" (Gen 32:36). This example is the touchstone of the paper which challenges the reader by saying, "The imprecatory words of the book of Psalms require wrestling on our part. And we are justified in demanding a blessing from them." This prepares the reader for a certain intensity required in considering or even wrestling with the proposals made in this article.

The author's helpful overview, at the conclusion of the introduction, of the topics that the paper will discuss includes:

- "The scriptural 'status' of the imprecatory psalms and psalmic words."
- "The poetic literary style of these psalms."
- "Various scholarly and ecclesial interpretations of imprecatory language in the Psalter."
- "The ethical dimensions of such language."
- "Options for reading and appropriating the imprecatory language of the Psalter into the life of believing communities today."

The "wrestling energy" of the paper is well sustained in the first section on the status of imprecatory words as a valued part of Jewish and Christian scriptures that transcend their original audiences to become "words about God for all communities of faith across all times and places." However, the article's emphatic statement that "we cannot summarily banish the imprecatory psalms and psalmic words to the periphery of the canon" (emphasis mine) is perhaps too strong of a statement since later examples given in the paper attest that the imprecatory psalms can indeed be exiled from faith communities for various reasons.

Additionally, ideas have not yet been explored as to why a faith community might want to ban these psalms. The reader may be meant to infer that the violent language of these psalms can be overwhelming and can even be considered as R-rated by some, but it would be helpful to explore the crux of the problem. This first section does helpfully note that imprecations are not confined to the psalms but appear in passages throughout the Old Testament and are often even quoted and included in the writings of the New Testament. Truly, such a widespread biblical use of imprecatory words argues for their acceptance and usefulness for early biblical audiences, and thus also for today's audiences.

The section on the poetic and literary style of the imprecatory psalms takes a wider view of Hebrew poetry that seems to dilute the "wrestling energy" building in the paper rather than intensifying it. The arguments in this section step back to address general academic principles of psalm interpretation such as the "rhythm" of the psalms and the parallel structure of biblical poetry without explaining their relevance to the interpretation of the imprecatory psalms. Yet, as mentioned previously, my own questions at this point are more specific to the literary elements and patterning of psalms in general and how this might affect the reader's expectations and interpretation of the imprecatory psalms, including:

- What is the normal, expected pattern of a Hebrew psalm?
- Do these expected elements of a psalm generally include "enemies" or "sinful people" against whom vivid imprecations might be made?
- What is the role of the contrast between "the sinful" and "the righteous" in these psalms and might this pattern of contrast encourage the dramatic speech of imprecation?
- Does the exaggerated speech of hyperbole play into the vivid and violent images created by the imprecatory psalms?
- How might cultural patterns seen in formulas of blessing and cursing play into this violent and hyperbolic imagery of imprecation?

By asking these specific questions, I suggest that the normal psalmic patterns may include elements of contrast, drama, and hyperbole that would help to explain the strong language of the imprecatory psalms. If these elements are simply an extreme application of an expected literary pattern, then educating readers about these patterns might help them to interpret and use the psalms more effectively, including the imprecatory psalms. Toward the end of the paper some of these literary elements are briefly mentioned, including that Hebrew poetry is "evocative, image-filled, and replete with hyperbole." It might be beneficial to offer such descriptions in this earlier literary section and to discuss other aspects of poetic patterning and their possible applicability to the imprecatory psalms.

Another literary point suggested by Robert Alter in *The Art of Biblical Poetry* is his suggestion that the psalms are vocative in character—acting with the force of direct address from the psalmist to God in contrast with the common address of prophetic poetry from God to the people.[1] This difference between the poetic speakers of the Bible and their immediate intended audience might shed further light on the passionate wording of the imprecatory psalms as the psalmist cries out to God. Speaking of prophetic poetry Alter states, "Since poetry is our best human model of intricately rich communication, not only solemn, weighty, and forceful but also densely woven with complex internal connections, meaning, and implication, it makes sense that divine speech should be represented as poetry."[2] In the context of this paper, it might also make sense that such deep human emotions as pain, anger, and a desire for justice through vengeance should be expressed through the vivid imprecatory wording of the psalms.

---

1. Robert Alter, *The Art of Biblical Narrative* (New York: Basic Books, 2011) 174–75.
2. Ibid., 176.

The third section on ecclesial and scholarly approaches to these texts addresses the history behind the first question of this paper, that of how imprecatory words and psalms are to be interpreted; yet it also touches on the second question of how the imprecatory psalms inform our understanding of God and God's relationship with humanity. This section contains several powerful examples of how the imprecatory psalms have been used and rejected in different contexts, including the story of a Carmelite prioress ministering in the former death camp of Dachau in post-war Germany. When the scripture readings were changed from being chanted in Latin to being heard in the vernacular, the prioress at Dachau ultimately decided that a vocal reading of the imprecatory psalms showed "the weaknesses of the psalms as prayer" and so eliminated them from the liturgy. Her reasons for this decision create a mighty wrestling match in my own mind as she reacts against people being unbearably stirred with violent emotions in public, and perhaps it is wrong of me to judge her from my comfortable distance from Dachau in time and place. Yet my soul asks: for her visitors, haven't these strong emotions already been stirred by the stark reality of the cruel and needless suffering of Dachau? Might it actually be helpful for them to cry out in community along with the psalmist for God to take vengeance against such evil rather than carrying it home to wrestle with within themselves?

The various scholarly views following this example range widely in their estimation of the usefulness of the imprecatory psalms. Perhaps purposefully, the paper tends not to evaluate these views; yet the progression from quotes of scholarly rejection toward those of acceptance subtly implies in this section that the paper calls for the acceptance and use of these powerful psalms. It would be helpful to have a paragraph of summary conclusion to evaluate the scholarship in this section.

The fourth section on "Ethical Dimensions of Psalmic Imprecatory Language" is more evaluative of the imprecatory psalms as well as of the scholarship that considers the ethical issues they raise. It feels like the reader and author are wrestling together with God over the various scholarly ideas about the ethical implications of the imprecatory psalms being used in the community of faith or conversely being ignored. Honesty in anger and lament is explored as a positive form of release for a community of faith, bringing possibilities for cathartic healing. Points about reading the imprecatory psalms in their wider liturgical and literary context are particularly helpful. This section seems to suggest an ecclesial setting in which to process the disturbing emotions of these psalms where learning, growth, and even self-reflection can occur rather than dealing with them in isolation.

Three characteristics of imprecatory psalms are given as a way "to include them in our own 'canons within canons' and to find within them insight into the nature of God":

- Here, the author explains that "the book of Psalms, not just the imprecatory psalms, is filled with references to 'the enemy' and 'the oppressor'"—desperate prayers prayed by a people who feel oppressed and threatened. This point speaks to my previous suggestion that imprecatory psalms use hyperbolic language to take the expected literary elements of a psalm to an extreme extent.

- The majority of imprecatory psalms are "expressing the voice of the gathered community of faith." This affirms that the original audiences wrestled with these strong emotions in a communal setting while not suggesting that the same is always true today.

- These are cries to God against injustice as "the psalm singers cry out to God in the midst of an unjust world—a world in which poverty, oppression, violence, and frightful indifference seem to be ever with them." The point might be made here that these cries express faith and trust in God as the ultimate and just judge who can act at His own discretion on behalf of His people.

In the final section on "Imprecatory Psalms in Twenty-first-century Faith Communities" questions are offered that help the reader to wrestle energetically with deep theological questions such as good vs. evil and theodicy—"questions of the source of, and solution for, evil in the world." Five proposals are offered to address how the imprecatory psalms might be appropriated by the people of God, each stressing the importance of leadership and teaching within faith communities in order to provide appropriate contexts for the use and application of these moving psalms:

- The importance of teaching these psalms in the church.

- An understanding of the psalter as poetry.

- Consideration of the possible historical contexts of these psalms as written in times of deep pain and suffering.

- "The words of the imprecatory psalms are words of giving over as much as they are words of crying out" so that the sharing of these words with God may decrease the destructive force of the powerful feelings behind them.

- About injustice as a source of anger and rage, the last and most important point asks, "When and to what extent do we act ourselves and what do we commit to the safekeeping of the God of all creation? Giving the outrage over to God does not mean giving the responsibility of the community over to God."

These words suggest that the community must learn to go beyond passionate words to respond to injustice, acting alongside God. Hearkening to Trible's illustration, the powerful conclusion of this paper brings the reader back to ponder the idea of continued wrestling with the imprecatory psalms. Dr. deClaissé-Walford answers her final question, "Should we read, study, pray, and preach the imprecatory psalms and the vengeance-filled words of so many of the psalms?" with a heartfelt "yes."

JESUS AND THE *LĒSTAI*: COMPETING KINGDOM VISIONS

Jesse Nickel

Introduction

At three points in the final hours of Jesus' life the Gospel writers set Jesus in direct contrast with *lēstai* ("violent revolutionaries" sing. *lēstēs*). It appears that the evangelists have intentionally drawn our attention to the fact that in these climactic events, Jesus is mistaken as, placed in direct comparison with, and suffers the punishment of a *lēstēs*. In this paper, I will explore the significance and theological implications of this particular component of these events. Having demonstrated the important role that eschatology played in motivating the violent seditious activity carried out by first-century Jewish *lēstai*, I will argue that the most significant effect of the evangelists' juxtaposition of Jesus and *lēstai* is to highlight the crucial contrasts between their competing visions for the inauguration of the kingdom of God.

Jesus not only rejected violence as a means of accomplishing his kingdom mission, he suffered horrific violence himself. However, according to the four Gospels' unanimous presentation of the final events of Jesus' life, it is precisely as a *lēstēs*—the very sort of individual who embraced such violent means of participating in God's eschatological victory—that Jesus was arrested, condemned, and killed. This must be taken into consideration in our reading and interpretation of this central and climactic moment of Jesus' ministry, as it has clear implications for our lives as followers of the crucified king.

The Texts and the Term

Before considering the significance of the evangelists' juxtaposition of Jesus with *lēstai*, we must examine (i) the manner in which this contrast is made (i.e., the texts in which it occurs), and (ii) the precise meaning of the lexeme *lēstēs* in these narrative contexts. Although *lēstēs* does occur (albeit infrequently) elsewhere in the Gospel narratives, its presence (and / or the presence of individuals who exemplify such

The Texts

The Arrest of a Lēstēs

The first occurrence of *lēstēs* in the passion narrative is found in the Synoptic accounts of Jesus' arrest in Gethsemane. Having been confronted by the "crowd with swords and clubs, from the chief priests, the scribes, and the elders" (Mark 14:43 parr.), identified to them by Judas' greeting and kiss, and following the ill-advised attempt of one of his followers to defend Jesus with the sword, Jesus turns and chastises those who have come to take him captive with the question, "Have you come out with swords and clubs to arrest me as though I were a bandit (*hōs epi lēstēn*)?" (Mark 14:48 // Matt 26:55 // Luke 22:52).[2] These words suggest that there is something deeply incongruous between the manner in which this mob has come to take Jesus captive and his true identity—and the rest of Jesus' statement (Mark 14:49 parr.) suggests that the adversarial group ought to have known better.

The Trial of a Lēstēs

In less explicit but nevertheless clear terms, Jesus is again set in contrast to a *lēstēs* in the Gospels' accounts of his appearance before Pontius Pilate. Three of the evangelists note that it was Pilate's custom to release a prisoner to the Jewish people at Passover each year (Mark 15:6 // Matt 27:15; John 18:39a).[3] Having examined Jesus, the Roman procurator therefore presented the gathered crowds with a choice: Jesus or Barabbas (Matt 27:17; Mark 15:8–9; John 18:39b; cf. Luke 23:18)?

---

1. *Lēstēs* occurs elsewhere (i) once in each of the Synoptic accounts of the Temple Act (Matt 21:13 // Mark 11:17 // Luke 19:46); (ii) twice in Luke's parable of the Good Samaritan (Luke 10:30, 36); and (iii) twice in the Johannine Jesus' discourse on the Good Shepherd (John 10:1, 8). Jesus' statement in John 10:10, that "the thief (*kleptēs*, picking up on "thieves [*kleptai*] and bandits [*lēstai*]" in v. 8) comes only to steal and kill and destroy," certainly emphasizes the violently negative attributes associated with individuals so described. On the significance of the use of *lēstēs* in the Temple Act, see Craig A. Evans, "Jesus and the 'Cave of Robbers': Towards a Jewish Context for the Temple Action," *BBR* 3 (1993) 93–110.

2. All biblical quotations are from the NRSV, unless otherwise indicated.

3. Cf. Luke 23:17, absent from MSS P75, B, and A. The historicity of the so-called *privilegium paschale* has been debated at length; see Raymond E. Brown, *The Death of the Messiah: From Gethsemane to the Grave: A Commentary on the Passion Narratives in the Four Gospels* (New York: Doubleday, 1994) 1:794–95, 814–20 (with thorough bibliography).

Beyond his depiction in the Gospels, nothing else is known about Barabbas.[4] However, the words of the evangelists leave little doubt about the type of man this was: Barabbas is described as a notorious (*episēmos*,[5] Matt 27:16) brigand who had been imprisoned for murder (*phonos*,[6] Mark 15:7; Luke 23:19, 25) and for his participation in a recent insurrection (*stasis*,[7] Mark 15:7; Luke 23:19, 25), and is associated with other seditious individuals (*stasiastēs*,[8] Mark 15:7).[9] John sums this all up by describing Barabbas with a single word: "Now Barabbas was a bandit (*lēstēs*)" (18:40).[10] Jesus is thus placed side-by-side with one who paradigmatically embodied the *lēstēs*-identity, suggesting that, from at least one perspective, the two were not so very different from one another.

4. F. F. Bruce, *New Testament History* (Garden City: Doubleday, 1972) 203n28, notes a marginal reading found in the Syriac Peshitta and in the text of Barṣalibi that indicates a variant identifying Barabbas as an *archilēstēs*—the term used by Josephus to describe the notorious revolutionary Hezekiah father of Judas (*J.W.* 1.204; *Ant.* 14.159). I am indebted to my colleague Michael Szuk for this reference.

5. Josephus uses *episēmos* to describe John of Gischala (*J.W.* 2.585): Brown, *Death of the Messiah*, 1:797. As many commentators observe, *episēmos* is a neutral term, meaning something along the lines of "notable"—any further connotations (positive or negative) must be inferred from the context in which it used; see D. A. Carson, "Matthew," in *Matthew & Mark*, vol. 9 of *The Expositor's Bible Commentary Revised Edition*, ed. Tremper Longman III and David E. Garland (Grand Rapids: Zondervan, 2010) 23–670 (636). R. T. France, *The Gospel of Matthew*, NICNT (Grand Rapids: Eerdmans, 2007) 1054, suggests that with *episēmos*, Matthew describes Barabbas as one who would have been "notorious" (NIV, NRSV, NJB) to the Roman authorities, but "well-known" (GNB, TNIV)—in a more positive sense—to those who saw him as a freedom fighter for Jewish liberation; cf. John Nolland, *The Gospel of Matthew: A Commentary on the Greek Text*, NIGTC (Grand Rapids: Eerdmans, 2005) 1168.

6. Cf. Mark 7:21 // Matt 15:19; Acts 9:1. On whether or not Mark's wording makes Barabbas *himself* out to be a murderer, see Craig A. Evans, *Mark 8:27–16:20*, WBC 34B (Nashville: Thomas Nelson, 2001) 481; cf. Robert H. Stein, *Mark*, BECNT (Grand Rapids: Baker Academic, 2008) 701.

7. Cf. Acts 15:2; 19:40; 23:7; 23:10; 24:5. Scholars have attempted to identify the insurrection mentioned by Mark and Luke with a known historical event from the period (often trying to connect it with one account or another in Josephus; e.g., *Ant.* 18.3–10, 60–62), without much success. See, e.g., James R. Edwards, *The Gospel According to Mark*, Pillar New Testament Commentary (Grand Rapids: Eerdmans, 2002) 460–61; William L. Lane, *The Gospel of Mark*, NICNT (Grand Rapids: Eerdmans, 1974) 554.

8. Mark 15:7 marks the only use of this word in either the OG/LXX or NT (cf. the use of the cognate *stasiazō* in Judg 7:15; 2 Macc 4:30; 14:6). Josephus, however, uses *stasiastēs* quite frequently to describe the "seditious" revolutionaries he deems responsible for the war against Rome; e.g., *Ant.* 17.214; 20.227; *J.W.* 1.10, 180; 2.9, 267, 289, 411, 423, 432, 441, 452, 455, etc.

9. See Mark 15:7; Matt 27:16; Luke 23:19; cf. Acts 3:14. For further discussion of the Gospels' presentation of Barabbas, see Brown, *Death of the Messiah*, 1:796–800; W. D. Davies and D. C. Allison, *A Critical and Exegetical Commentary on the Gospel According to Saint Matthew*, ICC (London: T&T Clark International, 1997) 3:585.

10. J. Ramsey Michaels, *The Gospel of John*, NICNT (Grand Rapids: Eerdmans, 2010) 927–28, makes the striking decision to translate *lēstēs* here simply as "terrorist" (*pace* Ernst Haenchen, *John 2: A Commentary on the Gospel of John Chapters 7-21*, trans. Robert W. Funk, Hermeneia [Philadelphia: Fortress, 1984] 180, who renders it as "robber"). Further helpful commentary on John's description of Barabbas as a *lēstēs* can be found in Marianne Meye Thompson, *John: A Commentary*, NTL (Louisville: Westminster John Knox, 2015) 381–82.

The Execution of a Lēstēs

Finally, Jesus is—in morbidly concrete fashion—"set alongside" *lēstai* in his crucifixion. Among the few details that the Gospels provide about the specific physical circumstances of Jesus' execution is the fact that Jesus was crucified with two others, individuals described by both Matthew (27:38, 44) and Mark (15:27) as *lēstai*.[11] Jesus' cross is set *between* the two others; thus he goes to his death flanked on each side by a *lēstēs*.

The Term

It is thus clear that in his arrest, trial, and execution, the Gospel accounts place Jesus in direct juxtaposition with *lēstai*. However, the precise meaning of *lēstēs* is much debated, especially with regard to its use during the first century CE.[12] For this reason, scholars who have commented on the use of the lexeme in the above-noted texts have offered a diversity of opinions on how it should be interpreted and what it should be understood to contribute to the narrative depiction of Jesus. We will first briefly discuss the semantic range of *lēstēs* before considering what the literary context suggests about its meaning within our focal texts.

The Semantic Range of Lēstēs

A simple consultation of the BDAG lexicon reveals two main options for the translation of *lēstēs*. The first of these is "robber, highwayman, bandit." *Lēstēs* was widely used to describe a criminal who stole from others, distinguished from a *kleptēs* by the willingness of the *lēstēs* to use violence to accomplish his deed.[13]

---

11. Luke describes the two men as "criminals" (*kakourgoi*) (23:32, 33, 39), whereas John simply mentions "two others" (*allous duo*) (19:18).

12. Brown, *Death of the Messiah*, 687, for example, argues that *lēstēs* was never used of violent revolutionaries during Jesus' time; and Thompson, *John*, argues that "In the LXX a *lēstēs* is a lawless or violent person, but certainly not a revolutionary, let alone a freedom fighter (Hos 7:1; Obad 5; Jer 7:11, 18:22; Ezek 22:9)" (222). However, W. J. Heard and K. Yamazaki-Ransom, "Revolutionary Movements," in *Dictionary of Jesus and the Gospels*, ed. Joel B. Green, Jeannine K. Brown, and Nicholas Perrin (Downers Grove, IL: InterVarsity, 2013) 790, chronicle the frequent instances of violent uprising throughout this period, and the use of "banditry" language to describe it; cf. France, *Gospel of Matthew*, 787, who claims that the use of *lēstēs* "by first-century Jews . . . usually has a more political angle, 'insurrectionist.'"

13. This use of the term is found in the New Testament both in Luke's parable of the Good Samaritan (10:30, 36) and in Paul's description of what he has suffered as an apostle (2 Cor 11:26). Given its use alongside *kleptēs*, one could argue that this is the sense with which *lēstēs* should be understood in John 10:1, 8, as well. See G. W. Buchanan, "Mark 11.15–19: Brigands in the Temple," *HUCA* 30 (1959) 169–77, for a thorough comparison of the usages of *kleptēs* and *lēstēs* across the LXX, NT, and other Second Temple Jewish literature.

The second option—for our purposes the more significant of the two—is "revolutionary, insurrectionist, guerilla." The most proliferous use of *lēstēs* in this sense is found in the works of Josephus. Although he does occasionally use *lēstēs* to refer to robbers, highway bandits, and the like,[14] Josephus far more often uses the term to refer to revolutionary individuals; more precisely, to refer to them in a derogatory manner.[15] For Josephus, *lēstēs* primarily connotes a seditious individual; one who was unhesitating in his willingness to use violent means to accomplish the goal of Jewish liberation from their Gentile overlords.

Josephus' polemical opinion of such revolutionaries is marked by deep animosity: he portrays them as a dissolute group of false Jews, "the dregs of society and the bastard scum of the nation" (*J.W.* 5.443;[16] see 442-445), driven to pursue independence from Rome by their impiety and greed.[17] Josephus places the entire blame for the disastrous uprising on these "brigands" (*lēstai*), the "seditious" (*hoi stasiazontes*), the "deceivers" (*goētai*) who acted as "tyrants" (*tyrannoi*) in compelling the unwilling Jewish populace to join them.[18] In his eyes, the atrocities they committed—most notably, their transgression of the Law (2.517-518) and defilement of the Temple (4.157, 323; 5.402, 412)—brought God's punishment upon the whole nation.[19]

Therefore, in examining Josephus' use of *lēstēs* we must be critically conscious of the ways in which his own perspective—shaped by his personal background, present agenda, and the revolt's catastrophic results—was at work.[20] However, despite the

14. E.g. *J.W.* 2.125, 228.

15. E.g. *J.W.* 2.253-54, 274-75, 585-87; 4.504; *Ant.* 14.159-60; 15.345-48; 17.285; 20.122-24, 160-61; and frequently elsewhere; see Michael F. Bird, "Jesus and the Revolutionaries: Did Jesus Call Israel to Repent of Nationalistic Ambitions?" *Colloquium* 38.2 (2006) 136; Evans, *Mark 8:27—16:20*, 425-26.

16. Josephus is here referring specifically to Simon bar Giora and John of Gischala. All quotations from Josephus' works are from the Loeb Classical Library translations.

17. Martin Hengel, *The Zealots: Investigations into the Jewish Freedom Movement in the Period from Herod I until 70 A.D.*, trans. David Smith (Edinburgh: T&T Clark, 1989) 16, see further 183-86; cf. Richard A. Horsley, "Josephus and the Bandits," *JSJ* 10.1 (1979) 37-63.

18. For *hoi stasiazontes*, see *J.W.* 1.27; 2.266, 274, 324, 422; 4.362; 5.30, 33; for *goētai*, see *J.W.* 2.264; for *tyrannoi*, see *J.W.* 1.10-11; 2.84, 88, 208; 5.5, 11, 439; 6.98, 129, 143, and frequently elsewhere. See Richard A. Horsley, "Ancient Jewish Banditry and the Revolt Against Rome, A.D. 66-70," *CBQ* 43.3 (1981) 409-32; cf. David M. Rhoads, *Israel in Revolution: 6-74 C.E. A Political History Based on the Writings of Josephus* (Philadelphia: Fortress, 1976) 12.

19. Although various revolutionary groups undoubtedly played an important role in both the initiation of the uprising and its continuation, it seems highly unlikely that Josephus is correct in attributing the entire responsibility for the revolt to such individuals. For one possible alternative hypothesis, see Martin Goodman, *The Ruling Class of Judaea: The Origins of the Jewish Revolt Against Rome, A.D. 66-70* (Cambridge: Cambridge University Press, 1987); see further the comments of James S. McLaren, "Resistance Movements," in *The Eerdmans Dictionary of Early Judaism*, ed. John J. Collins and Daniel C. Harlow (Grand Rapids: Eerdmans, 2010) 1138-39.

20. On the question of Josephus' value as a historical source, and the ways in which his background

polemical tone with which he describes such individuals, it remains the case that (i) the Josephan corpus is unparalleled by any other first-century literary work—Jewish or otherwise—in terms of the frequency with which *lēstēs* is used, and that (ii) for Josephus, *lēstēs* clearly connotes a violent, seditious individual.

Lēstai in the Passion Narratives

In determining how we ought to interpret the uses of *lēstēs* by the evangelists, we are of course not limited to the information found in lexicons and theological dictionaries. The lexeme does not stand alone; rather, details found in the narrative contexts shed considerable light upon what sort of individuals the evangelists intend their readers to envision when they speak of *lēstai*.

GETHSEMANE

Jesus' question to the armed crowd (Mark 14:48 parr.) is rhetorical. The circumstances surrounding this incident—the fact that this mob has come to confront Jesus and his followers (i) heavily armed, (ii) in numbers, (iii) in a secluded location, and (iv) at night—suggest that it is *precisely* "as though [he] were a *lēstēs*" that they have "come out . . . to arrest [him]." In other words, by sending this mob to arrest Jesus, the Jewish leadership has betrayed its suspicion that Jesus is, or will behave as, the leader of a popular movement whose adherents will not hesitate to use violence to defend their leader, or the cause for which they stand.[21] Because of this, the mob has, understandably, come prepared for a fight. There is no expectation either that Jesus himself will come quietly, or that Jesus' followers will passively allow him to be taken away.

Jesus' statement to this hostile group is emphatically *not* because, as one commentator has suggested, he "keenly felt the shame and humiliation of being treated as a common criminal."[22] It is not some sort of wounded pride that causes Jesus to rebuke his captors; it is his *disappointment*—disappointment that these, his fellow Jews, had failed truly to *listen* to what he had been saying ("Day after day I was with

---

and contexts influenced his writing, the work of Steve Mason is particularly valuable: see, e.g., "Contradiction or Counterpoint? Josephus and Historical Method," *Review of Rabbinic Judaism* 6.2 (2003) 145-88; "Of Audience and Meaning: Reading Josephus' *Bellum Judaicum* in the Context of a Flavian Audience," in *Josephus and Jewish History in Flavian Rome and Beyond*, ed. Joseph Sievers and Gaia Lembi, JSJSup 104 (Leiden: Brill, 2005) 71-100.

21. In support of this reading, see Darrell L. Bock, *Luke 9:51—24:53*, BECNT (Grand Rapids: Baker Books, 1996) 1772; Carson, *Matthew*, 614; Donald A. Hagner, *Matthew 14-28*, WBC 33B (Nashville: Thomas Nelson, 1995) 790; Stein, *Mark*, 672-73; cf. Edwards, *Gospel According to Mark*, 439; France, *Gospel of Matthew*, 1014.

22. Lane, *Gospel of Mark*, 526.

you in the temple teaching" Mark 14:48) and *see* what he had been doing, and as a result failed to understand the character of his ministry. By coming for him as if he were a *lēstēs*, and a leader of *lēstai*, they had made clear just what sort of "deliverer" they believed Jesus to be—despite everything he had said and done to distance himself from such an identity.[23]

Trial before Pilate

As shown above, John's declaration that Barabbas was a *lēstēs* (18:40) is filled out by the Synoptic evangelists' description of him (Mark 15:7; Matt 27:16; Luke 22:19, 25). We need not make any guesses about what sort of individual this was: neither a simple thief, nor a highway bandit, but a violent and seditious individual, well-known to the Jewish crowds, in prison—and, we presume, sentenced to be crucified—for committing murder in a recent, presumably well-known insurrection.

Golgotha

The Gospels offer minimal information about the two men crucified alongside Jesus, aside from their identification in Mark (15:27) and Matthew (27:38, 44) as *lēstai*.[24] That being said, three lines of reasoning suggest that the evangelists intend their readers to see these two as violent, revolutionary individuals.

First, we can infer a fair amount from the simple fact that they were *crucified*. Studies on crucifixion in the Roman world have demonstrated that this brutal means of execution was not a punishment handed out for just any crime.[25] Not only was

---

23. It is worth noting the tragic irony of the misguided action of one of Jesus' followers (Mark 14:47 parr.)—by going on the offensive, this disciple responded to the mob *exactly* as they expected Jesus and his followers to do.

24. Or *kakourgoi* (Luke 23:32, 33, 39). This aspect of Luke's account of Jesus' crucifixion is distinguished from that of the other evangelists not only by his use of this alternative term, but also by the unparalleled interaction between Jesus and the two crucified with him (23:39–43). Some commentators have suggested that Luke's use of the term is meant to make clearer the connection between Jesus' crucifixion and his citation of Isa 53:12 in Luke 22:37 (e.g. Bock, *Luke 9:51—24:53*, 1848; John Nolland, *Luke 18:35—24:53*, WBC 35C [Nashville: Thomas Nelson, 1993] 1138). A full consideration of Luke's purpose is beyond the scope of this paper; however, it is important to note that Luke is doing something subtly different with the crucifixion than his fellow Gospel writers, something that is connected to the complex critique of empire that runs throughout Luke-Acts, to which the apparent repentance of one of the *kakourgoi* contributes. The unique aspects of Luke's account, however, also function in support of the thesis of this paper, most notably in the words of the repentant *kakourgos* to his comrade, rebuking him for joining in the mockery of Jesus: "Do you not fear God, since you are under the *same sentence of condemnation (en tō autō krimati ei)*?" (23:40b)—explicitly equating the charge for which Jesus is crucified, with that for which the *kakourgoi* have met the same fate. Luke's description of the unmistakably political charges made against Jesus by the Jewish leaders (23:1–5) is also significant in this regard.

25. Some of the more significant recent studies include David W. Chapman, *Ancient and Christian*

crucifixion physically horrific, by all accounts an excruciating way to die;[26] moreover, its public nature made it particularly effective as a form of non-verbal communication. Crucifixion was therefore most commonly the sentence given to those guilty of some form of sedition: it allowed Rome to send a clear message to those under its control, demonstrating the consequences of any action that threatened the empire's rule.[27] This suggests that in designating the two crucified alongside Jesus as *lēstai*, it is unlikely that Matthew or Mark expected their readers to take this to mean that they were common thieves or even armed robbers.[28] Given the most common use of the term elsewhere, and the extreme punishment the two men were undergoing, it is better to read the Gospels' accounts to suggest that Jesus was hung on a cross between two violent revolutionaries.

Second, some commentators have gone further, considering the possibility that the two *lēstai* were comrades of Barabbas.[29] None of the evangelists offer any explicit support to this theory, but the facts that (i) Barabbas' death sentence had been commuted only hours earlier, (ii) Mark speaks of Barabbas having been imprisoned "with the rebels (*meta tōn stasiastōn*) who had committed murder during the insurrection" (15:7), and (iii) preparation had clearly been made for the execution of a group of *three* individuals together, suggest that a connection between Barabbas and the two crucified alongside Jesus is at the very least plausible.[30] If this is indeed the case, then the charges against, and characterization of, Barabbas can by extension (within reason) be applied to the two *lēstai*.

Finally, third, we may note that all three Synoptic evangelists report that, despite the fact that they themselves were in the same sorry state, the two crucified

---

Perceptions of Crucifixion (Grand Rapids: Baker Academic, 2010) (on what Jesus' crucifixion suggests about his identity, see 225-28); John Granger Cook, *Crucifixion in the Mediterranean World*, WUNT 327 (Tübingen: Mohr Siebeck, 2014); and Gunnar Samuelsson, *Crucifixion in Antiquity: An Inquiry Into the Background of the New Testament Terminology of Crucifixion*, WUNT 2/310 (Tübingen: Mohr Siebeck, 2011); the classic treatment is Martin Hengel, *Crucifixion in the Ancient World and the Folly of the Message of the Cross*, trans. J. Bowden (Philadelphia: Fortress, 1977).

26. Note Cicero's description of it as "the worst extreme of the tortures inflicted upon slaves" (*Verr.* 2.5.66.169; see further 2.5.64.165-66.170).

27. In support of this are the references to crucifixion found in Josephus' works (e.g., *J.W.* 2.253; 5.449-51; *Ant.* 17.295; cf. Philo, *Flaccus* 83-85), which clearly associate the practice with the Roman response to Jewish uprisings. See Joel Marcus, "Crucifixion as Parodic Exaltation," *JBL* 125.1 (2006) 73-87, for a particularly intriguing consideration of this almost propagandistic aspect of the practice of crucifixion.

28. Moreover, in Roman legal terms neither of these were capital offenses; see Lane, *Gospel of Mark*, 568.

29. E.g., Carson, *Matthew*, 636; R. T. France, *The Gospel of Mark: A Commentary on the Greek Text*, NIGTC (Grand Rapids: Eerdmans, 2002) 631.

30. The possibility that Jesus was therefore crucified on a cross that had originally been set up for Barabbas is theologically suggestive; see Davies and Allison, *Matthew*, 585.

alongside Jesus joined with passers-by in mocking the crucified Jesus (Matt 27:44; Mark 15:32b; Luke 23:39). Commentators have suggested that we can perhaps gain some sense of what motivated their hostile ridicule by considering the likely way that advocates of revolt would have viewed this ignominious end to Jesus' ministry.[31] Here was one who had demonstrated unparalleled authority and power, gaining the support of a large band of followers—one through whom the long-awaited deliverance from their idolatrous Roman overlords might come. Instead, Jesus, like so many before him, has ended up on a cross; just another gruesome victim of Rome's untouchable power. Worse still, Jesus did not seem to have even put up a fight.[32] This is, admittedly, a speculative, ultimately unprovable hypothesis about the mindset of the co-crucified; however, if these two men were committed to the violent overthrow of Roman power, and had given their own lives for that cause, disappointment leading to hostile mockery seems a plausible response to Jesus' crucifixion.

The *Lēstai* of the Passion Narratives

It is therefore clear that, notwithstanding the diversity of ways the term *lēstēs* could be used in the first century, in the Gospel passages discussed above it connotes an individual who was involved in violent seditious activity. It is precisely *this* sort of figure that Jesus was treated as in Gethsemane, placed in direct comparison with by Pilate, and suffered the punishment of on the cross.[33] Having thus demonstrated the *meaning* of the term, we can now turn our attention, in the second half of this paper, to the *significance* of this noteworthy component of the Gospels' portrayal of the events leading up to and including Jesus' death.

The Eschatological Motivation of Jewish *Lēstai*

In order fully to appreciate the significance of this intentional juxtaposition of Jesus with *lēstai* in the Gospels' passion narratives, we must first make clear a central component of Jewish revolutionary violence in the Second Temple period, of which

---

31. Craig A. Evans, *Matthew*, NCBC (Cambridge: Cambridge University Press, 2012) 454; France, *Gospel of Matthew*, 1072; I. Howard Marshall, *The Gospel of Luke: A Commentary on the Greek Text*, NIGTC (Grand Rapids: Eerdmans, 1978) 871.

32. This same sense of hopes arisen, only to be ruthlessly crushed, may go some way toward explaining the hostility Jesus faced from the crowd gathered outside Pilate's headquarters.

33. Some of the most important considerations of the ways in which Jesus compares to the various types of revolutionaries of his day include William Klassen, "Jesus and the Zealot Option," in *The Wisdom of the Cross: Essays in Honor of John Howard Yoder*, ed. Stanley Hauerwas et al. (Grand Rapids: Eerdmans, 1999) 131–49; and Richard A. Horsley, "Popular Messianic Movements Around the Time of Jesus," *CBQ* 46.3 (1984) 471–95.

lēstai were representative: namely, the motivational role played by the *eschatological expectations* that were prominent within Judaism during this period.[34]

Eschatology and Revolutionary Violence in Second Temple Judaism

Since the 1948 discovery of the Dead Sea Scrolls, many New Testament scholars have focused their attention on better understanding the complex world of Second Temple Judaism.[35] Many of its aspects have, as a result, come into clearer focus. Two that stand out for their relevance to the present study are: first, the significance of *eschatology* within the Jewish worldview;[36] and second, the relatively frequent outbreaks of violent revolutionary activity, undertaken by groups of Jews against their Roman overlords (or Rome's local representatives).[37] Of particular significance to our interests is the way that these two phenomena are *connected*. Did eschatological expectations shape or motivate the revolutionary violence with which many of Jesus' contemporaries were sympathetic—if not actively involved in—and if so, how?[38]

In this section of the paper, it will be demonstrated that both literary and historical evidence supports the hypothesis that the eschatological beliefs held by those Jews who rose up against their Gentile rulers played a role in motivating them to take up the sword. Because of what they believed about (i) what God had promised to do in the future *for* his people and *against* his/their enemies, (ii) how this would come about, and (iii) the role of God's faithful people in these climactic events, many Jews in the Second Temple period were led to engage in acts of revolutionary violence, believing that to do so was to demonstrate their identity as the "true" Israel. In order

---

34. For an overview of the role of eschatology in various movements of revolt in Second Temple Judaism, see Heard and Yamazaki-Ransom, "Revolutionary Movements," 791–93; see also at greater length Hengel, *Zealots*, 229–312.

35. It is beyond the scope of this paper to offer a comprehensive discussion of this development, or, more specifically, its impact on the study of the Gospels and the figure of Jesus at their center. I will therefore proceed with the assumption that readers of this paper will have at least a basic awareness of the considerable impact that the attempt to understand Jesus within the world of first-century Judaism has had upon Gospels scholarship, especially since the 1970s. For an insightful consideration of this topic, see Markus Bockmuehl, "God's Life as a Jew: Remembering the Son of God as Son of David," in *Seeking the Identity of Jesus: A Pilgrimage*, ed. Beverly Roberts Gaventa and Richard B. Hays (Grand Rapids: Eerdmans, 2008) 60–78.

36. See, among many others, E. P. Sanders, *Judaism: Practice and Belief, 63 BCE–66 CE* (Minneapolis: Fortress, 2016) 457–94; N. T. Wright, *The New Testament and the People of God* (Minneapolis: Fortress, 1992) 280–338.

37. For overview and bibliography, see Heard and Yamazaki-Ransom, "Revolutionary Movements"; McLaren, "Resistance Movements."

38. Much of what follows in this section constitutes a summarized version of chapters 2–3 of my unpublished PhD thesis, Jesse Nickel, "The Synoptic Jesus and Eschatological Violence" (University of St Andrews, 2016).

to demonstrate the legitimacy of this claim, we turn our attention to a brief overview of some of the most significant literary and historical evidence in support of it.

Literary Expressions of Eschatological Violence

An extensive body of Jewish literature from the Second Temple period expresses eschatological expectations of one form or another.[39] A survey of these texts reveals several elements in common, including passages which depict God fulfilling his promises to deliver his people from their enemies and establish his dominion over all creation, inaugurating a new era of blessing and righteousness. Although the *means* of this forthcoming deliverance is variously portrayed, these texts unanimously attest the expectation that *all* who opposed it—both human kingdoms as well as the cosmic forces that stood behind them—would be defeated.

Violence is consistently associated with the events envisioned in these texts.[40] In the book of Daniel we read that the suffering of the "holy ones of the Most High" (7:18) gives way to the beast being put to death and destroyed with fire (7:11, 22, 26); the "king of bold countenance" is broken (8:25), and the decreed end is poured out upon the desolator (9:27).[41] In the "Animal Apocalypse" (1 Enoch 85–90), the great battle between the "sheep" (God's faithful people) and the "birds" (their wicked pagan oppressors) reaches its conclusion when the sheep are given a "large sword," and go "out against all the wild beasts to kill them" (90:19), leading to the last judgment, in which sinners are condemned and cast into an abyss of fire (90:20–27).[42] Similarly, in the "Apocalypse of Weeks" (1 Enoch 93:1–10; 91:11–17), we read of "a sword" which is given "to all the righteous, to execute righteous judgment on all

---

39. Some of the most significant examples include Daniel, 1 Enoch, Jubilees, the Testament of Moses, the Psalms of Solomon, 4 Ezra, 2 Baruch, the Sibylline Oracles, and numerous texts from the Dead Sea Scrolls.

40. Some of the most prominent descriptions of such eschatological violence can be found in Jub. 23:9–32 (esp. 23, 30); T. Mos. 10.1–10; Pss. Sol. 17 (esp. vv. 22–25); 4 Ezra 11.1–12.3, 10–29; 13.1–13, 21–56; 2 Bar. 27.1–30.5; 36.1–40.4; 53.1–76.5; and Sib. Or. 3.669–701; 4.40–48; see Philip S. Alexander, "The Evil Empire: the Qumran Eschatological War Cycle and the Origins of Jewish Opposition to Rome," in *Emanuel: Studies in Hebrew Bible, Septuagint, and Dead Sea Scrolls in Honor of Emanuel Tov*, ed. Shalom M. Paul et al., VTSup 94 (Leiden: Brill, 2003) 19–20, for a list of relevant texts from the Dead Sea Scrolls.

41. Note also that according to Alexander, "Evil Empire," 21, Dan 11:1—12:3 was the "key text" behind the depictions of eschatological war in the Dead Sea Scrolls, Pss. Sol, 1 En., 4 Ezra, 2 Bar., Sib. Or., Ass. Mos., and Rev.

42. Quotations from 1 Enoch are from George W. E. Nickelsburg and James C. VanderKam, *1 Enoch: A New Translation based on the Hermeneia Commentary* (Minneapolis: Fortress, 2004). For introduction to and commentary upon the "Animal Apocalypse," see George Nickelsburg, *1 Enoch 1: A Commentary on the Book of 1 Enoch Chapters 1–36, 81–108*, Hermeneia (Minneapolis: Fortress, 2001) 354–63; see further Anathea Portier-Young, *Apocalypse Against Empire: Theologies of Resistance in Early Judaism* (Grand Rapids: Eerdmans, 2011) 346–81.

the wicked, and they will be delivered into their hands" (91:12), after which "all the deeds of wickedness will vanish from the whole earth and descend to the everlasting pit" (91:14).[43]

However, when it comes to lengthy and detailed description of violent conflict in the eschatological age, no other text compares to the *War Scroll* (1QM).[44] The *War Scroll* documents the eschatological conflict of the archangel Michael, the heavenly armies, and the human "sons of light," against the forces of evil, led by Belial, and the human "sons of darkness." It thus makes it clear that the *Yaḥad* (the sectarian Jewish community with whom this text is identified), believing itself to be the truly righteous community of God, expected to participate in battle against their foes in the eschatological culmination of the present age.

The abundant violence of this event is beyond dispute: it will involve "savage destruction before the God of Israel, for this will be the day determined by him since ancient times for the war of extermination against the sons of darkness" (I, 9–10).[45] The armies of the sons of light "shed the blood" of the wicked (VI, 17), and it is anticipated that God will "sharpen his weapons and will not tire until all the wicked nations are destroyed" (XVII, 1[46]). Elsewhere, God is implored to "place your hand on the neck of your enemies and your foot on the piles of slain! Strike the peoples, your foes, and may your sword consume guilty flesh!" (XII, 11–12; cf. XIX, 3–4). The "sons of light" expected to be the instruments of victory wielded by God's hand to bring about an end to wickedness. In this way, "the rule of the Kittim" would "come to an end," and "[God's] exalted greatness" would "shine for all the et[ernal] times, for peace, blessing, glory and joy" (I, 6, 8–9).[47] Thus, the *War Scroll* the describes the eschatological destruction of Belial and the "sons of darkness" in graphically violent language.[48]

---

43. For introduction to and commentary upon the "Apocalypse of Weeks," see Nickelsburg, *1 Enoch 1*, 438–50; see further Portier-Young, *Apocalypse Against Empire*, 313–45; Loren T. Stuckenbruck, *1 Enoch 91–108*, CEJL (Berlin: de Gruyter, 2007) 49–152.

44. Scholarship on 1QM abounds. A good introduction to the text can be found in Jean Duhaime, "War Scroll (1QM)," in *The Eerdmans Dictionary of Early Judaism*, ed. John. J. Collins and Daniel C. Harlos (Grand Rapids: Eerdmans, 2010) 1329–30; for much greater detail see Jean Duhaime, *The War Texts: 1QM and Related Manuscripts*, Companion to the Qumran Scrolls 6 (London: T&T Clark, 2004).

45. Unless otherwise noted, all translations will be taken from Florentino García Martínez and Eibert J. C. Tigchelaar, eds., *The Dead Sea Scrolls: Study Edition*, 2 vols. (Leiden: Brill, 1997).

46. Translation of Geza Vermes, *The Complete Dead Sea Scrolls in English*, rev. ed. (London: Penguin, 2011).

47. See Annette Steudel, "The Eternal Reign of the People of God—Collective Expectations in Qumran Texts (4Q246 and 1QM)," *RevQ* 17 (1996) 517, see further 517–24.

48. For further examples see 1QM III, 8; VIII, 8–9, 16–18; IX, 1–2; XVI, 7, 9; XVII, 12–13.

This brief selection of the literary evidence available thus demonstrates that Second Temple Jewish eschatological expectations almost unanimously include elements that can be described as "violent"[49] to one degree or another, and that such violence was primarily associated with two components of the eschatological fulfillment: (i) the judgment/destruction of the wicked; and (ii) the deliverance of God's faithful people. But did this expectation of future violence have any real-world consequences in the *present*? Did it make any difference to how Jews in first-century Palestine actually lived?

Eschatological Motivations in Jewish Revolutionary Violence

The impact of these eschatological expectations can be demonstrated by examining the historical sources which document outbreaks of Jewish revolutionary violence in the Second Temple period. Although such incidents appear to have been frequent,[50] three were of particularly large scale and impact: the Maccabean Revolt (167–164 BCE), the Jewish-Roman War (66–70 CE), and the Bar Kokhba Revolt (132–135 CE). The historical evidence for each of these conflicts—found in sources including the books of 1 and 2 Maccabees, the writings of Josephus, and a variety of epigraphic, numismatic, and archaeological data—suggests that eschatology functioned as a motivational and ideological factor in each one. In other words, the Jews who took up the sword against their Gentile oppressors did so, at least in part, because of what they believed about what would occur in the last days of the present age, and what the role of faithful Israel would be in these events: in the days to come, YHWH would fulfill his promises to deliver his people from the hands of their enemies, judge the wicked, and inaugurate the eternal age of blessing—and *righteous human violence* would be *integral* to these events coming to pass.

The motivational significance of eschatology in Second Temple Jewish revolutionary conflict is demonstrated by numerous elements of the historical sources. These include (i) the language of *sōteria* ("salvation, deliverance") coming about through the Maccabean victories (1 Macc 3:6; 5:62), given the eschatological

---

49. We should note here that "violent"/"violence" have become rather difficult terms to define, because of the flexibility with which they have been used in recent scholarship. A helpful discussion can be found in Thomas R. Yoder Neufeld, *Killing Enmity: Violence in the New Testament* (Grand Rapids: Baker Academic, 2011) 1–8.

50. Note Josephus, *J.W.* 6.329; *Ant.* 14.77. Tacitus' claim that *sub Tiberio quies* (*Hist.* 5.9, "under Tiberius all was quiet") should not be read to suggest the complete absence of revolutionary activity during Tiberius' reign, but rather the lack of any *major* conflict: see Wright, *New Testament*, 172. For a helpful overview of 164 BCE–66 CE (the years between the end of the Maccabean Revolt and the outbreak of the Jewish-Roman war), see Emil Schürer, *The History of the Jewish People in the Age of Jesus Christ (175 B.C.–A.D. 35)*, 3 vols. (Edinburgh: T&T Clark, 1973) 1:243–483.

associations of this term elsewhere;[51] (ii) the blessedness of the land under Simon's rule, described using "golden age" language (1 Macc 14:4-15; cf. Isa 17:2; 36:16; Mic 4:4; Zech 3:10);[52] (iii) Josephus' description of the "fourth philosophy" and its passion for *eleutheria* ("freedom") and the sole rule of God (*Ant.* 18.9-10, 23; cf. *J.W.* 2.118);[53] (iv) Josephus' identification of the *chrēsmos amphibolos* ("ambiguous oracle") as the foremost cause of the revolt against Rome (*J.W.* 6.312-13a);[54] (v) numerous passages in which Josephus refers to the people's expectation of "signs of deliverance" from God (*J.W.* 2.259; cf. 6.283-85); and (vi) the evidence that Bar Kokhba was hailed as Messiah.[55] Material remains dating to these events give the same impression: numismatic evidence attests the centrality of eschatologically-significant terms such as "freedom" and "redemption" to the revolutionary ideology,[56] and the association of the Hebrew title *nsy'* ("prince," cf. Ezek 37:25; 44-46) with Bar Kokhba suggests that he was acclaimed as the eschatological ruler who would defeat the enemies of God's people and usher in the age to come.[57]

Finally, we must not ignore the clear precedents for such violence found in the biblical narrative itself. 1 Maccabees 2:51-60 is instructive in this regard, drawing the revolt initiated by Mattathias into the history of Phinehas, Joshua, David and

---

51. E.g., Exod 15:2; Isa 12:2; 45:17; 46:13; 49:6; 49:8; 52:7; 52:10; and 59:11; see further John J. Collins, "Messianism in the Maccabean Period," in *Judaisms and Their Messiahs at the Turn of the Christian Era*, ed. Jacob Neusner et al. (Cambridge: Cambridge University Press, 1987) 103-4.

52. See Wright, *New Testament*, 429.

53. On *eleutheria* and its significance within revolutionary Judaism, see William Horbury, *Jewish War Under Trajan and Hadrian* (Cambridge: Cambridge University Press, 2014) 136-42, 146-49; cf. James S. McLaren, "Going to War Against Rome: The Motivation of the Jewish Rebels," in *The Jewish Revolt Against Rome: Interdisciplinary Perspectives*, ed. Mladen Popović, JSJSup 154 (Leiden: Brill, 2011) 129-53 (137-43). On the longing for the new manifestation of the rule of God in Israel, see Wright, *New Testament*, 302-7. For further discussion of the "fourth philosophy" and debates about its precise identity and association with other revolutionary groups active in the first century CE, see Heard and Yamazaki-Ransom, "Revolutionary Movements," 794-95.

54. For discussion of the possible referent of the "ambiguous oracle," see Anthony J. Tomasino, "Oracles of Insurrection: The Prophetic Catalyst of the Great Revolt," *JJS* 59.1 (2008) 92-94.

55. Most notably y. Ta'an. 4:8, 68d; see Horbury, *Jewish War*, 378-89; also Peter Schäfer, "Bar Kochba and the Rabbis," in *The Bar Kokhba War Reconsidered: New Perspectives on the Second Jewish Revolt Against Rome*, ed. Peter Schäfer, TSAJ 100 (Tübingen: Mohr Siebeck, 2003) 2-5.

56. See James McLaren, "Theocracy, Temple and Tax: Ingredients for the Jewish-Roman War of 66-70 CE" (paper presented at the Annual Meeting of the SBL, Atlanta, GA, November 21, 2004) 19-20, 23-24; also William Horbury, "Liberty in the Coin-Legends of the Jewish Revolts," in *On Stone and Scroll: Essays in Honor of Graham Ivor Davies*, ed. J. K. Aitken et al., BZAW 420 (Berlin: de Gruyter, 2011) 139-52; McLaren, "Going to War," 144-49; Ya'akov Meshorer, *A Treasury of Jewish Coins From the Persian Period to Bar Kokhba* (Jerusalem: Yad Ben-Zvi, 2001).

57. The title *nsy'* is found frequently on coinage from the first year of the revolt, as well as on documents discovered in the Judean desert: Schäfer, "Bar Kochba," 15; see further Horbury, *Jewish War*, 358-62; for description of the eschatological role of the *nsy'*, see CD VIII, 18-21; 1Q28b V, 20-22, 23b-29.

Elijah. This clearly shows that Jewish revolutionaries in the Second Temple period looked back not just to the Maccabees but, beyond them, to the tradition of *zeal for YHWH* that runs throughout the biblical narrative. Such zeal was often manifested in righteous acts of violence against the enemies of God and his people.[58]

Taken together, this evidence convincingly demonstrates that Second Temple Jews who took up the sword against their Gentile oppressors did so for more than simply "political" or "nationalistic" reasons. Integrated within the Jewish worldview, politics and nationalism were inseparable from beliefs about who God was, how he related to his people, and what he had promised them with regard to the days to come—that is, from *eschatology*. The formative role that eschatology played in determining how first-century Jews perceived and acted in the world therefore suggests that it was central to both (i) the motivation behind instances of violent uprising; and (ii) the ways in which these events were perceived at the time of their enactment.

Eschatological Violence in Second Temple Judaism, and *Lēstai* in the Gospels

Therefore, the literary and historical evidence leads me to argue that "eschatological violence"—that is, violent action motivated by eschatological expectations and/or oriented toward eschatological goals—was prevalent in the world of Second Temple Judaism; and, more specifically, in the first-century Palestinian world of Jesus and the Gospels.

The significance of this argument to the present study derives from the fact that *lēstai* such as those with whom Jesus is contrasted by the evangelists are *precisely* the sort of individuals for whom such "eschatological violence" would have been of central ideological significance. In other words, the historical and literary evidence surveyed above makes it likely that we should see these *lēstai* as representatives of the belief that to take up the sword in zealous violence against Rome was (i) to participate in the foretold eschatological judgment upon and destruction of the wicked, thus contributing to the inauguration of the age to come, and (ii) to mark oneself out as one of the holy, faithful, and righteous people of God, who, vindicated as such, would receive God's eschatological blessing.

---

58. Josephus frequently names "zeal" as a motivational factor in Jewish revolutionary activity (e.g., J.W. 2.230; 3.9; 5.21, 100; 6.79; 7.270). On the centrality of "zeal" to first-century Jewish revolutionary movements, see Hengel, *Zealots*, 146–228; Klassen, "Jesus and the Zealot Option," 136, 145–46. For further consideration of the trajectory of violence in the Old Testament, see John J. Collins, "The Zeal of Phinehas: The Bible and the Legitimation of Violence," *JBL* 122.1 (2003) 3–21; Jerome F. D. Creach, *Violence in Scripture*, Interpretation (Louisville: Westminster John Knox, 2013) 17–216.

Competing Kingdom-Visions: Jesus and the *Lēstai*

This paper has thus far demonstrated two main points: first, that in their passion narratives, the evangelists *explicitly* and *intentionally* contrast Jesus with *lēstai*—that is, violent revolutionaries; and, second, that the *lēstēs*-identity was rooted in a particular understanding of the Jewish eschatological hope, which resulted in certain expectations regarding the role of faithful Israel in the inauguration and fulfillment of these events. If these points are found to be convincing, how does this impact our understanding of the significance of the evangelists' explicit threefold juxtaposition of Jesus with *lēstai*, as well as its theological implications? It is to this question that we turn our attention for the rest of this paper.

Jesus as the Anti-*Lēstes* in the Passion Narrative

First, we must note the fact that the events leading up to and including Jesus' death stand in *direct* contrast to the eschatological hopes embraced by the *lēstai*. What is more, by making such explicit reference to *lēstai* at these three particular moments, the evangelists appear to have made an effort to make this contrast as clear as possible to their readers.

Gethsemane

When confronted by an armed band of adversaries, Jesus does not draw a weapon, shout something akin to the rallying cry of Mattathias—"Let everyone who is zealous for the law and supports the covenant come out with me!" (1 Macc 2:27b)—and enter the fray, invoking the armies of heaven to lend him assistance (cf. Matt 26:53). Instead of praising the bravery and zeal of the follower who struck the servant of the high priest, Jesus *rebukes* him, telling him to put away his sword; instead of dealing out injury and death to these apostate Roman-collaborators, Jesus *heals* the wounded one; instead of resisting, Jesus *submits*, acknowledging that "this is [their] hour, and the power of darkness" (Luke 22:53b).

Trial before Pilate

When Jesus is set alongside Barabbas, one who had fully embraced the *lēstēs*-identity and participated in eschatologically-motivated revolutionary violence, we are confronted by just how fundamentally distinct Jesus' character and actions were from those of this "notorious" prisoner. Barabbas, "the one who had been put in prison for insurrection and murder" (Luke 23:25), found the favor of the crowd, in whose eyes he represented a continued hope that their deliverance could be fought for; Jesus, on the other hand, received the fruit of the crowd's bitter disappointment: rejection and condemnation.[59]

Golgotha

Finally, Jesus is hung upon a Roman cross: the same end to which so many failed revolutionaries before him had come. Flanked by two *lēstai*, we are forced to confront the fact that this is an *end* for them: whatever they had hoped to accomplish by participating in the recent *stasis* ("insurrection") had failed, as they were now in the process of a slow, humiliating, painful death—a death that had come without seeing any sign of the kingdom's inauguration. Jesus dies alongside them, *as one of them*, crucified as one who posed a seditious threat to the empire, suffering the punishment for crimes of which he is entirely innocent.[60]

Contrasting Eschatological Visions

The presence of *lēstai* and all that they represent thus throws Jesus' identity into sharp relief. With this juxtaposition, the evangelists are not simply holding up two types of people next to one another. More significant than a contrast between one who embraced and advocated the nonviolent love of enemy and those who embraced and advocated revolutionary violence is the contrast between the eschatological vision each represented. In other words, by setting Jesus alongside *lēstai*, the evangelists juxtapose two visions of the inauguration of the kingdom of God, and the identity of those who belong to it.

Both Jesus and the *lēstai* firmly believed the promises YHWH had made to his people—that he would one day act in faithful righteousness to bring deliverance, vindication, and blessing for his people, and judgement upon their oppressors. What set them apart is the different way each would have answered two key questions: (i) How would this come about? and (ii) What would identify the truly faithful children of God?

---

59. For further consideration of the implications of and possible reasons for the choice made by the crowd, see France, *Gospel of Matthew*, 1050; Nolland, *Luke*, 1133; cf. Bock, *Luke 9:51—24:53*, 1833. Gerd Theissen's historical novel *The Shadow of the Galilean*, trans. John Bowden (London: SCM, 1987), offers an engaging imaginative portrayal of the different "ways" represented by Jesus and Barabbas, expressed most powerfully in Barabbas' letter to the protagonist Andreas (196-97).

60. France, *Gospel of Matthew*, 1068, is one of the few commentators who makes a similar observation about the manner of Jesus' execution, calling it a "harsh irony"; cf. Davies and Allison, *Matthew*, 616; France, *Gospel of Mark*, 594-95.

On the one hand were the *lēstai*, those Jews who, looking back at Israel's past, believed that when God made good on his word, it would involve the participation of those who were so zealous to preserve Torah and protect the holy name of YHWH that they were willing to kill or be killed for this cause. What is more, they hoped that such righteous action, as well as the shed blood of the saints, might contribute to the hastening of that great and terrible day of YHWH. When God *did* act, it would be those like themselves—those who would take up the sword in order to see the eschatological hopes of Israel fulfilled—that would be rewarded, recognized as the truly faithful children of God, and welcomed into God's kingdom.

On the other hand was Jesus, one whose entire public ministry had been oriented around his proclamation that "the kingdom of God has come near" (Mark 1:15); who suggested that in his ministry of healing and exorcism, the hopes of Israel were, in fact, being fulfilled *now*—for those with eyes to see (Matt 11:2–6). In the course of this ministry of mighty words and deeds, Jesus had steadfastly rebuked even the *suggestion* of engaging in violence against those who opposed him (see, e.g., Luke 9:51–56; 13:1–5; Matt 26:52–54), and taught his followers that it is the peacemakers, those who "love [their] enemies and pray for those who persecute [them]" who would thus identify themselves as the *true* "children of your Father in heaven" (Matt 5:44–45). Jesus made it clear that the enemy of the kingdom he was inaugurating was neither Rome nor any other human empire—since Jesus' kingdom-proclamation was ultimately not just for ethnic Israel, but for *all* who would hear and obey his teaching (Matt 28:19)—but the "ruler of this world" (John 12:31), the Satan, to whom had been given over the authority and power of all the kingdoms of the world (Luke 4:6). In order to play his part in the inauguration of the eschatological kingdom of God, and the victorious defeat of its enemies, Jesus did not shed the blood of the Gentile oppressors or their Jewish collaborators, but had his *own* blood shed, as he was executed with ruthless efficiency on a Roman cross. In that very moment—so his earliest followers tell us (e.g. Col 2:15)—Jesus won the crucial victory over the *true* enemy of God's kingdom. In so doing, Jesus provided an example for his followers, telling them that it is those who do likewise, "who take up their cross and follow me," "who lose their life for my sake, and for the sake of the gospel" (Mark 9:34, 35), who will inherit the kingdom.

Therefore, what distinguished Jesus from the *lēstai* was not simply their differing positions on violence, but their understanding of the *role* of such violence (or the lack thereof) in the inauguration of God's kingdom and identification of those who belong to it. Both Jesus and the *lēstai* believed themselves to be working toward, even contributing to, the inauguration of God's eschatological reign: the *lēstai* by engaging in seditious, violent activity against the Romans; Jesus by teaching, healing, casting out demons, and, ultimately, going to the cross.

The Victorious Jesus: A Failed *Lēstēs*

This last point—Jesus' crucifixion—is where this contrast makes itself most apparent, in no small part because of the evangelists' threefold reference to *lēstai* in the narrative leading up to and including this event. The juxtaposition between Jesus and the *lēstai* highlights one point more than any other: Jesus dies the death of a *lēstēs*—he suffers the punishment due to a violent revolutionary, the fate of one who embraced the ideology of eschatologically-motivated revolutionary violence. By holding Jesus up against such individuals in his arrest, trial, and execution, the evangelists confront their readers with the puzzling reality that, as he goes to his death, Jesus does so as one perceived as, compared to, and treated like a *lēstēs*. Executed on a Roman cross, *Jesus dies as a failed lēstēs*.

Yet the Gospels do not present Jesus' arrest, trials, and finally crucifixion as the *failure* of his kingdom mission. Rather, almost unbelievably, their accounts of this event make it clear that it is precisely in his submission to the powers of darkness, resulting in his death on the cross, that the decisive and climactic *victory* of Jesus' ministry is won.

This bears restating. As the events of the passion narrative draw ever closer to his death, the meaning of Jesus' crucifixion can be seen from two remarkably distinct perspectives: on the one hand, Jesus is shamefully treated by all those around him as a *lēstēs*—as one whose eschatologically-driven ethic contrasted with his own, in deeply significant ways: he is arrested, condemned, and unsentimentally hung on a cross to die. On the other hand, Jesus goes to his death trusting in God's will, without recourse to violence but instead taking violence upon himself, thus remaining faithful to and consistent with the character of his ministry from the beginning, and "obedient to death—even death on a cross" (Phil 2:8). What is more, *because of* this supreme act of faithfulness and self-giving love, Jesus is vindicated by God in his resurrection and rewarded in his exaltation to God's right hand (Phil 2:9–11).

In bringing the contrast between Jesus and the *lēstai* to the foreground in the events leading up to and including Jesus' crucifixion, the evangelists make it clear that, rather than this death representing the *failure* of an eschatological vision—as it did for any who would have seen Jesus in the guise of a *lēstēs*—it represented the climactic fulfillment of his ministry of the nonviolent inauguration of the kingdom of God, an act through which Jesus himself made peace for all of humanity, in his own flesh putting hostility itself to death (Eph 2:14–16). Jesus' crucifixion thereby put to death also the suggestion that God's eschatological victory would be in any way effected through the zealous violence of his followers against those they perceived to be the enemies of God, no matter how righteous they believed their own actions to be. Instead, Jesus' death as a *lēstēs* and alongside *lēstai* stands as the ultimate example of loving one's enemies, of being a peacemaker, and thus of being a true child of our Father in heaven (Matt 5:9, 44–45)—the paradigmatic embodiment of the character of the God whose kingdom this death inaugurated.

Conclusion

I have argued that in their accounts of Jesus' arrest, trial before Pilate, and crucifixion, the evangelists place Jesus in clear juxtaposition with *lēstai*; that is, with violent revolutionaries. Having demonstrated that Jewish revolutionary violence in the Second Temple period was eschatologically motivated, I then argued that this suggests that the threefold contrast between Jesus and *lēstai* at this climactic point of his ministry is intended to make explicit their distinct visions for the inauguration of the kingdom of God. How would this take place? What would it look like when God brought about the glorious fulfillment of his promises to forgive, free, redeem, and restore his people? Who *were* God's people, the true "children of God," those who would inherit this promised blessing? What would identify them? The crucial distinction between Jesus' answers to such questions, and the answers of the *lēstai*, was the role they saw violence playing in these eschatological events.

Therefore, the Jesus–*lēstai* juxtaposition, and the distinction it draws to our attention, serves to underscore the powerful mystery, irony, and wonder of the cross: Jesus, the one who proclaimed and inaugurated the kingdom of God without violence, who called his followers to be peacemakers, suffered the horrific violence of the cross, the punishment given to those who embraced violence as a means of participating in God's work of deliverance, and in this very act, the eschatological victory of God in Jesus was won—not by the sword, but by self-giving love.

RESPONSE TO NICKEL

Rebekah Eklund

I appreciated reading Dr. Nickel's thoughtful paper and wholeheartedly agree with his overarching claim that the gospels contrast Jesus' nonviolent, self-giving love with the way of violent revolution. I would, however, like to pose a few questions about the paths that the paper takes to arrive at that claim.

The Gospels' Portrayal of Jesus

Nickel claims that all four gospels intend to contrast Jesus with a *lēstēs*, that is, a "violent revolutionary." Nickel convincingly demonstrates that the semantic range of *lēstēs* includes that of a revolutionary, and that it is likely that the gospels sometimes (but not always) used the word in this way. At the same time, I wonder if Nickel occasionally stakes too much on this specific word, and if some attention to the different language used by the gospels may have strengthened his argument. For example, at the start of his paper Nickel cites a handful of key texts from three scenes in the passion narratives—the arrest of Jesus in Gethsemane, the trial before Pilate, and the crucifixion— not all of which use *lēstēs*. Each of these scenes deserves further attention in relation to the question of whether all four evangelists consistently intend to contrast Jesus with violent revolutionaries.

The Arrest of Jesus

Nickel proposes that the Jewish leaders arrest Jesus because they believe him to be a violent revolutionary, an argument that stems in part from Jesus' question to them in Gethsemane, as reported in the three Synoptics: "Have you come out against me as a *lēstēs*, with swords and clubs . . . ?" (Matt 26:55; Mark 14:48; Luke 22:52). This retort alludes to Jesus' earlier accusation against these very leaders, also made in the three Synoptics, that *they* have made the temple into a den of *lēstai*—namely, a den of thieves who are extorting the people they are meant to be protecting (Matt 21:13; Mark 11:17; Luke 19:46). In this latter case, *lēstēs* does not appear to indicate a violent revolutionary. Earlier, the three Synoptic evangelists have suggested that the Jewish leaders arranged to have Jesus arrested at night to avoid provoking the *people*—the leaders seem to be worried about the crowds starting a riot, not Jesus or his disciples (Matt 26:3–5; Mark 14:1–2; Luke 22:2). In John, similarly, the chief priests fear that Jesus' popularity with the people might attract Rome's attention and lead to the destruction of the whole nation (11:47–50; 18:14).[1] These details imply that the Jewish leaders do fear Jesus (and the possibility of violence), but not that they view Jesus as a violent rebel.

Barabbas

In the scene where Pilate offers a choice between Jesus and Barabbas, Matthew refers to Barabbas as a "notorious prisoner" (*desmion epismon*) (Matt 27:16); Mark groups Barabbas with "the rebels [*stasiastai* . . . during the insurrection [*stasis*]" (Mark 15:7); Luke says that Barabbas was in prison for "an insurrection [*stasis*]" in the city (Luke 23:19);[2] and John calls Barabbas a *lēstēs* (John 18:40). Even without using the term *lēstēs* (for the Synoptics do not), all four gospels certainly present Barabbas and Jesus as two contrasting options, even as opposites. Indeed, scholars like Adela Yarbro Collins have argued on historical grounds that the people's embrace of Barabbas echoes the history of the Jewish-Roman War by pointing to their rejection of the nonviolent way espoused by Jesus and their acceptance of leaders like Barabbas who "led them into a brutal and destructive war."[3]

Crucifixion

But do all four gospels likewise present the two men crucified alongside Jesus as representatives of that polar choice?[4] On a historical level, Nickel shows that it is *possible* that the other two are being crucified as rebels, since crucifixion was "most commonly the sentence given to those guilty of some form of sedition," but as he also notes it is certainly not the *only* reason for crucifixion.[5] At a narrative level, the four evangelists describe the two co-crucified men in significantly different ways.

---

1. D. Moody Smith, *John Among the Gospels* (Columbia: University of South Carolina Press, 2001) 220–21. Historically speaking, Markus Bockmuehl proposes that Jewish opposition to Jesus likely stemmed not from fears that he was fomenting a revolt but from his supposed crimes of sorcery and false prophecy; see Bockmuehl, "Resistance and Redemption in the Jewish Tradition," in *Redemption and Resistance*, ed. Markus Bockmuehl and James Carleton Paget (New York: T&T Clark, 2009) 65–77.

2. For an exploration of which insurrection Luke may have in mind, see Joel Marcus, *Mark 8–16*, AB 27A (New Haven: Yale University Press, 2009) 1029–30.

3. Adela Yarbro Collins, *Mark*, Hermeneia (Minneapolis: Fortress, 2007) 721.

4. Nickel is careful to say that "none of the evangelists offer any explicit support" to the theory that the two bandits are not only *lēstai* but are also companions of Barabbas.

5. So Bockmuehl, "Resistance and Redemption in the Jesus Tradition," 69 n12 and n13.

Matthew and Mark call them *lēstai* (Matt 27:38; Mark 15:27); Luke uses "criminals" (*kakourgoi*) (Luke 23:33, 39); and John doesn't identify them at all, calling them only "two others" (*allous duo*) (John 19:18). Thus, while John is the only evangelist to use the specific word *lēstēs* to describe Barabbas, he applies it neither to Jesus (at his arrest) nor to the two other crucified men. In Luke's Gospel, the evangelist appears to be drawing a different comparison: Luke's description of the two co-crucified men as "criminals" or "evil-doers" (Luke 23:33, 39) provides the backdrop to the centurion's confession of Jesus as *dikaios*—the righteous or innocent one (Luke 23:47).

Eschatology and Violence

This brings us to Nickel's second claim, that *lēstai* were eschatologically motivated, and sought to use violent means to usher in the kingdom of God. This advances a similar claim made by Martin Hengel, who painted a sharp contrast between the Zealots and the Jesus movement (a contrast later popularized through the influence of John Howard Yoder). Hengel writes, "In Zealotism and early Christianity, two eschatological messianic movements were firmly opposed to each other."[6]

I will pose two questions in relation to this second claim:

1. How strong is the evidence that eschatological views did motivate violent action?

2. What was the intended and actual function of Jewish apocalypses?

Eschatological expectations of that era were notoriously varied and complex. Nickel does a thorough job exploring several texts that presume and perhaps even advocate for violence in the eschatological end-times. It's less clear, however, that these same texts—or the types of ideas contained in them—led in a direct way to actual revolt in practice. The *War Scroll* (1QM), for example, emerged from the Qumran community, a sectarian community who had withdrawn to the desert and, as far as we know, did not engage in any form of violent uprising. While the Maccabean revolt had obvious *theological* underpinnings, it did not necessarily have *eschatological* motivations.[7]

Nickel makes a stronger case that it is possible to find eschatological motivation in the uprisings of 66–70 CE and 132–135 CE. On the other hand, as Martin Goodman writes in relation to the Bar Kokhba revolt, "None of the contemporary

---

6. Martin Hengel, *The Zealots* (Edinburgh: T&T Clark, 1989) 301; see also Bockmuehl, "Resistance and Redemption in the Jesus Tradition," 66.

7. John J. Collins, "Messianism in the Maccabean Period," in *Judaisms and their Messiahs*, ed. Jacob Neusner, William S. Green, and Ernest Frerichs (Cambridge: Cambridge University Press, 1987) 103–4.

evidence ... unequivocally suggests eschatological fervor."[8] Similarly, evidence in Josephus's "ambiguous oracle" is similarly, well, ambiguous. While Goodman focuses on messianic hopes in particular, rather than eschatological beliefs more generally, he concludes, "evidence is negligible that messianic hope had any political effect in Judaea over the sixty years between 70 and 130."[9]

Therefore, it is not impossible that eschatological views sometimes did motivate violent uprisings. But it seems just as likely that some violent uprisings, and therefore some *lēstai*, had no eschatological hopes that their actions would usher in the kingdom of God, and could be motivated, say, by "zeal for Yahweh" or the restoration of kingly rule (a theological concern but not necessarily an eschatological one). Additionally, many of those who longed for eschatological vindication—perhaps even some of those who penned the apocalyptic literature cited by Nickel—chose other, nonviolent paths of resistance.

Jewish Apocalypses of Resistance

For this latter claim, I appeal to Anathea Portier-Young's *Apocalypse against Empire*, which Nickel cites in his discussion of 1 Enoch. For Portier-Young, "The first Jewish apocalypses emerged as a literature of resistance to empire," with a "message of faithfulness and hope."[10] Portier-Young is clear that she finds not one apocalyptic theology of resistance in the texts but rather multiple theologies of resistance.[11] For example, the writer of Daniel "advocated a stance of faithful waiting for God to act" through "nonviolent resistance and covenant obedience," whereas another group, represented in the Apocalypse of Weeks and the Book of Dreams (in *1 Enoch*), "expected that when God intervened, God would also arm the righteous remnant for victory against their oppressors."[12] Even in the case of *1 Enoch*, however, it is not clear whether the righteous take matters into their own hands to usher in the

---

8. Martin Goodman, "Messianism and Politics in the Land of Israel, 66–135 C.E.," in *Redemption and Resistance*, ed. Markus Bockmuehl and James Carleton Paget (New York: T&T Clark, 2009) 156 (149–57).

9. Ibid., 154. Goodman further speculates, "[U]ncertainty about the nature of the messianic age may have prevented hopes for a messiah providing the driving force for political action except in the most extreme circumstances and among self-selected groups" (157). On Josephus' "ambiguous oracle" see ibid., 151–53; for Shimon Bar Kosiba (alternatively Bar Kokhba), see ibid., 155–56.

10. Anathea Portier-Young, *Apocalypse against Empire: Theologies of Resistance in Early Judaism* (Grand Rapids: Eerdmans, 2011) xxii.

11. Ibid., 4.

12. Ibid., 219.

kingdom, or whether they "wait on God's future action to equip them for their work of judgment."[13]

There is another book that may be relevant to our exploration of the function of apocalyptic literature, and that is a Jewish-Christian apocalypse: the book of Revelation. Like the apocalyptic literature cited by Nickel, it contains graphic depictions of end-time violence, both angelic and human. Yet it is not (in my view) proposing that the faithful will inaugurate the kingdom through their own violent actions—quite the contrary!—and it did not inspire revolutionary violence among its original readers. Rather, one of its main purposes seems to be precisely one of the functions of Jewish apocalypses as identified by Portier-Young: to undermine and relativize the rule of the empire, to show its contingency in relation to the eternal rule of God.[14] For example, Portier-Young argues that Daniel's visions reassured the faithful that, despite Antiochus's desecration of the temple, "there had been no interruption in the provident care of God . . . for service before God's heavenly throne had not ceased."[15] Substitute "Domitian" for "Antiochus," and that could be an apt description of Revelation. I wonder, then, if it might strengthen Nickel's argument to situate Jesus within this complex set of apocalyptic thought, by seeing him as inheriting one strand of Jewish apocalyptic resistance and rejecting another.

Conclusion

Nickel's paper raises so many important questions that I have hardly done justice to any of them. Even if the Jewish authorities didn't mistake Jesus for a *lēstēs*, the gospels indicate that they were nervous about Roman reprisals toward any signs of trouble in the province. The disciples themselves persistently misunderstand Jesus' mission—jockeying for places of honor in the heavenly throne room, showing up with swords to Jesus' arrest,[16] and nursing their disappointed hopes about the redemption of Israel after his crucifixion. Perhaps some of Jesus' contemporaries did misinterpret Jesus as a violent revolutionary, but the evangelists—and Nickel—have made sure that we do not make the same mistake.

---

13. Ibid., 340.
14. Ibid., 168.
15. Ibid., 155.
16. This is a notable detail preserved in all four accounts. Why did at least one of Jesus' disciples bring a sword to Gethsemane? (Luke's Gospel suggests that Jesus may even authorize the disciples to bring two swords with them, although the phrase *hikanon estin* in Luke 22:38 is notoriously difficult to translate.) Did the disciples themselves misunderstand Jesus to be a potential revolutionary, or do they simply intend to defend their master against anyone who tried to arrest or harm him?

PAUL AND VIOLENCE

Seyoon Kim

Paul as a Violent Person according to a Modern Comprehensive Definition of "Violence"

What Is "Violence"?

In his fine book, *Killing Enmity,* T. R. Yoder Neufeld observes how dramatically the concept of "violence" has broadened in modern discussion.[1] It is now used to refer not only to acts that cause physical harm or damage, but also to words that hurt the feelings of others. It is applied not only to personal relationships among individuals, but also to various systems and structures of society and to various trends of culture that affect our lives. Furthermore, what constitutes violence is often determined by the perception of the one who experiences it, regardless of the intent of the perpetrator. So, any act or language of individuals or groups or any social and cultural system or structure that anyone feels to be oppressive or abusive of his/her personhood or well-being may be perceived as violence.

In discussing violence in the Scriptures, the reader- or victim-centered perception of violence means that "a text becomes violent if the interpreter or reader experiences or employs it as such."[2] The NT contains no actual teaching for Christians to exercise physical violence toward others. But there are plenty of criticisms, accusations, and condemnations of Jewish and gentile persecutors, of false teachers or prophets within the church, and of misbehaving members of the church. Not only is such negative language seen as implying or inciting violence, but also the following teachings of the NT: the household codes that teach submission of a wife to a husband or a slave to a master; the division between believers in Christ as those who are to be saved and unbelievers as those who are to be judged;[3] teachings on or

---

1. T. R. Yoder Neufeld, *Killing Enmity: Violence and the New Testament* (Grand Rapids: Baker Academic, 2011) 1–8.

2. Ibid., 4.

3. See J. S. Vos, "Splitting and Violence in the New Testament: Psychoanalytic Approaches to the Revelation of John and the Letters of Paul," in *Destructive Power of Religion: Violence in Judaism, Christianity, and Islam*, vol. 2 of *Religion, Psychology, and Violence*, ed. J. H. Ellens (Westport, CT: Praeger,

warnings about God's judgment; (potentially intolerant) claims of revelatory truth;[4] metaphors of warfare and weapons;[5] and so forth. Even the whole notion of atoning sacrifice in the Bible is seen as imbuing violence, and especially that of Christ's atoning sacrifice on the cross is condemned as "a metaphor of the worst kind of violence, infanticide or child sacrifice."[6]

Then Paul Is a Violent Person

If "violence" is so defined, Paul clearly is a violent person. For in his letters he uses such language and imparts such teachings that are deemed as evoking violence. So, for example, in Galatians, expressing his strong disappointment and anxiety about the Galatian Christians deserting his gospel and "turning to a different gospel" (1:6; 4:20), he calls them "bewitched" and "fools" (3:1, 3).[7] He strongly denounces his Judaizing opponents as hypocrites who do not keep the law themselves but, out of their ulterior motives, are "forcing" his Galatian converts to get circumcised and keep the law (6:12–13). He even curses them as false teachers or prophets who "trouble" the young Christians in Galatia by preaching a "perverted gospel of Christ," "a different gospel," which is in fact no gospel (1:6–9), and so mislead them, the Spirit-endowed children of God (4:1–7), back into the camp of the fleshly children of the slave woman Hagar (4:21–31). Rehearsing his quarrel with Cephas and Barnabas over the question of table fellowship with gentile Christians in Antioch, Paul likewise condemns even his fellow apostles as "hypocrites" (2:11–14).[8] Just as Paul devalues the circumcision of the Judaizing opponents in Galatia as mere mutilation (*apokoptein*) of their bodies and castigates them as doomed to God's judgment for unsettling the faith of the Christians there with their false gospel that requires circumcision (Gal 5:10, 12), so also he vilifies the Judaizing opponents in Philippi as "dogs" (reversing the typical Jewish vilification of the gentiles) and devalues their circumcision (*peritomē*) as mere mutilation (*katatomē*) as well as threatening them

---

2004) 191–94; Yoder Neufeld, *Killing Enmity*, 7.

4. Yoder Neufeld, *Killing Enmity*, 5.

5. See Yoder Neufeld, *Killing Enmity*, 122–49; C. J. Roetzel, "The Language of War (2 Cor 10:1–6) and the Language of Weakness (2 Cor 11:21b—13:10)," in *Violence, Scripture, and Textual Practice in Early Judaism and Christianity*, ed. R. S. Baustan, A. P. Jassen, and C. J. Roetzel (Leiden: Brill, 2010) 87–88.

6. J. H. Ellens, "Religious Metaphors Can Kill," in *The Destructive Power of Religion: Violence in Judaism, Christianity, and Islam*, vol. 1 of *Sacred Scriptures, Ideology, and Violence*, ed. J. H. Ellens (Westport, CT: Praeger, 2004) 263.

7. Biblical quotations are from the NRSV except for the occasional use of the author's own translations.

8. See F. Tolmie, "Violence in the Letter to the Galatians?," in *Coping with Violence in the New Testament*, ed. P. Williams and J. W. Henton (Leiden: Brill, 2012) 74–75.

with destruction at the last judgment (Phil 3:2, 19). Although it is usually neglected in the context of discussing the issue of violence, it needs to be pointed out that not just these harsh words but that which Paul defends with them, namely, his gentile mission itself, must have been a violent act to most Jews of his time, in fact, a far more "violently" offensive behavior than uttering these words.

In the Corinthian correspondence, he also strongly chastises the Corinthian Christians for their various misdeeds such as rivalry and division (1 Cor 1–4), sexual vices (1 Cor 5–6), litigation (6:1–8), and so forth. He warns the knowledge-boasters of their risky involvement in idolatrous practices, using the example of the Exodus generation of Israelites who were destroyed for their idolatry and immorality (1 Cor 10:1–12). He scolds some rich members who abuse the Lord's Supper in a manner that shames their poor brothers and sisters, and he threatens them with God's judgment that already manifests itself in physical illness and death (1 Cor 11:17–22, 27–34). He directs the Corinthian church to "deliver" an incestuous man in their midst "to Satan for the destruction of the flesh" (1 Cor 5:1–5). Calling his unruly Corinthian converts to a life of conscientious self-discipline on the way to the eschatological consummation of their salvation, he holds up his own "pommel[ing]" and "subdue[ing]" of his "body" as a model for their imitation (1 Cor 9:24–27). In 2 Cor 10–13, his anger explodes in bitter and most sarcastic polemic against both his opponents, who deny his apostolic legitimacy and slander his financial practices, and his Corinthian converts who are swayed by those opponents to treat him with suspicion, the opponents whom he compares even with Satan (2 Cor 11:12–15).[9] Having strongly expressed his disappointment at his Corinthian converts' misdeeds, he threatens to come to them with his apostolic or fatherly authority in order to examine and discipline them, if necessary, with a rod (1 Cor 4:21; 2 Cor 13:1–4, 10).

Quite apart from such "violent" language, Paul's various teachings have also been perceived by some critics as evoking intolerance and violence. To begin with, he claims that by God's revelation he received the gospel of the crucified Jesus as the risen Lord, the Messiah and God's Son (Gal 1:11–17; 1 Cor 9:1; 15:3–8), which means that all human beings, Jews and gentiles, are justified or saved through faith in that gospel of God's righteousness (i.e., covenant faithfulness or grace) apart from the works of the law (Rom 1:3–5, 16–17; Gal 2:16; 3:2, 5, 10). So there is a clear division between Christians who have been transferred from the kingdom of Satan into the kingdom of God and his Son Jesus through faith in the gospel and pledge to render "the obedience of faith" to the Lord Jesus, God's Son and viceroy (e.g.,

---

9. See Roetzel, "Language of War," 84–91, who characterizes Paul's polemic in 2 Cor 10:1–6 as "martial rhetoric" *comparable to* the examples of some war narratives of the Hellenistic and Roman literature.

Rom 1:3–5; 10:9–10; Col 1:13–14; 1 Thess 1:9–10), and those who have not been, the "outsiders" to God's kingdom or church (1 Thess 4:12), who "do not know God" and "do not obey the gospel of our Lord Jesus" (1 Thess 4:5; 2 Thess 1:8).[10] The latter, the unbelievers, are such people because their minds are blinded by Satan, "the god of this age," so they do not understand the gospel of God's Son Jesus Christ's decisive victory over Satan in his death and resurrection and his present process of destroying the satanic forces with God's kingly power for the consummation of God's kingdom (1 Cor 15:20–27; 2 Cor 4:4). So they (especially those who persecute Christians) will receive God's "vengeance" or "punishment of eternal destruction" (2 Thess 1:8–9; 2:10–12; 1 Thess 5:3; Phil 1:28) at God's judgment at the parousia of the Lord Jesus Christ, while the believers will have the consummation of their justification, their deliverance from God's wrath, and participation in his glory (Rom 5:6–11; 8:31–39; 1 Thess 1:10; 5:9–10; 2 Thess 1:5; 2:13–14). Warning Christians that at God's last judgment even they will be judged according to their works (e.g., Rom 2:1–11; 14:10; 2 Cor 5:10), Paul strongly exhorts them to stand fast in the Lord, rendering the obedience of faith to him, so as not to fall back into the satanic kingdom (e.g., Rom 11:22; 1 Cor 10:12; Col 1:21–23; 1 Thess 3:8) and suffer God's vengeance at the last judgment (1 Thess 4:3–8). So he urges the Philippian Christians to "work out their salvation with fear and trembling" (Phil 2:12). In order to underline the seriousness of Christian discipleship in the present phase of justification on the way to its consummation at the last judgment, Paul describes it as a process of spiritual warfare in which believers are to render their body parts to God as "weapons [*hopla*] of righteousness" in order to reap "eternal life" (the life of the age to come, i.e., of God's kingdom), rather than to sin (a metonym for Satan) as "weapons [*hopla*] of wickedness" so as to reap death (Rom 6:12–23; see also 2 Cor 6:6–7; Eph 6:10–17; 1 Thess 5:8 for further metaphors of weapons for Christian discipleship and mission). Hence, Paul warns: "If any one does not love the Lord, let him be accursed [*anathema*]" (1 Cor 16:22).

It is well known that of the two moments of the saving event of Christ Jesus, Paul focuses more on his death than on his resurrection. So he repeatedly explains his gospel in terms of Christ Jesus' death on the cross as a sacrifice of vicarious atonement that God provided for remission of our sins and for our salvation (e.g., Rom 3:24–26; 4:25; 5:6–10; 6:2–11; 8:3–4, 32; 1 Cor 15:3; 2 Cor 5:14–21; Gal 1:4; 2:20; 3:13; Col 1:20, 22; 1 Thess 5:9–10). Hence, he calls the gospel simply "the word of the cross" (1 Cor 1:18; see also Phil 3:19, where he calls the opponents to the [or

---

10. See also Paul's negative presentation of Judaism in such texts as Gal 3–4 and 2 Cor 3, which is criticized as his "caustic interpretation of Scripture" by C. T. Davis III, "The Evolution of a Pauline Toxic Text," in *The Destructive Power of Religion: Violence in Judaism, Christianity, and Islam*, vol. 1 of *Sacred Scriptures, Ideology, and Violence*, ed. J. H. Ellens (Westport, CT: Praeger, 2004) 200–202.

his?] gospel "the enemies of the cross of Christ") and says that in his founding mission to the Corinthians he proclaimed nothing but "Jesus Christ and him crucified" (1 Cor 2:1–2; see also Gal 6:14). To the Galatians he says that during his founding mission to them he "placarded before [their] eyes Jesus Christ as crucified" (Gal 3:1). For Paul, Christ's self-sacrifice on the cross is significant not only as an event for our atonement, but also as a model for our imitation (Phil 2:5–11; 1 Cor 10:31—11:1; see also Rom 15:7–9). Thus, since Paul's theology is so much focused on Christ's death on the cross, scholars like to characterize it as *theologia crucis*. For those who see the whole idea of atoning sacrifice in the Bible as evoking or inciting violence, Paul's portrayal of Christ Jesus as crucified for our atonement through his blood is clearly the most extreme form of violence. When Paul stresses through his sending- and delivering-formula that it was God himself who sent and delivered his Son Jesus to such a death of bloody sacrifice (Rom 3:24–26; 4:25 [note the divine passive verbs]; 8:3–4, 32; 2 Cor 5:21; see also Rom 5:8), he may be seen as heightening the degree of the cruelty involved in Christ's death on the cross.

So, according to such a modern definition of violence as described above, Paul clearly is a violent person and his teaching is quite violent.

Problems with the Modern Definition of Violence

So is Jesus also a violent person, even though he regards even anger with or abuse of neighbor as tantamount to murder (Matt 5:21–22), and forbids vengeance and teaches love of one's enemy (Matt 5:38–48). For, as the bearer of God's kingdom, he not only mightily fights against the kingdom of Satan, subduing Satan and casting out his demons (e.g., Mark 3:22–27; Matt 12:22–30; Luke 11:14–23), but he also imparts similar teachings as Paul's, often picking debates with Pharisees, scribes, and Sadducees, and he eats and drinks with sinners and tax collectors, offending most of his fellow Jews (just as his apostle Paul later associates himself with gentiles). Then, he even predicts the destruction of the temple with a violent sign-act (Mark 11:15–19 parr.).[11]

But then, according to such modern definition of violence as described above, can there be a human being who is not violent? If anyone who makes claims to truth or righteousness and criticizes falsehood or evil is perceived as intolerant and violent, who can be spared the charge of violence? I imagine that some monists who believe there is no real good or evil (but only apparent good and evil) may have no notion of fighting and eradicating falsehood and evil. But the religious conflicts

---

11. See Ellens, "Religious Metaphors Can Kill," 258; J. H. Ellens, "The Violent Jesus," in *The Destructive Power of Religion: Violence in Judaism, Christianity, and Islam*, vol. 3 of *Models and Cases of Violence in Religion*, ed. J. H. Ellens (Westport, CT: Praeger, 2004) 22–32.

in the predominantly Hindu India suggest that in reality even monistic Hinduism would not tolerate rival religious claims that do not subscribe to its fundamental monistic assumption. In my Korean experiences, even many Buddhists who have a fundamentally monistic worldview make efforts to propagate their views of true knowledge, suppress personal vices and social evils, and promote personal and social good. I do not know whether they are able to express such efforts without the use of such language as "suppressing," "fighting," or "eradicating" falsehood or evil, which is said to evoke violence. But I imagine that just as they cannot avoid doing violence to plants in order to sustain their own existence, even though they strenuously maintain vegetarianism in order to avoid killing animal life, they cannot avoid suppressing personal vices and social evils, even if they might hesitate to use such terms. In fact, they are also keen for social justice and often actively support social underdogs fighting against unjust politico-socio-economic systems. The same holds true, I would think, for gender-justice feminists fighting male-dominant culture and patriarchal family systems. I do not know how many people of racial minorities and the socially underprivileged succeed in avoiding such language in their efforts to secure their human rights and establish social justice. I imagine that even absolute pacifists will not be able to avoid the thought of struggling or fighting against oppressive and exploitive systems and cultures. If they want to avoid any violent language for such efforts, what language should they use to express that thought? I wonder whether some who sharply criticize Paul or Jesus for their "violent" teachings and language are not themselves proving to be violent in doing so. In reality, can there be any authentic human existence that is not violent according to the contemporary expanded definition of violence?

Furthermore, is it desirable to abandon all efforts to criticize (i.e., to distinguish true and false or right and wrong, and sometimes also to blame the false or wrong side), to judge and condemn falsehood and evil, and to punish their perpetrators? If we abandon the whole idea of judging and condemning, how are we to establish justice, order, and peace in society, how are we to prevent society from falling into anarchy, and how are we to protect the weak and the good from the powerful and wicked, the peaceful from the violent? Pointing out how, in his efforts "to establish a thoroughgoing peaceable ethic based on the Sermon on the Mount," Glenn Stassen recognizes "the need for constraints and even a modicum of force in the interests of protection," Yoder Neufeld comments that "putting a mugging and a forceful pulling of a person out of danger into the same category" could be seen as "undercutting meaningful ethical discernment and debate."[12] Some extreme anti-violence perspec-

---

12. Yoder Neufeld, *Killing Enmity*, 7. He refers here to the works of G. Stassen, *Living the Sermon on the Mount: A Practical Hope for Grace and Deliverance* (San Francisco: Jossey-Bass, 2006); and G.

tives may regard even the acts of "discernment and debate" as violence because they involve "criticism"—analyzing right or wrong, and making (at least value) judgments about them. But think of what consequences to personal and societal well-being the failure to condemn "mugging" and commend "a forceful pulling of a person out of danger" would bring. If, for fear of perpetrating violence in its new expanded sense, we avoid such common parlance as "we have to fight political corruption and eradicate all sorts of social evil" and abandon the efforts to curb such evils forcefully with the legal means sanctioned in a democratic country, we would actually be contributing to the growth of real violence in society that harms a much greater number of people in much more serious ways than such common parlance can ever hurt some sensitive souls of society.

It is necessary to ask those who object to Paul's and Jesus' teachings about God's last judgment as violent teachings whether they then also object to the whole justice system and justice process of any country or society as a violent system and process. One may object to Paul's insistence that the criterion of God's judgment is "the obedience of faith" to the Lord Jesus Christ. We may or must condemn a bad justice system and process that delivers unjust judgments and so strengthens injustice rather than justice in society. We must work toward making our justice system just. But if we reject the whole idea of judgment as violence and therefore reject the justice system in principle, how are we to see justice and order established in our society and have the weak protected from the violence of their powerful oppressors? The binding force of the justice system is often felt as restrictive and even offensive—that is, "violent" according to the modern definition of violence. Are we therefore to abolish it altogether and let our society fall into total anarchy? As a society, is it not better to have a small or mild form of "violence" in the justice system than its large and severe form in anarchy?

As long as one believes in a transcendent God who rules over his creation and history and holds his human creatures responsible for their deeds, the idea of his judgment over their deeds is unavoidable. His laws or statutes as well as the mention of his judgment often feel inhibitive and even threatening, i.e., "violent" according to the current definition. But the believer takes them as less "violent" than the

---

Stassen with M. W. White, "Defining Violence and Nonviolence," in *Teaching Peace: Nonviolence and the Liberal Arts*, ed. J. D. Weaver and G. Biesecker-Mast (Lanham, MD: Rowman & Littlefield, 2003) 17-37. But see W. Wink, "Beyond Just War and Pacifism: Jesus' Nonviolent Way," in *The Destructive Power of Religion: Violence in Judaism, Christianity, and Islam*, vol. 4 of *Contemporary Views on Spirituality and Violence*, ed. J. H. Ellens (Westport, CT: Praeger, 2004) 53-76 (esp. 67-68), who argues that in Matt 5:38-42 Jesus teaches a "coercive" and yet "nonviolent" resistance to evil, which is the third way that overcomes the weakness of the theories of both just war and absolute pacifism (= nonresistance). However, would such nonviolent "coercive" resistance not still be a form of violence according to the modern expanded definition of that word?

consequences that his/her neglect of them would eventually bring about for him/herself as well as for others. So, then, should we criticize Paul for teaching about God's judgment and warning Christians to live a life of true belief and righteous conduct in view of it? Can we not see such a warning, in fact, as an act of love as it can lead some people to refrain from doing evils that would hurt others and might plunge themselves into the lot of those who turn their back on God's saving grace offered in Christ? Depending on one's own belief or worldview, one may hold the whole notion of God's judgment as mistaken or criticize Paul for teaching about it in a wrong way. But is it right to criticize him for teaching as a theist God's judgment *per se* as a violent act? If it is, is not such a criticism or judgment also a form of intolerance or violence for a belief that is different from one's own? Certainly, some of the language that Paul employs for God's judgment ("vengeance," "punishment of eternal destruction," etc.) is harsh and violent (see heading below, "How Successful is Paul . . ."). But once his belief in God's eschatological judgment is granted, may such language not be understood as his traditional way of expressing the fundamental hope for God's ultimate eradication of evil and a stern warning for people not to exclude themselves from God's grace? Or for that hope and that warning are we just to state blandly that "God will resolve the problem of evil at the end" and that "it will be bad to be excluded from God's grace at the end"—without using any metaphor for it out of fear of inciting violence?[13]

All these considerations show that there must be some limit in applying to Pauline Epistles and other scriptural texts the modern expanded understanding of violence that has been developed from the subjective perspective of the reader. In order to determine whether or not some teachings and language of Paul and others in the New Testament are violent, we must take into consideration not just some (not always intelligent) readers' feelings about them, but also other factors such as

---

13. In Rom 1:18–32 Paul speaks of God's wrath being revealed against all ungodly and wicked human beings in terms of God giving them up (see especially vv. 24, 26, 28) to their debased mind and to their passion and lust, so that they may go on with their inclination to suppress truth and worship idols rather than God, as well as with their impure and evil deeds. In contrast to this, Paul speaks of God's righteousness being revealed to those who believe in the gospel in terms of his justifying them to have salvation and life (1:16–17). Just as God's righteousness or justification begins at present and will be consummated at the last judgment, so also God's wrath or condemnation begins at present and will be consummated at the last judgment. Seeing Paul speak of God's present judgment on ungodly and wicked human beings thus, some sensitive modern readers may regret that he does not likewise speak of God's last judgment on them just in terms of God giving them up to reach the end of their self-chosen path of rejecting his saving grace in Christ, instead of "violently" describing that act as God's "vengeance," "punishment of eternal destruction," etc. But anticipating that God's judgment is not far away, Paul is more concerned to issue a stern warning both for believers and unbelievers not to turn their back on God's grace and meet an unsavory end, than to consider the possible linguistic sensitivity of his readers in a remote future.

whether the teachings and language are justified, and whether they serve a positive purpose more than yielding a negative effect.

How Did Paul Change from a Violent "Zealot" to a "Pacifist" Christian and Apostle?

Aside from concerns about a subjective definition of "violence," my main purpose in this paper is to consider the question, How did Paul change from a violent "zealot" to a Christian and an apostle who teaches the ways of loving neighbor and achieving peace? Among those who discuss Paul's teaching, language, and conduct in terms of violence, this question or perspective appears largely neglected.

The Gospel of Reconciliation and Peace

In his own confession, before his conversion Paul was a Pharisee and "zealot" who "persecuted the church of God excessively and tried to destroy her" out of his incomparably great zeal for his ancestral traditions in Judaism (Gal 1:13-14; Phil 3:6; see also Acts 22:3-4; 1 Cor 15:9). Apparently he regarded the believers in Jesus as the Messiah as blasphemous to God and his law since for him Jesus' death on the cross clearly proved that he had died under God's curse declared by his law (Deut 21:23; see also Gal 3:13).[14] So, following the tradition of the "zeal" of Phinehas (Num 25:1-5), Elijah (1 Kgs 18:36-40; 19:10-18), the Maccabees (1 Macc 2:15-28), and others for the honor of God and the integrity of God's law, he violently persecuted the church.[15]

---

14. James D. G. Dunn and other adherents of the New Perspective on Paul have popularized the view that the pre-conversion Paul persecuted the church because by preaching the gospel to gentiles without requiring observance of such laws as circumcision, Sabbath, and purity it was infringing upon the integrity of Israel as God's holy people. See J. D. G. Dunn, "Paul's Conversion—A Light to Twentieth Century Disputes," in *Evangelium, Schriftauslegung, Kirche: Festschrift für Peter Stuhlmacher zum 65. Geburtstag*, ed. J. Adna, S. J. Hafemann, and O. Hofius (Göttingen: Vandenhoeck and Ruprecht, 1997) 90; J. D. G. Dunn, *The Partings of the Ways between Christianity and Judaism* (Philadelphia: Trinity, 1991) 121-22; etc. But it is unrealistic to play down the provocation of the Christian proclamation of the crucified Jesus as the Messiah to the "zealotic" Pharisee Paul (see 1 Cor 1:22-23) and to focus only on the supposed preaching of the "Hellenists" to gentiles. See S. Kim, *Paul and the New Perspective: Second Thoughts on the Origin of Paul's Gospel* (Grand Rapids: Eerdmans, 2002) 2-19.

15. The party of Zealots to which Josephus refers in his *Jewish War* (4:161, 225; 7:268-70; etc.) may have been formed during the Jewish War of AD 66-70, but it is generally agreed that the ideology of "zeal" also inspired many other individuals like Paul and those of the anti-Roman resistance groups before the Jewish War. See W. R. Farmer, *Maccabees, Zealots, and Josephus* (New York: Columbia University Press, 1956); M. Hengel, *The Zealots: Investigations into the Jewish Freedom Movement in the Period from Herod I until 70 AD* (Edinburgh: T&T Clark, 1989); R. A. Horsley and J. S. Hanson, *Bandits, Prophets, and Messiahs* (Minneapolis: Winston, 1985); D. Rhoads, "The Zealots," *ABD* 6:1043-54; M. R. Fairchild, "Paul's Pre-Christian Zealot Associations: A Re-Examination of Gal 1.14 and Acts 22.3," *NTS* 45 (1999) 514-32.

But while traveling on the road to Damascus, according to Luke, in order to persecute the Christians there (Acts 9:1–18), Paul saw the crucified Jesus appearing as the risen Lord and God's Son (1 Cor 9:1; 15:8; Gal 1:15–16). In 2 Cor 5:11–21, against some Jewish Christian opponents who took issue with his past as a persecutor of the church and questioned the legitimacy of his appeal to the Damascus vision of Christophany for his apostleship (note especially the use of *exestēmen* in 2 Cor 5:13),[16] Paul provides an autobiographical account of the theological revolution that the Christophany wrought in him.[17] He implicitly admits that before the Damascus vision of the glorified Lord Jesus Christ (see 2 Cor 3:6, 18; 4:1, 6) he rejected Christians' claim of Jesus as the Messiah and persecuted them for it. For Jesus had not fulfilled the Jewish messianic expectation of restoring the Davidic dynasty, destroying or subjugating the nations, and ushering in for Israel an everlasting era of justice and peace,[18] but instead died a criminal's death under God's curse. But through the revelation of the crucified Jesus as the Messiah, God's Son and the Lord, Paul realized that on the cross Jesus bore God's curse on our sins in our stead and on our behalf (2 Cor 5:21; Rom 8:3–4; Gal 3:13) and that that was his true messianic act, which was confirmed by God's resurrecting him from the dead and exalting him to his right hand in heaven. So, through the Damascus revelation, Paul realized that Jesus' true messiahship consisted precisely in his death of vicarious atonement for our sins, which was to make sinners righteous, that is, to restore them to the right relationship with God (2 Cor 5:14–15, 21). Thus, the Damascus revelation made him turn his back on Jewish messianism as a "fleshly" understanding (2 Cor 5:16) and accept the Jerusalem church's gospel as enshrined in such formulae as those quoted in Rom 1:3–4 and 1 Cor 15:3–5 (or its Semitic equivalent in Rom 4:25). And it made him avail himself of Christ Jesus' atonement by faith in the gospel and so become a "new creation," for whom all his sins, including his hostility to Christ Jesus and his persecution of his church, had "passed away" and a "new reality [had] come into being" (2 Cor 5:17; see also Isa 43:18–19).

---

16. Note also the marginal annotation in Nestle-Aland 26th and 27th eds. of 2 Cor 12:1ff. and 1 Cor 14:2 as parallels to this verse (28th ed. replaces the reference to 2 Cor 12:1ff. with that to 1 Cor 14:15, 28f.). See also Acts 26:24–25; and especially the *Kerygmata Petrou* 17:13–19, where "Peter" rejects the appeal of Simon [*alias* Paul] to a vision as a means of the revelation of God's Son Jesus as well as of his apostolic call.

17. For the details of and the supporting arguments for the following interpretation of the passage, see S. Kim, *The Origin of Paul's Gospel* (Tübingen: Mohr Siebeck, 1981; 2nd ed. 1984; Grand Rapids: Eerdmans, 1982) 311–15; also S. Kim, "2 Cor 5:11–21 and the Origin of Paul's Concept of Reconciliation," *NovT* 39 (1997) 360–84, reprinted in Kim, *Paul and the New Perspective*, 214–38.

18. See J. J. Collins, *The Scepter and the Star: Messianism in Light of the Dead Sea Scrolls*, 2nd ed. (Grand Rapids: Eerdmans, 2010) 77–78, for the view that this constituted "the common core of the Jewish messianism around the turn of the era."

This theological revolution made Paul realize that the Messiah Jesus had decisively defeated our real foe that brings us the ultimate *Unheil*, that is, not an enemy nation like Rome but the kingdom of Satan who reigns over us in sin and death (i.e., by making us commit sin or transgress against God's kingship and paying us with death as our wages—Rom 6:23).[19] So Paul realized that the gentile nations were the objects not of destruction or subjugation but of redemption. God has exalted the Davidic Messiah as his Son at his right hand, investing him with his kingly power or lordship (Rom 1:3–4), not to destroy the nations but to go on with his mopping-up operation against the satanic forces (1 Cor 15:23–28) and to redeem Israel and the nations from the satanic kingdom. Paul was commissioned as an apostle to proclaim this victorious Messiah Jesus, God's Son, to all the nations and to bring them to render "the obedience of faith" to his lordship (Rom 1:5), so that they might be transferred or redeemed from Satan's kingdom into the kingdom of God and his Son and obtain salvation in it (Col 1:13–14).

In the autobiographical account of his conversion and apostolic call at the Damascus Christophany, Paul makes it clear that Christ's death of vicarious atonement has resulted in our obtaining God's righteousness (2 Cor 5:21). But especially in view of his opponents' insinuation of his past enmity to Jesus Christ (which is

---

19. So, unlike the author of Revelation, Paul did not yet see Rome as the incarnation of Satan or its empire as the embodiment of Satan's rule. Therefore, in spite of his critical attitude to its negative side (its idolatry, military oppression, exploitation, decadence, etc.), as part of the present evil world under the sway of Satan, he did not seek to subvert it, but by conducting his gentile mission, taking advantage of its positive side (political unity, the rule of law, relative justice and peace, fast and secure roads and sea routes, etc.), he tried to redeem the peoples within the empire by the gospel of the kingdom of God and his Son, Jesus Christ. Contra N. T. Wright, *Paul and the Faithfulness of God* (Minneapolis: Fortress, 2013) 1271–1319, see S. Kim, "Paul and the Roman Empire," in *God and the Faithfulness of Paul: A Critical Examination of the Pauline Theology of N. T. Wright*, ed. C. Heilig, J. T. Hewitt, and M. F. Bird (Tübingen: Mohr Siebeck, 2016) 277–308; also S. Kim, *Christ and Caesar: The Gospel and the Empire in the Writings of Paul and Luke* (Grand Rapids: Eerdmans, 2008) 3–71. Since Christ Jesus the Lord is engaged in a mopping-up operation not against the gentile nations but the satanic forces, not against "the flesh and blood, but . . . against the spiritual hosts of wickedness in the heavenly places" (Eph 6:12), in urging Christians, his people, to fight the holy war as his troops, Paul "spiritualizes" or "moralizes" the holy war tradition of the Old Testament and Judaism and teaches them to win the war against the satanic forces with the weapons of truth, righteousness, faith, love, hope, the gospel of *peace*, the word of God, and prayer (Rom 6:13–23; 1 Thess 5:8; Eph 6:10–20; see also 2 Cor 6:6–7; 10:1–6). See Yoder Neufeld, *Killing Enmity*, 138–49 (esp. 142: "Does the violence in the warfare imagery Paul employs in this exhortation valorize violence, or does it by being fused with the exercise of faithfulness, love and hope—virtues that have their most intense demonstration in the ministry, death and resurrection of Jesus—subvert, redefine, and finally undo the violence of war? Is it enmity that kills or enmity that is killed? In my view the answer is the latter"; see also 147). But still there may be some readers who feel violence is being advocated even in such metaphors of war and weapons as Paul's, just as there are some readers who read Eph 6:10–20 as teaching a shamanistic "spiritual warfare" of exorcism, etc. If they insist that we should avoid such metaphors in order not to incite violence, then they should teach us how else we should more irenically, but still effectively, speak of the Lord Jesus Christ's work and our task of removing or resolving the most serious problem of evil in our lives and in the world.

also an enmity to God who sent him and delivered him up to his atoning death; Rom 8:3–4, 32; Gal 4:4–5, etc.) as well as of his past persecution of the church, Paul introduces "reconciliation" as a new soteriological term for God's giving Christ up as an atoning sacrifice: "in Christ God was reconciling the world to himself, not counting their trespasses against them" (2 Cor 5:19a). And Paul testifies to his own experience of this grace of God in Christ's atoning death thus: "God reconciled us to himself through Christ" (2 Cor 5:18a; the "we/us" in 2 Cor 5:18–20 being, in the first place, a literary plural for Paul himself). Then, with his opponents' rejection of his apostleship in view, he goes on to affirm that "God g[ave] us the ministry of reconciliation" (v. 18b) and "entrust[ed] to us the message of reconciliation" (v. 19b). So as an apostle of Christ, he is an "ambassador for Christ" who delivers God's message of reconciliation to the Corinthians as well as to other gentile nations, making an appeal, "Be reconciled to God" (v. 20). So the gospel is God's "message of reconciliation," and the apostle Paul is God's or Christ's envoy of peace!

Such a great theological revolution from the nationalistic and even militant Jewish messianism to the messianism of God's grace of atonement and reconciliation, which began at the Damascus Christophany, led him to develop from the Jerusalem gospel (Rom 1:3–4) his gospel of justification by God's grace and through our faith (Rom 1:16–17).[20] In Rom 1:1–4, Paul defines "the gospel of God" as concerning God's Son whom God sent to "be born of the seed of David" (see Gal 4:4; Rom 8:3), gave up to a death of vicarious atonement for our sins (see Rom 4:25; 8:3–4, 32; Rom 3:24–26; 2 Cor 5:21), and raised from the dead and installed as his Son to exercise his power on his behalf (see 2 Sam 7:12–14; Ps 2:7; Ps 110:1).[21] The saving act of God announced or narrated in the gospel is the fulfillment of the promises that God had made through his prophets in the Scriptures (Rom 1:2; 15:7–12). So in the gospel, God's righteousness (his faithfulness to his covenant to care for Israel and all the nations) is revealed (Rom 1:17; see also Rom 3:21–26). Therefore, whoever believes in the gospel, that is, accepts the gospel (see 1 Cor 15:1–5), avails him/herself of God's righteousness, that is, his grace of sending and offering Christ as the eschatological sacrifice of atonement for his/her sins and installing him as his/her Lord, so that he/she is forgiven or acquitted of his/her trespasses, restored to the right relationship with God, and so transferred from the kingdom of Satan to the kingdom of God, which his Son Jesus Christ the Lord rules on his behalf at present (see 1 Cor

---

20. See Kim, *Origin of Paul's Gospel*, 268–311; also S. Kim, *Justification and God's Kingdom* (Tübingen: Mohr Siebeck, 2018) 15–71.

21. For a justification of thus seeing the Jerusalem gospel of Rom 1:3–4 with Paul's eyes, that is, in terms of the sending- and delivering-formulae (Gal 4:4–5; 2:20; Rom 4:25; 8:3–4, 32; etc.) implicit in it, see Kim, *Justification*, 53–55.

15:23-28; Col 1:13-14). Therefore, the gospel is "the power of God for salvation to everyone who believes [it]" (Rom 1:16).

By formulating this gospel in the most striking terms of "Christ's death for the ungodly" (Rom 5:6) and "God justifying the ungodly" (Rom 4:5),[22] or "God reconciling his enemies to himself" (Rom 5:10; 2 Cor 5:19), as well as stressing God's love for us, his rebellious creatures (Rom 5:8; 8:32; 2 Cor 5:14; etc.), Paul tries to express the unimaginable wonder of this gospel. Considering his nationalistic and militant messianism in Judaism, we can well appreciate the awe that he feels over this gospel of Christ that resolves the conflict and enmity between God and his creatures and establishes peace between them (Rom 5:1; Col 1:20; Eph 2:14-16).

The gospel of justification by God's grace and through our faith (without the works of the law) establishes a relationship of righteousness and peace not only between God and human beings but also among human beings. For that gospel nullifies all forms of discrimination according to race, gender, social class, intellectual attainment, moral achievement, and so on. Before God all human beings are just sinners, regardless of what they were born with or have achieved in the flesh (see Phil 3:3-4; 1 Cor 1:26-31), and, as ungodly sinners and God's enemies, they are all justified or reconciled to God by his grace in Christ. Hence Paul declares that the gospel is "the power of God for salvation to everyone who has faith, to the Jew first but also to the Greek" (Rom 1:16), and that as the apostle to the gentiles he has an obligation to preach it "both to Greeks and to barbarians, both to the wise and to the foolish" (Rom 1:14). In the course of arguing for his gospel of "justification not by works of the law but through faith in Jesus Christ" (Gal 2:16), he declares even more comprehensively, "There is neither Jew nor Greek, there is neither slave nor free, there is neither male nor female; for you are all one in Christ Jesus" (Gal 3:28; see also Rom 3:22, 28-30; 10:12; 1 Cor 12:13; Col 3:11). This understanding of the gospel provided him with the theological justification for his gentile mission, a revolutionary undertaking within the Jewish context. So he was able to preach the gospel to the gentiles and make efforts to bring them along with Jews into the kingdom of God and his Son or the family of Abraham and God. Then, later in Eph 2:11-22, the fruits of his gentile mission with the gospel of justification by grace alone and through faith alone, that is based on Christ's atoning sacrifice on the cross (Eph 2:1-10, 14-15), are celebrated in terms of bringing about reconciliation and peace between Jews and gentiles as well as between God and human beings and of bringing Jews and gentiles united together into the household of God. The same understanding of the gospel also enabled Paul to treat men and women as equals,

---

22. This formulation is even contrary to the fundamental understanding of God's law in the OT and Judaism (see Exod 23:7; Prov 17:15; Isa 5:23; CD 1:19).

exhorting husband and wife to submit to each other (1 Cor 7:1–16; see Eph 5:21) and recognizing a woman's right to lead worship services in the church (provided that she observes the proper dress code; 1 Cor 11:2–16). Furthermore, the gospel of justification by grace and through faith led Paul to exhort free persons and slaves to transcend in the Lord this worldly distinction (1 Cor 7:20–24; Philemon), a truly revolutionary teaching in the ancient world. These examples show how his gospel of justification by grace and through faith effects God's salvation or healing even here and now by removing or reducing the conflicts, oppression, and violence between different races, genders, and social classes,[23] and how that gospel as a post-Easter soteriological form of Jesus' gospel of God's kingdom realizes the "justice, peace, and joy [or wellbeing/happiness]" of God's kingdom (Rom 14:17) here and now, albeit in the form of its first fruits.[24]

Christ Jesus' Victory Over the Satanic Powers through His Self-Sacrifice

In speaking of Christ's defeat of the satanic forces, Paul does not depict a cosmic war as in some apocalyptic literature. Instead, he simply asserts that Christ's death of vicarious atonement for our sins on the cross was the means for defeating "the rulers and authorities" and redeeming us from "the elements of the universe" (Gal 3:13—4:11; Col 2:8–23). Sometimes Paul attributes this victory to the initiative of God, who sent Christ Jesus his Son and delivered him to a death of vicarious atonement for us (e.g., Gal 4:1–7; Rom 3:24–26; 4:25; 8:3–4, 32; Col 2:13–15). Other times he expresses this truth by stressing Christ as the initiator of his own redemptive work: "[Christ] gave himself for our sins to deliver us from the present evil age" (Gal 1:4; see also, e.g., Gal 2:20; Rom 5:6–11; 2 Cor 5:14–15. "The present evil age" is the age ruled by "the god of this age"; 2 Cor 4:4; see also 1 Cor 2:6–8). Accordingly, Paul stresses the love of God (Rom 5:5, 8; 8:31–32) or the love of Christ (Rom 8:35; 2 Cor 5:14; Gal 2:20). As the former was actually shown in the latter (Christ's death of vicarious atonement), both refer to the same reality, and so Paul also speaks of "the love of God in Christ" (Rom 8:39).

So Paul's gospel proclaims that God or Christ has won victory over the satanic forces through his love, which is Christ's self-giving or God's giving of his Son. Thus, the gospel proclaims the truth that the self-giving love of God or Christ overcomes or resolves the sin of Adamic humanity's self-assertion or self-seeking under Satan's

---

23. So whenever in history the church preached that gospel aright and believers lived in a manner worthy of it, it advanced human rights and promoted freedom, justice, and peace in many nations; regrettably, though, often by preaching a distorted gospel, the church produced instead "the works of the flesh" (Gal 5:19–21).

24. See Kim, *Justification*, 117–39.

instigation (see Gen 3:1-5), the sin that lies behind every act of oppression and violence. Only self-giving love resolves the problem of hate and aggression. Only the divine love of self-giving out of God's divine fullness (*plēroma*) can redeem all human beings from the ills of their self-seeking, which is driven by human finitude (i.e., want). Crucifixion was the cruelest form of execution in the ancient Mediterranean world. So, Christ crucified represents both the ultimate expression of human violence, the most forceful form of human self-assertion, and the ultimate revelation of the divine essence as self-giving love that has overcome it.

Therefore, it is quite ironic for some writers to condemn Paul's gospel of Christ's atonement as inciting violence. J. H. Ellens provides a good example.[25] Seeing the gospel in terms of the OT-Jewish cult of offering sacrifice to God as a propitiation for sins, he condemns it as "a metaphor of the worst kind of violence, infanticide or child sacrifice." Claiming that the Hebrew system of atonement is "exactly opposite to the Hebrew tradition of the covenant of grace," he asserts that the gospel of Christ's atoning sacrifice on the cross also "radically contradicts the grace ethic it purports to express and cuts its taproot by the dominant model of solving ultimate problems through resort to the worst kind of violence." But unfortunately Ellens never properly reflects on the revolutionarily new idea of the gospel, namely, that it is not human beings but *God* who offers Christ Jesus his Son as a sacrifice of atonement for human sins.[26] Nor does he ever properly appreciate what is actually conveyed through that message: God's love for the fallen humanity or his will to reconcile his rebellious creatures (his "enemies") to himself. Nor does he show how we can speak about the event of Christ's crucifixion as God's saving event in a way that avoids the kind of charges that he lays at Paul's door. The question here is simply whether there is a way of referring, metaphorically or however else, to the indisputable historical *fact* of Jesus' crucifixion, the cruelest form of violence, without evoking an association of violence. Just as some readers manage to read Eph 6:10-20 as encouraging violent warfare or an enthusiastic exorcism, there will be some readers who fail to understand and appreciate the meaning of the gospel of Christ crucified as a message of God's love and reconciliation and instead regard it as an encouragement to solve problems through resort to violence. But the existence of such readers is no reason for abandoning the gospel of Christ's atonement on the cross and the war metaphors.

---

25. Ellens, "Religious Metaphors Can Kill," 255-72. The following three quotations from him are from 263. See also J. G. Gager, with E. L. Gibson, "Violent Acts and Violent Language in the Apostle Paul," in *Violence in the New Testament*, ed. E. L. Gibson and S. Matthews (New York: T & T Clark, 2005) 13-21 (esp. 16-19).

26. See R. G. Hamerton-Kelly, *Sacred Violence: Paul's Hermeneutic of the Cross* (Minneapolis: Fortress, 1992) 80.

The Church as the Troops of the Lord Jesus Christ: Keeping "the Law of Christ" and Imitating Christ

Having decisively defeated Satan through his atoning death on the cross and his resurrection, the risen Lord Jesus Christ, God's Son, goes on mopping-up the satanic forces with God's kingly power entrusted to him (1 Cor 15:23–28). He does this by reigning over us, the justified and redeemed, that is, by leading and enabling us through his Spirit (God's Spirit) to obey his reign and bear "the fruit of the Spirit/ righteousness" (Gal 5:22–23; Phil 1:11; 2 Cor 9:8–10; Rom 6:12–22; 7:4–6; 8:1–16; Col 1:10; 1 Thess 4:3, 7), instead of obeying Satan's reign and producing "the works of the flesh" (Gal 5:19–21). In practical terms, this means that at each moment of moral choice the Lord Jesus Christ directs and enables us through his Spirit to do his will or to obey his law ("the law of Christ" [1 Cor 9:21; Gal 5:14; 6:2], namely, his double command of love: to love God and neighbor [Mark 12:28–34 parr.]) and so to bear "the fruit of righteousness" (Phil 2:12–15), instead of succumbing to the temptation of Satan to satisfy the desires of our flesh and so to bear the fruit of evil.[27]

This is the way the Lord Jesus Christ, God's Son, continues redeeming us from the kingdom of Satan at present toward the consummation of our salvation at his parousia. To view it from another perspective, this is the way the Lord Jesus Christ, God's viceroy, is going on destroying the satanic forces and bringing God's kingdom to its consummation at his parousia (again 1 Cor 15:23–28). Therefore, we, those who have been justified, that is, transferred from the kingdom of Satan into the kingdom of God and his Son (Col 1:13–14),[28] are the Lord Jesus Christ's troops employed in his holy war against the satanic kingdom. So we are to offer our body not to sin (a metonym for Satan) as a "weapon [*hopla*] of wickedness" but to God (or his Son, the Lord Jesus Christ, who reigns on his behalf at present) as a "weapon [*hopla*] of righteousness" (Rom 6:12–23). Thus, as his troops we have to fight the holy war "against the wiles of the devil . . . against the rulers and authorities of this present darkness, against the spiritual hosts of wickedness in the heavenly places" with the weapons of truth, righteousness, faith, love, hope, the gospel of peace, the word of God, prayer" (Eph 6:10–20; see also 2 Cor 6:6–7; 10:1–6; 1 Thess 5:8), and participate in the Lord Jesus Christ's work of realizing God's kingdom of "justice, peace,

---

27. Note the contrast between the peace and peace-engendering virtues that Paul mentions in the illustration of "the fruit of the Spirit" ("love, joy, peace, long-suffering, kindness, goodness, faithfulness, gentleness, self-control") and the violence-engendering vices of "the works of the flesh" ("strife, jealousy, anger, rivalry, dissensions, party spirit, envy, drunkenness") (Gal 5:19–23; see also 2 Cor 6:4–7). So, reigning over us, the justified and redeemed, through his Spirit, the Lord Jesus Christ God's Son goes on realizing God's kingdom of "justice, peace, and joy" (Rom 14:17), overcoming the evils of self-seeking, conflict, and violence in the satanic kingdom.

28. See Kim, *Justification*, 59–71, for justification as lordship-transfer.

and joy" (Rom 14:17) here and now. Then at his parousia, the Lord Jesus God's Son will consummate his victory over the satanic forces by destroying the last enemy, death, and raising the dead (1 Cor 15:26; 1 Thess 4:13–18) and by consummating our justification through his intercession before the judgment throne of God as well as by redeeming the whole world from the satanic power of death (Rom 8:17–39), so that God's kingly reign may prevail over all his creation and universal shalom be established (1 Cor 15:28; Rom 16:20).[29]

Paul's lengthy discussion of eating idol food, directed toward ending the Corinthians' dispute about the issue and restoring their communal peace (1 Cor 8–10), illustrates well the way he thinks Christians should obey the Lord Jesus Christ's reign through observance of "the law of Christ" in their daily life and establish justice and peace. This is already suggested by his framing of his whole treatment of the issue by an *inclusio* with the demands for love of God and love of neighbor in 8:1–2 and 10:31–33 (in chiastic structure: 8:1 // 10:32–33; 8:2 // 10:31). Paul's specific instruction on the question of eating idol food may be summarized in three points:

1. Basically, Christians have the freedom of eating meat bought from the market or offered on the table of a non-Christian neighbor's home (10:25–27).

2. Yet the knowledge-boasting Corinthians should avoid the danger of idolatry involved in participation in pagan temple meals, etc. (10:1–22, esp. vv. 14–22).

3. They also must sacrifice their right to eat the meat offered at the market or on a neighbor's table for the sake of the "weak" brothers and sisters, in order not to lay a stumbling block before them if they object to eating it (8:7–13; 10:23–24, 28–30).

With the first point, Paul makes it clear that Christians are no longer bound to the Mosaic law. Then, with the second and third points, he indicates that he has in mind, respectively, Jesus' command to love God wholeheartedly, which excludes any form of idolatry (see 8:2 // 10:31), and his command to love neighbor as oneself, which requires caring for the neighbor's interest (see 8:1 // 10:32–33). In the middle of imparting this teaching, namely in ch. 9, Paul supports this teaching with his own example of self-sacrificing apostolic service for others (love of neighbor): his foregoing of his apostolic right to claim financial support from the church (9:1–18) as well as his missionary policy of "making [himself] a slave to all, that [he] might win the more," both to the Jews under the law and to the gentiles outside the law (9:19–23). In that context, implicitly treating the purity regulations of Moses as *adiaphora*, he declares that he is "not under the law [of Moses]" (9:20), and that he is "in the law

---

29. For more details of this summary statement about the present saving reign of the Lord Jesus Christ, God's Son, see Kim, *Justification*, 73–91.

of Christ," suggesting that in that way he really fulfills the legal obligation toward God (9:21), i.e., the obligation to love God. Here it is especially noteworthy that in explaining his missionary policy of "making myself a slave to all, that I might win the more" (9:19), he echoes Jesus' ransom saying in Mark 10:45 // Matt 20:28. It is equally noteworthy that he concludes his extended teaching on the question of eating idol food over three chapters with a double exhortation, first, to love God wholeheartedly ("do all things to the glory of God," 10:31), and then to love neighbor, which he expresses through the words that strongly echo the same ransom saying of Jesus (10:[32–]33: "just as I try to *please all people* in everything I do, *not seeking my own advantage, but that of many, that they may be saved*") as well as Jesus' stumbling-block saying (10:32: "Give no offense to Jews or to Greeks or to the church of God"; Mark 9:42–50 // Matt 18:6–9 // Luke 17:1–2; see also 1 Cor 8:13).[30] Seeing all these, we can affirm that Paul is exactly right to reach the grand conclusion to his extended teaching with this instruction, "Be imitators of me, as I am of Christ" (1 Cor 11:1).[31] Thus, 1 Cor 8–9 shows how Paul teaches the Corinthian believers to resolve their communal conflict about the issue of idol food by observing "the law of Christ" (the double command of love), which is the way to obey the Lord Jesus Christ's reign, as well as how he determines his own apostolic stance in obedience to that law.

This discussion shows also that imitating Christ is a way of obeying the Lord Jesus Christ's rule through observance of his law. Paul's apostolic ministry in obedience to "the law of Christ" is actually to imitate the Christ of the ransom saying (1 Cor 9:19; 10:33). Paul exhorts the Corinthians to fulfill the "the law of Christ" likewise by imitating the Christ of the ransom saying (1 Cor 10:33), following his own imitation of him (1 Cor 11:1). According to the Synoptic witnesses (Mark 10:35–45 // Matt 20:20–28; see also Luke 22:24–27), Jesus spoke the ransom saying about his self-sacrificing service for others, in contrast to the gentile rulers' domination over others, in order to teach his disciples to give up their self-seeking and domineering impulses and to follow his own example. Paul appreciates the saying not only as an explanation of Christ's self-surrender for our atonement on the cross (e.g., Gal 1:4; 2:20), but apparently also as the best example of neighbor-love (see John 15:13; Rom 5:7–8). So, he fundamentally determines his own self-sacrificing apostolic stance

---

30. See also Rom 15:1–6, where Paul similarly concludes his extended treatment of the dispute about eating meat (Rom 14:1–23) with an exhortation using words reminiscent of the spirit of the ransom saying: for "the strong" not to seek their own interest but the interest of "the weak" in imitation of Christ (Rom 15:1–3) and so to establish peace and harmony in their church (Rom 14:19; 15:5), glorifying God together (Rom 15:6; see also 14:5–9, 13).

31. For more details of this summary presentation, see S. Kim, "*Imitatio Christi* (1 Corinthians 11:1): How Paul Imitates Jesus Christ in Dealing with Idol Food (1 Corinthians 8–10)," *BBR* 13 (2003) 193–226, which also shows some more aspects of Jesus' conduct and teaching that Paul imitates; see also Kim, *Justification*, 82–85 (esp. n. 12).

according to that saying (besides 1 Cor 9:19; 10:33, see also 1 Thess 2:5–9), and also exhorts the Corinthians to practice self-sacrifice for the interest of others according to that saying (1 Cor 10:33). It is quite likely that the picture of the Godlike Christ's self-emptying to take the form of a slave, and self-humbling to be obedient to God unto death on a cross (Phil 2:6–8), echoes the ransom saying. Even if the Philippians hymn (2:6–11) is pre-Pauline, in view of his appreciation of the ransom saying, it is highly likely that Paul understands the hymn as portraying the Christ of the ransom saying. Paul offers that hymn to the Philippian Christians in order to exhort them to end their communal dissension and achieve unity through humility and self-sacrificing love for one another after the example of Christ (Phil 2:1–11). He further supports this exhortation through the examples of Timothy and Epaphroditus, who imitate Christ in their sacrificial service (Phil 2:19–30), as well as his own example of willingness to sacrifice himself for the sake of the Philippians (Phil 2:17). If Euodia and Syntyche and the people around them achieve unity of mind "in the Lord," that is, in obedience to the reign of the Lord Jesus, in observance of his law to love neighbor (Phil 4:2), or in imitation of Christ's (and Paul's) self-sacrifice to serve others, the Philippian church will have peace and joy (Phil 3:1; 4:4–9).[32] Such a life of imitation of Christ will make us "be transformed into his image from one degree of glory to another" (2 Cor 3:18) until the consummation at his parousia (Phil 3:20–21; Rom 8:29; 1 Cor 15:49). The church, as the community of the people who confess Jesus as Lord, should work toward realizing the justice, peace, and joy of his kingdom inside and outside by living such a life of obedience to his reign or of imitation of him.

The ransom saying may be the best illustration of Christ's law of neighbor-love. However, other sayings of Jesus also provide concrete examples of it (e.g., the stumbling-block saying [Mark 9:42–50 // Matt 18:6–9 // Luke 17:1–2] echoed in Rom 14:13, 20; 1 Cor 8:13; 10:32). Among them, Jesus' commands in the Sermon on the Mount/Plain (Matt 5:38–48 // Luke 6:29–36) not to take revenge on one's enemies but to love them are the most striking. In Rom 12:14—13:10, Paul alludes to them and expands on them (see also 1 Cor 4:12–13; 1 Thess 5:15), explicitly referring to the neighbor-love commandment as the summary of all the commandments in the second table of the Ten Commandments (Rom 13:8–10).[33] Paul's purpose there is to exhort the Roman Christians to "live peaceably with all" (Rom 12:18; see also

---

32. Note how in 1 Cor 6:1–8 Paul rebukes the Corinthians for a member of the church suing a fellow member in a worldly court: "It is already a complete defeat for you that you have lawsuits at all with one another. Why do you not rather suffer wrong? Why do you not rather be defrauded?" (v. 7). Paul is clearly lamenting the Corinthian Christians' lack of willingness to give up self-seeking in obedience to Christ's command to love neighbor as oneself.

33. See M. Thompson, *Clothed with Christ: The Example and Teaching of Jesus in Romans 12.15—15.3* (Sheffield: Sheffield Academic, 1991) 90–160; D. Wenham, *Paul: Follower of Jesus or Founder of Christianity?* (Grand Rapids: Eerdmans, 1995) 250–70.

1 Thess 5:13, 23) by practicing neighbor-love to all, even to their persecutors and enemies, including the Roman rulers (Rom 13:1–7).

Thus, the church as the troops of the Lord Jesus Christ, God's Son, carry out his holy war against the kingdom of Satan and win victory over Satan's power of sin through the "obedience of faith" to Christ's reign, which in practice means observance of his law, the double commandment of love, to bear "the fruit of righteousness," and to realize the "righteousness/justice, peace, and joy (or wellbeing)" of his kingdom. Christians observe "the law of Christ" by sacrificing themselves to serve others in imitation of Christ Jesus who gave himself as "ransom for many." So just as Christ Jesus decisively defeated Satan through his self-giving love for all sinners on the cross, so also his disciples or troops are to go on mopping up the still-active satanic forces by their self-giving love for others. The self-assertion or self-seeking of the race of the first Adam under Satan's reign can be beaten only by the self-giving love of the race of the last Adam that has been redeemed into the kingdom of God and his Son Jesus Christ the Lord. The unrighteousness/injustice, conflicts (or violence), and suffering that the former engenders can be overcome only by the latter.

How Successful Is Paul in Practicing His Own Teaching of Self-Giving Love, Even for Enemies?

How successful is Paul then in practicing his own teaching of self-giving love for others that overcomes conflicts and violence and promotes reconciliation and peace? We have already seen above how he fundamentally defines his apostolic role in terms of a self-sacrificing ministry for the church according to Jesus' ransom saying and how conscientiously he conducts his ministry in imitation of the ministry of the Christ of that saying (see also 2 Cor 12:13–18, esp. v. 15).

We have also considered his teaching about God's last judgment. There, from his theological perspective, we acknowledged its necessity and tried to appreciate its positive intent to encourage Christians to persevere in faith and love until the consummation of their salvation at the eschaton. However, it is quite clear that his language about the destruction of unbelievers and persecutors of Christians at the last judgment is excessively harsh and evocative of violence for modern sensitivity. Paul's use of such language is traditional, often echoing OT texts or the Jewish tradition (e.g., Rom 12:19, 20;[34] 1 Thess 2:14–16; 5:3; 2 Thess 1:6–9). Nevertheless, had

---

34. If the quotation from Prov 25:21–22 ("you will heap burning calls upon his head") is to be negatively interpreted in terms of God's condemnation at the last judgment (see K. Stendahl, "Hate, Non-Retaliation, and Love, 1 QS x, 17–20 and Rom. 12:19–21," *HTR* 55 [1962] 343–55), although a positive interpretation in the sense of "God will make the enemy into your friend" appears more plausible (see J. G. D. Dunn, *Romans 9–16*, WBC 38B [Dallas: Word, 1988] 750–51).

he borne in mind his own teachings about loving enemies rather than revenging them and about blessing persecutors rather than cursing them (Rom 12:14–21), he certainly could have at least moderated his language about the opponents of the Christian faith and expressed the fate of unbelievers less harshly.[35]

Paul lashes out in particularly harsh or even violent condemnation against two kinds of people:

1. His Christian opponents (the Judaizers or "false teachers" in the Galatian church and the "super apostles" in the Corinthian church) whom he regards as distorting the gospel and denying his apostleship and thus leading his converts astray from the right faith (see "How Did Paul Change . . . ?" above);

2. Non-Christian persecutors who hinder his gospel preaching and force his converts to give up their faith in the gospel (e.g., 1 Thess 2:14–16; 2 Thess 1:6–9; see also Phil 1:28–29 and 3:18–19 [?]).

To these two groups of people, Paul is not ready to apply his own teaching of enemy love. However, he expresses his love in a moving way to the Corinthian church that was misled by the "super apostles" to doubt the genuineness of his apostleship and his collection scheme for the Jerusalem church but then repented of their wrongs (2 Cor 1–9). He expresses his forgiveness of the one particular member of the church who apparently pained him especially severely, and he asks the whole church to forgive him and love him (2 Cor 2:5–11). So it appears that Paul thinks he cannot apply his teaching of enemy love to the "false apostles/teachers" and the non-Christian persecutors so long as they persist in leading Christians astray from the right faith or in preventing others from coming to faith in the gospel of God's saving grace—because the duty of neighbor-love requires him to fight such people rather than to forgive them for their sinful acts, which would be actually to condone them. Even so, Paul's violent language against "false teachers/apostles" must have contributed much to the rise of the tradition of harsh theological polemic and especially the violent treatment of "heretics" in the history of the church. Nevertheless, it is also to be noted that even in his sharpest denunciations of "false apostles/teachers" or persecutors he never suggests exercising physical violence against them.

In this connection, it is noteworthy that in the catalogues of his suffering (1 Cor 4:9–13; 2 Cor 4:7–10; 6:4–10; 11:23–27; 12:10; see also 2 Cor 1:3–11; Phil 1:12–18) Paul expresses little feeling of resentment toward his persecutors and even less of vengeance. In this, he apparently practices his own teaching: "Beloved, never avenge yourselves, but leave it to the wrath of God" (Rom 12:19).[36] Some may point to

---

35. See n.12 above.

36. Note that in one of the catalogues Paul says that he responds to his persecutors with the

1 Thess 2:14–16 to counter this observation. In that passage Paul does express some resentment toward the Jews who persecuted him and hindered him from preaching the gospel to the gentiles. However, that sentiment is to be understood as part of his lament over their present unbelief in their Messiah Jesus, which he sees as the culmination of their long history of disobedience to God and of persecution of his true prophets (see Rom 9–11). Furthermore, it is to be appreciated that even in that Thessalonians passage in which he is speaking of the Jews who, in alliance with the pagan persecutors, "drove [him] out" of Thessalonica only a few months ago, and gave him such great anxiety about the budding church that he had left behind like "orphans" in Thessalonica (1 Thess 2:17–3:10), he simply leaves them to God's wrath, with no more than a tinge of resentment. Note also that even while speaking of God's "destruction" of unbelievers and the persecutors of the church at his last judgment, unlike some apocalyptic literature (e.g., Rev 19:11—20:10) or even the imprecatory Psalms (e.g., Ps 69:23–25; 109:8–11; 140:8–11), Paul has no interest in elaborating on that destruction by drawing a gruesome picture of it. Clearly with the idea of the "destruction" of the enemies of God at the last judgment, he is interested more in affirming that God will clear his creation of all evils and establish universal shalom than in taking comfort in the thought that God will take revenge on those who are enemies on our behalf.[37]

Clearly Paul is not perfect in practicing his own teaching of enemy love. However, here we need to ask, "How many of us can claim to respond to our persecutors better than Paul?" In spite of all the negative or even "violent" statements about God's judgment of unbelievers and evildoers, in his lack of a spirit of vengeance toward his enemies we can recognize the remarkable degree of influence that Jesus' prohibition of vengeance and his exhortation of enemy love had upon him—the erstwhile Jewish "zealot," a passionate man who apparently had a temper as a personality trait.[38]

Conclusion

Paul hurls harsh and violent condemnations against the "false apostles/teachers" who lead his converts astray from the right faith, as well as against the opponents of the Christian faith who persecute him, hoping that he will cease to preach the gospel of Christ Jesus and persecute his converts, hoping that they will give up their

"weapons of righteousness" such as "purity, knowledge, forbearance, kindness, the Holy Spirit, genuine love, truthful speech, and the power of God" (2 Cor 6:6–7), i.e., with the peace-promoting "fruits of the Spirit" rather than the violence-promoting "works of the flesh" (Gal 5:19–23; see also Phil 4:8–9).

37. See Vos, "Splitting and Violence," 193–94.
38. See G. Bornkamm, *Paul* (trans. D. M. G. Stalker; Minneapolis: Fortress, 1995) 239.

Christian faith. It is possible for some readers of his letters to focus just on this aspect of his life and teaching and to feel justified in using similarly violent language toward their opponents or even consider themselves inspired to attack them physically, something that Paul never suggests.

But such a focus ignores Paul's gospel of God's salvation through his and his Son's self-giving love and his energetic exposition of it in terms of "justification" and "reconciliation," the metaphors that express most effectively the truth that God's salvation establishes righteousness/justice and peace not only between God and human beings but also among human beings. It also ignores his impressive apostolic life of self-sacrificing service for others, as well as his emphatic teaching for Christians to live in a manner "worthy of the gospel of Christ" (Phil 1:27), that is, to practice self-giving love for neighbors (including enemies) in imitation of Christ, and in imitation of his own apostolic example.

It is the responsibility of exegetes, theologians, and pastors to teach their flock not to focus only on the opening words of Eph 6:10–20 and get encouraged to justify a violent war or inspired to conduct a shamanistic kind of "spiritual warfare," but to look at the whole text (and do that in light of the whole gospel) to get the real meaning and method of "spiritual warfare." Likewise, it is their job to teach their flock not to focus just on Paul's violent language, but to consider his teaching and ministry as a whole to judge whether he remained a violent "zealot" even after he became a Christian,[39] or whether, as he claims, he was created anew to be an envoy of God and his Son Jesus Christ for reconciliation and peace to all the nations (2 Cor 5:14–21).

---

39. So Gager, with Gibson, "Violent Acts and Violent Language," 13–21.

RESPONSE TO KIM

Julien C. H. Smith

Introduction

I am largely persuaded by both halves of Professor Kim's argument: that describing Paul as a violent person under the comprehensive definition Kim provides is not ultimately useful; and that Paul should be understood rather as an emissary of the gospel whereby we are enabled by the Spirit to fulfill Christ's law of neighborly love. Behind Kim's historical and exegetical work, I detect a normative concern: can Paul be regarded as a touchstone of Christian theology and ethics if, as Kim notes, he is "perceived by some critics as evoking intolerance and violence?" In response, I pose three questions, each of which aims to extend the implications of Kim's argument in a way that addresses this larger normative question. First, prior to his Damascus Christophany, was Paul actually a violent persecutor of the church? Second, does Paul envision the church as the "troops of the Lord?" And third, in what rhetorical context should we place Paul's allegedly violent speech?

Was Paul a Persecutor of the Church?

Having addressed the charge of Paul's allegedly violent rhetoric, Kim turns to his major question of interest: "How did Paul change from a violent 'zealot' to a Christian and apostle who teaches the ways of loving neighbor and achieving peace?" Kim's evidence that Paul "persecuted the church excessively and tried to destroy her" is from the apostle's own hand (Gal 1:13–14). Paul's phrase, *kath' hyperbolēn ediōkon*, is rendered "I was *violently* persecuting" in the NRSV. Other translations render the adverbial phrase as "beyond measure" (AV) or "intensely" (NIV) but all agree that the verb connotes the action of persecution. Here, Kim understands Paul to be following in the footsteps of Phinehas, Elijah, and the Maccabees, defending what he terms the "honor of God and the integrity of his law" through violence. Thus, Kim locates Paul prior to his Damascus Christophany within "nationalistic and even militant Jewish messianism." I must add that Kim is not alone here: the claim that Paul violently persecuted the church enjoys wide scholarly support.[1]

Yet to what extent did Paul participate in the physical violence commonly associated with the ideology of "zeal?"[2] Much seems to hang on what we think he means by the verb *diōkō*. LSJ does indeed list *persecute* as one of the attested meanings; more commonly the verb means *pursue, chase away*, and as a legal term, *prosecute*.[3] The other evidence Kim cites from Paul's own hand, Phil 3:6, unfortunately does not provide more helpful context. There we learn simply that Paul was *kata zēlos diōkōn tēn ekklēsian*.[4] On this slender evidence, it seems to me, we could equally imagine Paul *pursuing* the church as *persecuting* it. At first blush, such a translation seems nearly meaningless. However, in contexts such as the Psalms (LXX) where the verb *diōkō* apparently connotes persecution, this meaning is clearly derived metaphorically from the concrete image of a hunter pursuing his quarry.[5] While subjectively the quarry might well describe such pursuit as persecution, we can imagine contexts in which pursuit is aimed at some other purpose. Consider the pursuit of an uncooperative witness in order to serve a subpoena to testify in court, or the pursuit of a fugitive by law enforcement agents. If Paul understood himself to be pursuing the church in this sense, the question then becomes, what do we imagine Paul did when he caught it?

Luke gives us some indication, and I admit the words he puts in Paul's mouth in Acts 22:3–4 do not initially seem to support my reticence to view Paul as a violent persecutor of the church. Before an angry mob in Jerusalem Paul defends himself:

> I persecuted this Way *up to the point of death* [*achri thanatou*] by binding both men and women and putting them in prison, as the high priest and the whole council of elders can testify about me. From them I also received letters to the

---

1. Seyoon Kim, *The Origins of Paul's Gospel*, 2nd ed., WUNT 2/4 (Tübingen: Mohr Siebeck, 1984) 44–50; E. P. Sanders, *Paul: The Apostle's Life, Letters, and Thought* (Minneapolis: Fortress, 2015) 76–81; N. T. Wright, *Paul and the Faithfulness of God* (Minneapolis: Fortress, 2013) 1:194. Both Sanders and Wright regard Paul's persecution of the church as an accepted fact. Sanders, however, claims that Paul's persecution of the church cannot be located within behavior characteristic of the historical Pharisees.

2. On the evidence of his letters, I think we can safely infer that Paul engaged in violent *rhetoric* directed against the church. I am interested in the narrower question of what we can infer about his allegedly violent *actions*. On whether violent rhetoric constitutes persecution, see n6 below.

3. H. G. Liddell, R. Scott, and H. S. Jones, *A Greek-English Lexicon*, 9th ed. with revised supplement (Oxford: Clarendon, 1996). Curiously, LSJ provides only NT texts—John 5:16 and Matt 5:10—as witnesses for the meaning of "persecute."

4. 1 Cor 15:9 gives us simply *ediōxa tēn ekklēsian*.

5. See the discussion in Albrecht Oepke, "*diōkō*," in *Theological Dictionary of the New Testament*, 10 vols, ed. Gerhard Kittel and Gerhard Friedrich, trans. Geoffrey William Bromiley (Grand Rapids: Eerdmans, 1964). In Ps 7:2, 6 (LXX), the image is of a lion pursuing its prey. But note that the verb *katadiōkō*, which Oepke notes commonly denotes persecution in the Psalms, is used in Ps 23:6 (22:6 LXX) metaphorically to present goodness and mercy in hot pursuit of the psalmist.

> brothers in Damascus, and I went there in order to bind those who were there and to bring them back to Jerusalem for punishment.

We could, of course, observe that this is Luke's characterization of Paul and not the apostle's own words. But, for the sake of argument at least, let us take Luke at his word here. It is hard to think of a more violent turn of phrase than Paul's *achri thanatou*. But note that whatever Paul is doing—persecuting, pursuing, or prosecuting—his object is "the Way," not the men and women who are adherents of the Way. To be sure, he binds such persons and brings them back to Jerusalem for punishment, yet he does so clearly in his capacity as an authorized agent of the high priest and council of elders. The picture we have is of a man who has been given the legal authority to investigate individuals suspected of religious infractions and, if warranted, arrest and transport them to the religious authorities for adjudication.

If we see Paul as an authorized agent tasked with issuing and enforcing subpoenas to appear before the council, his self-understanding as being involved in the *pursuit* of a deviant religious sect for the purpose of legal *prosecution* rather than extra-judicial *persecution* seems more plausible.[6] But what about his frank admission in Gal 1:13 that he was endeavoring to *destroy* the church? This sounds awfully like persecution. Perhaps, but as Paul makes clear at the end of this autobiographical section, it was *the faith* he was seeking to destroy (Gal 1:23). We can, of course imagine Paul's *modus operandi* to have been the violent extermination of all adherents to the faith, but is it not more plausible to think that Paul's weapons of choice were not swords but rather words? The strongest evidence pointing in this direction is indeed Paul's own letters. That is, can we not imagine that Paul was *en route* to the synagogue in Damascus intending to "destroy arguments and every proud obstacle raised up against the knowledge of God," just as was his practice in the church at Corinth (2 Cor 10:4–5)? Might it be the case that Paul's "violence" was not so much transformed as redirected? But before further examining Paul's allegedly violent rhetoric, I wish to explore his martial imagery.

---

6. From the vantage point of a modern western democratic society like the USA, in which is enshrined the separation of church and state, we might insist that any efforts to curtail individual religious freedom should be regarded as illegitimate, and hence as persecution, even if sanctioned by recognized religious authorities. Yet we cannot hold Paul to a standard of behavior based upon a distinction between civil and religious authority that was unknown in Mediterranean antiquity. On the religious and civil authority vested in the council of elders and high priest, see Shaye J. D. Cohen, *From the Maccabees to the Mishnah*, 2nd ed., reprint, 1987 (Louisville: Westminster John Knox, 2006) 101–3; James C. VanderKam, *An Introduction to Early Judaism* (Grand Rapids: Eerdmans, 2001) 176–85.

Troops in the Lord's Army?

As a result of his Damascus Christophany, Paul comes to see Jesus as Messiah, whom God has exalted and invested with kingly power for the purpose of what Kim describes as a "mopping-up operation against the Satanic forces" (1 Cor 15:23–28). Jesus engages in this task by reigning over the church, enabling obedience through the Spirit to the "law of Christ" (Gal 5:14; 6:2), that is, the command to love God and neighbor. For Kim, it thus follows that the church has been enlisted as "the Lord Jesus Christ's troops employed in his holy war against the Satanic kingdom." Yet is this a necessary inference? Must the church see itself—even if only metaphorically—as troops in the Lord's army?

This is not merely a logical inference for Kim but depends rather on Paul's use of martial imagery. We are to offer our bodies not as "weapons [*hopla*] of wickedness" but as "weapons [*hopla*] of righteousness" (Rom 6:13). Here I believe "instruments" would serve better as a translation for *hopla* since there is nothing in the passage that connotes a martial context.[7] There are, of course, instances in which Paul does indeed use the term to denote weaponry (2 Cor 6:7; 10:4) and armor (Rom 13:12; Eph 6:11, 13). Yet, do his metaphorical references to his own or the church's use of weaponry and armor belie a deeper belief that the church must see itself as the Lord's troops engaged in battle—admittedly nonviolently, as Kim makes clear—with Satan's kingdom? Kim takes Paul's most extensive use of martial imagery, in Eph 6:10–20, as evidence for the affirmative—the church is enjoined to "fight the holy war" against the "wiles of the devil" (referring to Eph 6:11). And yet, Paul does not command the church to fight. Rather, having clothed themselves with armor, they are to *stand firm* against the devil's deception and aggression (Eph 6:11, 13, 14). This sounds rather more like civil defense than military combat.[8]

There is only one instance I am aware of in which Paul unambiguously uses the term *hopla* as weapons to be used aggressively and destructively in warfare: 2 Cor 10:3–6.[9] Yet even here, he seems to be describing his own behavior, or perhaps

---

7. Interpreters are divided on this question: C. E. B. Cranfield, *Romans: A Shorter Commentary* (Grand Rapids: Eerdmans, 1985) 138–39; Frank J. Matera, *Romans*, Paideia Commentaries on the New Testament (Grand Rapids: Baker Academic, 2010) 154; N. T. Wright, "Romans," in *Acts–First Corinthians*, NIB 10 (Nashville: Abingdon, 2002) 542, opt for the translation "instruments"; Ernst Käsemann, *Romans*, trans. Geoffrey W. Bromiley (Grand Rapids, MI: Eerdmans, 1980) 177, opts for "weapons."

8. Andrew T. Lincoln, *Ephesians*, WBC 42 (Dallas: Word, 1990) 442, indicates that the injunction to "stand firm" (*stēnai*) implies a defensive posture: "It involves standing firm, holding one's position, resisting, not surrendering to the opposition but prevailing against it." So also Ernest Best, *A Critical and Exegetical Commentary on Ephesians*, ICC (Edinburgh: T&T Clark, 1998) 591: "emphasis lies on the need of holding on to a position and not of advancing or attacking."

9. In 2 Cor 6:7 Paul speaks of having commended himself to the Corinthian believers "with the

that of fellow apostles, rather than exhorting the Corinthian church to follow him. More importantly, Paul seems to be using the term *hopla* to refer to an arsenal of *verbal* weaponry. These *hopla* are the means by which Paul aims to "destroy arguments and every proud obstacle raised up against the knowledge of God," taking "every thought captive to obey Christ" (2 Cor 10:4b–5). And here we return to the evidence I adduced earlier that Paul's "violent" behavior, both prior to and following his Damascus Christophany, is perhaps best understood as verbal warfare. My third and final comment reflects upon the ancient context within which we might best understand this sort of rhetoric.

"Violent" Speech and Forensic Rhetoric

Paul's allegedly violent rhetoric seems alarming and reprehensible to us, but I suspect it would have seemed rather conventional to his contemporaries. As L. T. Johnson has observed, the rhetoric of slander was equally at home in intra-Jewish polemic and Hellenistic philosophical debate.[10] The majority of extant *progymnasmata*, preliminary composition exercises, provide instruction in the use of invective (*psogos*), an attack seeking to blame a particular individual.[11] Although it is doubtful that Paul received advanced rhetorical training, his facility with invective is evident from his lively characterization of his opponents in passages such as 2 Cor 11:13–15; Phil 3:18–19; and 1 Thess 2:15–16.[12] By suggesting that Paul's use of violent rhetoric was conventional, I by no means intend to imply that Paul meant nothing by it. My point is not that Paul's violent speech was, as we might say, *purely* conventional and hence of no concern to contemporary readers of Paul. Rather, the descriptor "conventional" implies that a speaker (or writer) and audience understood and agreed upon the appropriateness of certain forms of speech to certain occasions. It is in-

---

weapons [*dia tōn hoplōn*] of righteousness for the right hand and for the left," yet the reference seems decidedly ambiguous. Frank J. Matera, *II Corinthians: A Commentary*, NTL (Louisville: Westminster John Knox, 2003) 153, takes Paul to mean "the weapons that *are* righteousness." Victor Paul Furnish, *II Corinthians*, AB 32A (Garden City, NY: Doubleday, 1984) 346: "having weapons that God's righteousness has provided." Margaret E. Thrall, *A Critical and Exegetical Commentary on the Second Epistle of the Corinthians*, 2 vols., ICC (London: T&T Clark International, 2004) 1:462: "weapons consisting of (human) righteousness."

10. Luke Timothy Johnson, "The New Testament's Anti-Jewish Slander and the Conventions of Ancient Polemic," *JBL* 108 (1989) 419–41.

11. Invective is treated in the *progymnasmata* of Theon, Aphthonius, and Nicolaus. Hermogenes only treats encomium, the antithetical pair of invective. See George Alexander Kennedy, ed. and trans., *Progymnasmata: Greek Textbooks of Prose Composition and Rhetoric*, WGRW 10 (Atlanta: Society of Biblical Literature, 2003).

12. On the extent of Paul's training in rhetoric, see Stanley E. Porter, "Paul of Tarsus and His Letters," in *Handbook of Classical Rhetoric in the Hellenistic Period (330 B.C.–A.D. 400)*, ed. Stanley E. Porter (Leiden: Brill, 1997) 533–38.

structive to observe that we largely no longer consider violent rhetoric appropriate in the contexts that Paul and his audience would have. We do not, for example, send our children to school to learn how to craft invective, as was commonplace in the pedagogical milieu of Paul's day.[13] Such observations should lead us carefully to consider what sort of rhetorical context Paul might have understood himself to be operating within.

Paul often directs his sharp words toward individuals, even those for whom he cares deeply (Gal 3:1). Yet it is, above all, the *beliefs* and *practices* that he regards as antithetical to the gospel upon which Paul pours forth contempt and vitriol (Gal 1:6). It is, as he insists to the Corinthian church, *arguments* that he is keen to destroy (2 Cor 10:4b). And, in Paul's world as in ours, the law court was the venue *par excellence* where arguments were advanced, defended, and attacked with violence.[14] Paul was clearly not a lawyer, and yet the urgency—and at times violence—with which he often argues compares favorably to that profession. And so, my suggestion is this: might we not helpfully see the context of Paul's violent language as appropriate to the task of prosecution and defense, language that aims not to incite further violence but rather to serve the process of justice, that violence may be constrained?[15]

Conclusion

These three questions aim to address what I take to be the normative question behind Kim's argument: can we read and teach Paul today in a way that doesn't take his violent rhetoric as the paradigm for our interaction with others? To this end, I question whether, prior to his Damascus Christophany, Paul violently persecuted the church. If Paul was engaged in pursuit and prosecution rather than persecution, we may imagine that the "weapons" he employed to this end remained consistent before and after Damascus: verbal arguments rather than physical violence. Second, I propose that when Paul employs martial imagery, his goal is to encourage a defensive, rather than aggressive, posture among his audience. Finally, I suggest that Paul's violent rhetoric is appropriate to certain venues where such language may be

13. Mastering the skill of crafting encomium and invective, as well as the other preliminary exercises, was crucial because they functioned as the building blocks from which declamations were composed. See the example related to the use of invective in Raffaella Cribiore, *Gymnastics of the Mind: Greek Education in Hellenistic and Roman Egypt* (Princeton: Princeton University Press, 2001) 237.

14. George A. Kennedy, "The Genres of Rhetoric," in *Handbook of Classical Rhetoric in the Hellenistic Period (330 B.C.-A.D. 400)*, ed. Stanley E. Porter (Leiden: Brill, 1997) 48, observes that the rhetorical schools primarily trained students for careers in deliberative and judicial oratory.

15. Kim makes the salutary point that the very notion of justice implies some level of violence, and that if we are categorically opposed to violence, we would then be obliged to reject the notion of a system of justice, accepting the anarchy and violence that would result. Most of us, ancient and modern alike, regard the system of justice to be an indispensable element of a flourishing society.

appropriately employed to destroy arguments. But this also means, as Kim rightly observes in his conclusion, that it is "the responsibility of exegetes, theologians, and pastors to teach their flock" that Paul's violent rhetoric must not be used in contexts today in which it is likely to do violence not to arguments but rather to people.

"I WILL PUT ENMITY BETWEEN YOU ..."[1]: SCRIPTURAL ARCANA IN CARL SCHMITT'S POLITICAL THEOLOGY

Kyle Gingerich Hiebert

Introduction

If political theory thrives in times of crisis it is a small step to suggest that political theology does likewise. In our contemporary climate, the "newly arisen apocalyptic tone" that Jacques Derrida spoke of in 1980 has seeped into the cultural imaginary to such a degree that any crisis whatsoever—from global environmental degradation to genocide and much more besides—can be given new urgency by describing it as apocalyptic.[2] Long before Derrida, Friedrich Nietzsche memorably described the shattering of Enlightenment dreams of perpetual peace as nothing less than the advent of nihilism: "For some time now, our whole European culture has been moving as toward a catastrophe, with a tortured tension that is growing from decade to decade: restlessly, violently, like a river that wants to reach the end."[3] In Nietzsche's wake, then, perhaps it is unsurprising that there has been an explosion of interest in the work of Carl Schmitt (1888–1985), the paradigmatic modern apocalyptic theorist of the emergency. This is due in no small part to the work of the Italian philosopher Giorgio Agamben who uses Schmitt's work to develop a powerful critique of our contemporary biopolitical situation.[4] However, despite his appropriation in philosophy and political theory, there is almost no theological work that rigorously

---

1. Gen 3:15, as quoted in Carl Schmitt, *The Concept of the Political*, trans. George Schwab (Chicago: University of Chicago Press, 1996) 68. All biblical quotations are taken from the NRSV.

2. Derrida's original lecture took place in 1980 at a conference on his work at Cerisy-la-Salle. For an English translation see Jacques Derrida, "Of an Apocalyptic Tone Recently Adopted in Philosophy," *Semeia* 23 (1982) 63–97.

3. Friedrich Nietzsche, *Will to Power*, trans. and ed. Walter Kaufmann and R. J. Hollingdale (New York: Vintage, 1968) 3.

4. See Giorgio Agamben, *Homo Sacer: Sovereign Power and Bare Life*, trans. Daniel Heller-Roazen (Stanford: Stanford University Press, 1998); Giorgio Agamben, *State of Exception*, trans. Kevin Attell (Chicago: University of Chicago Press, 2005). Other significant treatments of Schmitt in contemporary philosophy are Jacques Derrida, *The Politics of Friendship*, trans. George Collins (New York: Verso, 2005); and Chantal Mouffe, ed., *The Challenge of Carl Schmitt* (London: Verso, 1999).

and charitably engages in any significant way Schmitt's development of political theology or its legacy. This is particularly curious because Schmitt is universally recognized as the "godfather of political theology" and for reintroducing the very term "political theology" into the lexicon of modern discourse.[5] To cite but one recent example, Elizabeth Philips mentions Schmitt's ongoing influence on political theology, and even obliquely (and intriguingly) suggests a constructive influence on the work of William Cavanaugh, but does not explore this and quickly sets him aside as a controversial background figure.[6]

To be fair, Schmitt's work is difficult and provokes notoriously different and even opposing interpretations, owing at least in some measure to his role as crown jurist for the Third Reich. Indeed, many interpreters understand Schmitt's involvement with the Nazi Party, of which he was officially a member from May 1933 to December 1936, to be the decisive locus around which his political theology is to be interpreted.[7] The rhetorical force of such accounts reach their crescendo in Schmitt's opening address at a 1934 conference on "Judaism and Jurisprudence": "But the most profound and ultimate meaning of this battle, and thus also of our work today, lies expressed in the Führer's sentence: 'In fending off the Jew, I fight for the work of the Lord.'"[8] Coupled with Schmitt's infamous essay entitled "The Führer Protects the Law,"[9] which provided juridical support for the bloody purge of 30 June 1934, the so-called "Night of the Long Knives," it is not unreasonable to argue that anti-Semitism is not an indirect result of Schmitt's political theology but an intrinsic element.[10] Therefore, if Schmitt's work is mentioned in theological discourse at all it

---

5. See, for example, Michael Hollerich, "Carl Schmitt," in *The Blackwell Companion to Political Theology*, ed. Peter Scott and William T. Cavanaugh (Malden: Blackwell, 2004) 107.

6. See Elizabeth Philips, *Political Theology: A Guide for the Perplexed* (London: T&T Clark, 2010) 4–5. For a notable exception see Michael Northcott, *A Political Theology of Climate Change* (Grand Rapids: Eerdmans, 2014) especially 210–43.

7. For one such account see Derek Simon, "The New Political Theology of Johann Baptist Metz: Confronting Schmitt's Decisionist Political Theology of Exclusion," *Horizons* 30.2 (2003) 227–54.

8. Carl Schmitt, "Eröffnung der wissenschaftlichen Vorträge durch den Reichsgruppenwalter Prof. Dr. Carl Schmitt," in *Die deutsche Rechtswissenschaft im Kampf gegen den jüdischen Geist* (Berlin: Deutscher Rechtsverlag, 1936) 14.

9. See Carl Schmitt, "Der Führer schützt das Recht: zur Reichstagsrede Adolf Hitlers vom 13. Juli 1934," in *Positionen und Begriffe im Kampf mit Weimar-Genf-Versailles 1923–1939* (Berlin: Duncker & Humblot, 1994).

10. The issue of whether and to what extent Schmitt's work in the Weimar period can be directly linked to his subsequent involvement in the Nazi Party is one of the looming questions taken up in the massive and contentious scholarship on Schmitt. At its most basic, the fault line can be drawn between Hannah Arendt, who claims that Schmitt was a "convinced Nazi," and Jacob Taubes, who claims that Schmitt merely "flirted with the Nazis." See Hannah Arendt, *The Origins of Totalitarianism* (New York: Meridian, 1958) 339; and Jacob Taubes, *The Political Theology of Paul*, trans. Dana Hollander (Stanford: Stanford University Press, 2004) 100.

is invariably used as a negative foil against which a robustly Christian political theology must be boldly asserted. Anyone acquainted with the beginnings of political theology in Germany in the 1960s will undoubtedly be familiar with plethora of rather vague assertions, such as that of Johann Baptist Metz, who claims that "the notion of political theology is ambiguous, hence exposed to misunderstanding, because it has been burdened with specific historical connotations."[11] Supporting Metz's insistence that any specifically Christian political theology must use the qualifier *new*, Jürgen Moltmann argues for the need to distinguish political theology from the "pseudo-religiosity" of Schmitt's political theology, which he suggests is better understood as political religion.[12] Despite the uncovering of the theological element in Schmitt's work begun by Heinrich Meier—an element that is still being contested—the underlying and largely unarticulated assumption within the discipline of theology seems to be, very simply, that Schmitt's political theology is little more than thinly veiled ideological legitimation of Nazi policy and, when it comes right down to it, is conspicuous in its avoidance of substantive theological statement and, therefore, is not worthy of any sustained theological engagement beyond outright denunciation.[13]

I have argued elsewhere in some detail that the legacy of the effects of Schmitt's political theology continues to haunt contemporary debates in largely unacknowledged and unexpected ways and that the discipline of theology in general has prematurely bid *adieu* to Schmitt to its own detriment.[14] What follows is an attempt to deepen and expand that argument by exploring what I call the scriptural arcana in Schmitt's political theology. The task of re-examining the effects of Schmitt's legacy is arguably becoming more urgent, particularly given recent renewed calls to simply "forget Schmitt!" that are made alongside continuing explicit acknowledgement of the foundational nature of his work and its underrepresentation within the discipline of theology.[15] At least part of this impulse is understandable to anyone

---

11. Johann Baptist Metz, *Theology of the World*, trans. William Glen-Dopel (New York: Herder and Herder, 1969) 107.

12. See, for example, Jürgen Moltmann, "Christian Theology and Political Religion," in *Civil Religion and Political Theology*, ed. Leroy S. Rouner (Notre Dame: University of Notre Dame Press, 1986) 41–58.

13. For Meier's work see Heinrich Meier, *The Lesson of Carl Schmitt: Four Chapters on the Distinction Between Political Theology and Political Philosophy*, trans. Marcus Brainard (Chicago: University of Chicago Press, 1998). For a recent contestation of the extent to which the theological element is central in Schmitt see Aaron B. Roberts, "Carl Schmitt—Political Theologian?" *The Review of Politics* 77 (2015) 449–74.

14. See Kyle Gingerich Hiebert, *The Architectonics of Hope: Violence, Apocalyptic, and the Transformation of Political Theology* (Eugene, OR: Cascade, 2017). This essay draws on this work in places throughout.

15. See Carl Raschke, "Forget Schmitt! Political Theology Must Follow Agamben's 'Double Paradigm' of Sovereignty," *Political Theology* 19.1 (2018) 1–3.

who has attempted to read Schmitt; his work, as I alluded to above, is difficult and easily provokes conflicting interpretations. The difficulty Schmitt presents us with, however, lies less in the constructions of the positions he critiques and the explicit recommendations he makes and more in the multiple allusions and hidden resonances with which he intentionally saturates his texts. Indeed, in *Roman Catholicism and Political Form*, Schmitt suggests that "to every great politics belongs the 'arcanum'" and Schmitt's texts themselves employ a vast array of literary and cultural allusions, unexplained and obscure references, bold prognostications and cryptic insinuations.[16] In a manner not dissimilar to his own description of reading Hobbes, Schmitt too has a taste for "esoteric coverups," reveals his thoughts only in part, and acts "as people do who open a window only for a moment and close it quickly for fear of a storm."[17] Just as in the case of reading Hobbes, then, all of this makes reading Schmitt simultaneously exhilarating and frustrating. Doubling this difficulty is the undeniable fact of Schmitt's support for the Nazi party, which forces upon us an abyssal question: how is it possible that such a creative and formidable mind could find something to endorse in National Socialism? Such a question admits of no straightforward answer and that Schmitt rallied to the Nazi cause is no insignificant detail. However, when read carefully Schmitt's work resists any easy *reductio ad Hitlerum* and this fact needs to be wrestled with in the discipline of theology as it has been to a much greater extent in the case of Martin Heidegger, who joined the Nazi party on the very same day as Schmitt. In what follows, then, I will address this double difficulty firstly by offering a reading of Schmitt's political theology outside of his relation to Nietzsche, Heidegger, and the Third Reich and secondly by turning to an account of the biblical figures, texts, and allusions—what I will collectively refer to as scriptural arcana—that are mysteriously invoked to support some of Schmitt's most (in)famous arguments.

Defamiliarizing Schmitt's Political Theology

It is prudent that any engagement with Schmitt's thought should frankly acknowledge that such an endeavor must "think both *with* and *against* Schmitt."[18] Such an acknowledgement allows us to recognize that Schmitt's questions continue to be

---

16. Carl Schmitt, *Roman Catholicism and Political Form*, trans. G. L. Ulmen (London: Greenwood Press, 1996) 34.

17. Carl Schmitt, *The Leviathan in the State Theory of Thomas Hobbes: Meaning and Failure of a Political Symbol*, trans. George Schwab and Erna Hilfstein (Chicago: University of Chicago Press, 2008) 26.

18. Chantal Mouffe, "Introduction: Schmitt's Challenge," in *The Challenge of Carl Schmitt*, ed. Chantal Mouffe (London: Verso, 1999) 6.

relevant today, especially in our age of post-political liberal tolerance, and that it would be a mistake to dismiss him simply because of his inextricable involvement with the Nazi Party. Moreover, as I indicated above, it is also necessary to acknowledge that there is no reigning scholarly consensus on the interpretation of Schmitt's political theology, so much so that scholars are even able to come to opposite conclusions in their interpretations.[19] Schmitt's work is notoriously difficult to decode, especially with respect to its theological inflections, and at least part of the reason for this has to do with his Christian background in general and with his fraught relationship with Catholicism in particular, all of which is important for understanding his political theology and the scriptural arcana found within it.

Schmitt was born in 1888 to Catholic parents in Plettenburg, Westphalia, which was predominantly Protestant, and at age eleven was sent to a nearby Catholic boarding school where he found himself in the midst of a Catholic majority.[20] Against his mother's wishes, he decided not to study theology and opted instead for law, studying at the universities of Berlin, Munich and completing his doctorate at the University of Strasbourg in 1910 and his *Habilitation* in 1916. He held teaching appointments at the universities of Strasbourg, Munich, Greifswald, Bonn, and Berlin, published in Catholic journals, and came into contact with many notable Catholics including, amongst others, Karl Eschweiler, Jacques Maritain, Erich Przywara, Erik Peterson, and Hans Barion to whom he dedicated *Political Theology II*. Schmitt was excommunicated from the Roman Catholic Church in February of 1926 because his attempts to have his first marriage nullified failed.[21] Some have seen this event as sufficient evidence of a decisive break with the Roman Catholic Church, however, the evidence we have indicates neither that the so-called "early Schmitt" was particularly devout nor that he "broke with the church in the mid-twenties."[22] Indeed, as is the

---

19. One particularly salient example of this problem are the opposing interpretations of Renato Cristi and Heinrich Meier on the question of rationality in Schmitt's use of the Roman Catholic Church in his explication of the exception. Cristi argues that, for Schmitt, the church embodies a form of rationality while Meier argues that Schmitt's political theology emerges within a fundamental aporia that demands a leap of faith that is not rational. See Renato Cristi, *Carl Schmitt and Authoritarian Liberalism* (Cardiff: University of Wales Press, 1998) esp. 75; and Meier, *Lesson of Carl Schmitt*, esp. 122–23.

20. There are a number of excellent biographies of Schmitt. For the following account I have relied primarily on Reinhard Mehring, *Carl Schmitt: A Biography*, trans. Daniel Steuer (Malden: Polity, 2014). See also Joseph W. Bendersky, *Carl Schmitt: Theorist for the Reich* (Princeton: Princeton University Press, 1983).

21. For further details about Schmitt's two marriages see Reinhard Mehring, "A 'Catholic Layman of German Nationality and Citizenship'?: Carl Schmitt and the Religiosity of Life," in *The Oxford Handbook of Carl Schmitt*, ed. Jens Meierhenrich and Oliver Simons (Oxford: Oxford University Press) esp. 77–78.

22. See, for example, John McCormick's very brief assessment in *Carl Schmitt's Critique of Liberalism: Against Politics as Technology* (Cambridge: Cambridge University Press, 1999) 86–87.

case most often with Schmitt, the matter is far more complex and while there is not space here to explore Schmitt's relationship to Catholicism it is clear that a unique Catholic sensibility continues not only in Schmitt's work itself but also in his own self-understanding, even if this emerges as a tactical attempt to rehabilitate his work after 1945.

Turning to Schmitt's texts themselves, then, the most oft cited passages in his entire oeuvre come from *Political Theology* (1922) and *The Concept of the Political* (1927). Schmitt reintroduced the term "political theology" in 1922 and famously argued that "all significant concepts of the modern theory of the state are secularized theological concepts not only because of their historical development but also because of their systematic structure, the recognition of which is necessary for a sociological consideration of these concepts."[23] As is the case throughout Schmitt's work, he writes to counter what he sees as a grave problem, in this case the legal positivism of Hans Kelsen, a prominent Austrian jurist and legal scholar who appointed Schmitt to his chair at the University of Bonn. Kelsen sought to develop a pure theory of law, devoid of any subjective elements and based on norms that could be universally valid.[24] Against this strong neo-Kantian tendency in German legal theory, Schmitt claims that "all law is situational law" and that Kelsen merely "solved the problem of sovereignty by negating it."[25] The problem for Schmitt is that this kind of legal positivism is, quite simply, tautological. More specifically, the problem lies in the fact that the state has been reduced to nothing other than the legal order itself and when this happens it is incapable of addressing those emergencies that lie outside the law and thereby also incapable of thinking about the source of its own political legitimacy. Simply put, for Schmitt, positivism cannot think the ground of its own rationality. This brings to the fore perhaps the most significant concept that is taken up from Schmitt's work, namely his argument that "sovereign is he who decides on the exception."[26] With reference to the Danish philosopher and theologian Søren Kierkegaard, Schmitt claims that "the exception is more interesting than the rule. The rule proves nothing; the exception proves everything. In the exception the power of real life breaks through the crust of a mechanism that has become torpid by repetition."[27] It is easy to make too much of this bold assertion by claiming, as

---

23. Carl Schmitt, *Political Theology: Four Chapters on the Concept of Sovereignty*, trans. George Schwab (Chicago: University of Chicago Press, 1985) 36.

24. See Hans Kelsen, "God and the State," in *Essays in Legal and Moral Philosophy*, trans. Peter Heath (Dordrecht: Reidel, 1974) 61–82.

25. Schmitt, *Political Theology*, 13 and 21.

26. Ibid., 5.

27. Ibid., 15. See also Søren Kierkegaard, *Fear and Trembling and Repetition*, trans. Hong and Hong (Princeton: Princeton University Press, 1983) esp. 225–28.

Jürgen Habermas does, that this focus on the exception and the need for a genuine decision "results in the violent destruction of the normative as such," thereby making political discourse unintelligible.[28] Schmitt's own rhetoric may go some of the way toward helping us to understand Habermas's critique, after all he does claim that "the norm is destroyed in the exception,"[29] however it misses the sense in which Schmitt's political theology is precisely a sustained struggle to think through the paradox of sovereignty in a manner that maintains rational order. Indeed, Schmitt has been aptly described as a "fanatic of order."[30]

In what may be read as the companion volume to *Political Theology*, Schmitt writes in *Roman Catholicism and Political Form* (1923) of the kind of thinking that belongs intrinsically to the Roman Catholic Church, differentiating it from the kind of instrumental rationality and "economic-technical thinking that prevails today."[31] At work in the background here is Schmitt's worry that his one-time teacher, Max Weber, was right that the modern state had actually become a huge industrial plant in which the political is eclipsed by the economic and technical-organizational, thereby paralyzing the decision in endless discussion. Opposed to this, Schmitt appeals to the rationalism of the Roman Catholic Church, whose "argumentation is based on a particular mode of thinking whose method of proof is a specific juridical logic and whose focus of interest is the normative guidance of human social life."[32] Schmitt is very clear that "the Church has its own rationality" that exists as a *complexio oppositorum*, a complex of opposites, which is able to hold together opposing forms of life without reducing one to the other nor synthesizing them in a kind of Hegelian fashion to some "higher third."[33] Indeed, Schmitt claims of the Roman Catholic Church that "there appears to be no antithesis it does not embrace. It has long and proudly claimed to have united within itself all forms of state and government; to be an autocratic monarchy whose head is elected by the aristocracy of cardinals but in which there is nevertheless so much democracy that . . . even the least shepherd of Abruzzi, regardless of birth and station, has the possibility to become this autocratic sovereign."[34]

---

28. Jürgen Habermas, *The New Conservatism: Cultural Criticism and the Historians' Debate*, trans. Shierry Weber Nicholsen (Cambridge: MIT Press, 1989) esp. 133–37.

29. Schmitt, *Political Theology*, 12.

30. Jens Meierhenrich and Oliver Simons, "'A Fanatic of Order in an Epoch of Confusing Turmoil': The Political, Legal, and Cultural Thought of Carl Schmitt," in *The Oxford Handbook of Carl Schmitt*, ed. Jens Meierhenrich and Oliver Simons (Oxford: Oxford University Press) 12.

31. Ibid., 65.

32. Schmitt, *Roman Catholicism and Political Form*, 12.

33. Ibid., 8–9 and 13.

34. Ibid., 7.

Schmitt's fascination with the so-called counter-revolutionaries helpfully illuminates his discussion of the exceptional nature of sovereignty, which stands at the very core of his initial articulation of political theology. For Schmitt, the significance of the conservative authors of the counter-revolution, specifically the Catholic political philosophers Louis de Bonald, Joseph de Maistre and Juan Donoso Cortés, is rooted in their attempts to think sovereignty with the aid of analogies from Christian theology. The critical link here is between sovereignty and the decision, that is, the recognition that the very idea of the decision as such had been thrust into the center of the political philosophy of the counter-revolution. Schmitt's discussion of Cortés in particular brings these connections into view most sharply and begins to shed light on his virulent attack on liberalism.

> Donoso Cortés considered continuous discussion a method of circumventing responsibility and of ascribing to freedom of speech and of the press an excessive importance that in the final analysis permits the decision to be evaded. Just as liberalism discusses and negotiates every political detail, so it also wants to dissolve metaphysical truth in a discussion. The essence of liberalism is negotiation, a cautious half measure, in the hope that the definitive dispute, the decisive bloody battle, can be transformed into parliamentary debate and permit the decision to be suspended forever in an everlasting discussion.[35]

What is important to note here is that in the development of the nineteenth-century theory of the state there are two intertwined processes at work that Schmitt sees as decisive for thinking about the nature of the political, namely "the elimination of all theistic and transcendental conceptions and the formation of a new concept of legitimacy."[36] The significance of the counter-revolutionaries for Schmitt lies precisely in their recognition that the historical unfolding of these two principles paralyzed the political "in a paradisiacal worldliness of unproblematic concreteness," a heightened moment that could only be met with an "absolute decision created out of nothingness."[37] For Schmitt, the modern age is nothing but an outworking of the consequences of this historical unfolding, a veritable "onslaught against the political" that can only be met with one solution: dictatorship.

Here, as everywhere, Schmitt's understanding of dictatorship is far more complex than a simple a form of arbitrary despotism. Indeed, in what he himself

---

35. Schmitt, *Political Theology*, 63.

36. Ibid., 51.

37. Ibid., 65 and 66, respectively. Schmitt's endorsement of the political philosophy of the counter-revolutionaries stands in marked contrast to what he calls political romanticism, embodied for Schmitt in the figure of Adam Müller, whose theory of the state embodied the liberal indecisiveness of the bourgeoisie and was primarily a matter of aesthetics. See Carl Schmitt, *Political Romanticism*, trans. Guy Oakes (Cambridge: MIT Press, 1991) 115–43.

considered one of his own major works, Schmitt gives us an historical analysis of the legal concept of dictatorship and argues for a transformation from what was a commissary dictatorship—one that suspends the constitution in order to protect it—to a sovereign dictatorship—one that suspends the constitution in order to create the possibility for another that is yet to come.[38] For our purposes, the distinction between commissary and sovereign dictatorship that Schmitt draws here is less important than the fact that, in whatever form, dictatorship is understood as a nonarbitrary exception to a norm. As Schmitt puts it in his preliminary remarks, "Paradoxically, dictatorship becomes an exception to the state of law by doing what it needs to justify; because dictatorship means a form of government that is genuinely designed to resolve a very particular problem."[39] This understanding of dictatorship as the exception or suspension of law prefigures and anticipates much of Schmitt's later work and even here is not without theological overtones.[40]

Making the theological connection more explicit, Schmitt claims that "the exception in jurisprudence is analogous to the miracle in theology."[41] Here we can begin to see the structural analogy that Schmitt draws between theology and jurisprudence and the importance of what he calls the sociology of juristic concepts emerging in his initial articulation of political theology. Schmitt is concerned to investigate the historical development of the philosophical idea of the modern state, a story that he sees as inextricably linked to the rise of a rationalist metaphysics that rejects the exception in all its forms. Schmitt explains that the sociology of juristic concepts "aims to discover the basic, radically systematic structure and to compare this conceptual structure with the conceptually represented social structure of a certain epoch."[42] Thus defined, we should not be surprised that his thinking is thereby pushed into the theological realm (where else could it have gone?) since the metaphysical image a particular epoch has of itself is structurally analogous to the shape of its political formation. Going back, then, to Schmitt's reliance on the Roman Catholic Church as an exemplary form of political representation, the question is not how to apply Roman Catholic theology to juridical problems but rather how to think through modern jurisprudence to find the root of its own metaphysical assumptions. Schmitt comes back to this again in the postscript to *Political Theology II* (1970) and helpfully articulates exactly what is at stake, namely "the classical case

---

38. See Schmitt, *Dictatorship*, trans. Michael Hoelzl and Graham Ward (Malden, MA: Polity, 2014) esp. 112–31.
39. Ibid., xliii.
40. See ibid., 120–21.
41. Schmitt, *Political Theology*, 36.
42. Ibid., 45.

of a transposition of distinct concepts which has occurred within the systematic thought of the two—historically and discursively—most developed constellations of 'western rationalism': the Catholic *church* with its entire juridical rationality and *the state of the ius publicum Europaeum*."[43] For Schmitt, "the scientific conceptual structure of both these faculties [theology and jurisprudence] has systematically produced areas in which concepts can be transposed, among which harmonious exchanges are permitted and meaningful."[44]

In addition to his reliance on the conservative Catholic political philosophy of the counter-revolution, Schmitt turned to the English political philosopher Thomas Hobbes (1588–1679), who was for him the "true teacher of a great political experience; lonely as every pioneer; misunderstood as is everyone whose political thought does not gain acceptance among his own people; unrewarded, as one who opened a gate through which others marched on; and yet in the immortal community of the great scholars of the ages, a sole retriever of an ancient prudence."[45] Reflecting the enduring influence of Hobbes on his thinking, Schmitt articulates the importance of the *Leviathan* for his own political theology by explaining that "even during the Reformation of the Christian church in the sixteenth and seventeenth centuries, what had began as Christologo-political conflict over the *ius reformandi* [the right to reform] became a politico-theological revolution. Thomas Hobbes *brought the Reformation to a conclusion* by recognizing the state as a clear alternative to the Roman Catholic Church's monopoly on decision-making."[46] What Hobbes managed to do in the seventeenth century was precisely what Schmitt was attempting to do in the twentieth century and in the immense wake of Hobbes, Schmitt's thinking can be read as a political theology of the mortal god. Summarizing Hobbes, Schmitt claims that "the terror of the state of nature drives anguished individuals to come together; their fear rises to an extreme; a spark of reason (*ratio*) flashes; and suddenly there stands in front of them a new god."[47] As Hobbes himself states, "this is the generation of that great *Leviathan*, or rather (to speak more reverently) of that *Mortall God*, to which wee owe under the *Immortal God*, our peace and defence."[48] What is clear from this reading is that the ontological primacy of violence borne out of the fear of death is at work in the background and feeds the thoroughly negative theological anthropology

---

43. Schmitt, *Political Theology II: The Myth of the Closure of any Political Theology*, trans. Michael Hoelzl and Graham Ward (Malden, MA: Polity, 2008) 117.

44. Ibid., 109.

45. Carl Schmitt, *Leviathan in the State Theory of Thomas Hobbes*, 86.

46. Schmitt, *Political Theology II*, 125–26.

47. Schmitt, *Leviathan in the State Theory of Thomas Hobbes*, 31.

48. Thomas Hobbes, *Leviathan*, ed. Richard Tuck (New York: Cambridge University Press, 1996) 120.

that drives much of Schmitt's thinking.[49] Moreover, despite the fact that Hobbes's project was a model for Schmitt, it was a project that ultimately failed insofar as it set the stage for the development of liberalism. Hobbes's introduction of a distinction between public and private reason in his discussion of belief in miracles opened up a crack in *Leviathan* that ultimately became "a sickness unto death" that destroyed the mortal god from within by transforming the administration of state power into a technical instrument. Indeed, Schmitt claims that "the *legislator humanus* became a *machina legislatoria*."[50] By allowing for private beliefs, Hobbes unwittingly paved the way for the introduction of a radical individualism and the positivist hostility to all metaphysics indicative of modern liberalism, the very historical processes that he claims have led to the modern eclipse of the political.[51]

Scriptural Arcana in Schmitt

With the foregoing introduction to Schmitt's political theology in mind, then, we are now in a position to turn more explicitly to the scriptural arcana—the biblical figures, texts, and allusions—that mysteriously appear in some of Schmitt's most (in)famous arguments. For reasons of length, it is not possible to give a comprehensive account of all the scriptural arcana in Schmitt. However, three examples will not only serve to highlight how Schmitt employs these texts and figures but will also further illuminate the shape of the unique affinity between theology and jurisprudence in Schmitt's work.

Undoubtedly amongst the most well-known of Schmitt's arguments is his contention that "the specific political distinction to which political actions and motives can be reduced is that between friend and enemy."[52] In the course of making this argument, Schmitt recognizes that the most significant challenge to this vision of the political is found in the words of Jesus to "love your enemies" (Matt 5:44 // Luke 6:27), yet he writes that in this biblical statement "no mention is made of the

---

49. See Ibid., esp. 75–85 and 117–20. See also Pierre Manent, *An Intellectual History of Liberalism*, trans. Rebecca Balinski (Princeton: Princeton University Press, 1994) esp. 20–38. Further supporting Schmitt's argument that theories of the state are secularized theological concepts, Manent helpfully notes the sense in which Hobbes's definition of Leviathan's power is structurally analogous to Anselm's famous ontological argument for the existence of God.

50. Schmitt, *Leviathan in the State Theory of Thomas Hobbes*, 65.

51. It is interesting to note at this point that Schmitt lays the blame for this catastrophic failure not with Hobbes but rather with the Jewish philosopher Benedict de Spinoza who opens up this crack in the theoretical justification of the state in Benedict de Spinoza, *Theological-Political Treatise*, trans. Michael Silverthorne and Jonathan Israel (Cambridge: Cambridge University Press, 2007) esp. 238–59. The complex issue of Schmitt's anti-Judaism foregrounded here is treated in Meier, *Lesson of Carl Schmitt*, esp. 151–56.

52. Schmitt, *Concept of the Political*, 26.

political enemy. Never in the thousand-year struggle between Christians and Moslems did it occur to a Christian to surrender rather than defend Europe out of love toward the Saracens or Turks."[53] Of course, Schmitt's confident historical gloss here is definitively repudiated by Michael Sattler, a former Benedictine monk and early Anabaptist leader who, at the trial where he was condemned to death, proclaimed that "if the Turk comes, he should not be resisted, for it stands written: thou shalt not kill. We should not defend ourselves against the Turks or our other persecutors, but with fervent prayer should implore God that He might be our defense and resistance."[54] Nevertheless, in the space of one short paragraph, Schmitt points to a distinction in Plato's *Republic* between *hostis* and *inimicus*, that is between a public enemy and a private foe, as sufficient evidence that Jesus's words are to be interpreted as private, spiritual, and not politically relevant.[55] Alongside other forms of human activity that depend on fundamental distinctions, namely between beautiful/ugly in art, good/evil in morality, and profitable/unprofitable in economics, what is most important for Schmitt is the sense in which the political antithesis between friend and enemy remains decisive because it denotes the ultimate degree of intensity. In fact, Schmitt argues that every other domain of life—e.g., art, morality, economics, etc.—is incapable of generating genuine enemies and suggests that "in the domain of economics there are no enemies, only competitors, and in a thoroughly moral and ethical world perhaps only debating adversaries."[56] Indeed, for Schmitt the friend/enemy distinction is not a symbol or a metaphor but rather the concrete, existential, and ever-present possibility of extreme conflict, that is, the site where life itself is at stake and this alone is what makes it genuinely political. Put another way, it is precisely in a situation of extreme enmity that the political emerges since this alone is the concrete situation wherein the real possibility of physical killing must be adjudicated. Despite the stark nature of these reflections, Schmitt is careful to qualify them and suggests that his definition "neither favors war nor militarism, neither imperialism nor pacifism."[57] What is of the utmost importance for Schmitt is the structure or form of the political and not the concrete content of any particular decision that may be made in a situation of extreme enmity because, as Schmitt writes, "these cannot be decided by a previously determined general norm nor by the judgement of a disinterested and therefore neutral third party. Only the actual participants can correctly recognize, understand, and judge the concrete situation

---

53. Ibid., 29.
54. John Howard Yoder, *The Legacy of Michael Sattler* (Scottdale: Herald Press, 1973) 72.
55. Schmitt, *Concept of the Political*, 28–29 and n9.
56. Ibid., 28.
57. Ibid., 33.

and settle the extreme case of conflict."[58] This qualifier notwithstanding, it is clear that what fascinates Schmitt most in all of this are the antagonistic moments where the political emerges as a meeting place for lethal violence. For while he is careful to say that the political enemy "need not be morally evil," he is concerned, above all, with what Jürgen Habermas has called "the aesthetics of violence."[59]

It is particularly interesting to note the sense in which Schmitt's reasoning here is not immune to the dualistic sickness he accuses Hobbes of instantiating. Indeed, Schmitt's articulation of the political can be read as a modern liberal construction insofar as he too relies on the public/private distinction to relativize Jesus's formidable challenge to his definition of the political. Moreover, it seems to represent a departure from some of his earlier statements on the concrete and visible form of the Roman Catholic Church that stands in the background of his definition of the political: "The great betrayal laid to the Catholic Church is that it does not conceive Christ as a private person; does not conceive Christianity as a private matter, something wholly and inwardly spiritual, but rather has given it form as a visible institution."[60] For Schmitt, the Roman Catholic Church stands as a true visible public, that is, an authentically political bulwark against the disastrous consequences of Protestant inwardness. Underscoring this point, Schmitt claims that "just as Christ had a real body, so must the Church have a real body. . . . Every religious sect which has transposed the concept of the Church from the visible community of believing Christians into a *corpus mere mysticum* basically has doubts about the humanity of the Son of God."[61] So even if Schmitt's recourse to a dualistic public/private reading of Jesus's injunction to "love your enemies" is understood as a shift, his earlier work on the public and visible nature of the Roman Catholic Church at the very least indicates why he sees Jesus's words as the most significant challenge to his own definition of the political.[62] Moreover, it allows us to see why Schmitt must argue that Jesus's words are in no way intended to dissolve the political antithesis between friend and

---

58. Ibid., 27. Schmitt also explicitly states (ibid., 26) that the friend/enemy distinction "provides a distinction in the sense of a criterion and not as an exhaustive definition or one indicative of substantial content."

59. See ibid., 27; and Habermas, *New Conservatism*, 137, respectively. Schmitt sees his argument about the nature of the enemy to be continuing in the wake of Hegel, not Nietzsche, as he makes plain in Schmitt, *Concept of the Political*, 62–63.

60. Schmitt, *Roman Catholicism and Political Form*, 31–32.

61. Carl Schmitt, "The Visibility of the Church: A Scholastic Consideration," in *Roman Catholicism and Political Form*, trans. G. L. Ulmen (London: Greenwood Press, 1996) 52.

62. It may well be possible to understand Schmitt's reading of Jesus's injunction to "love your enemies" as a "ghastly confusion" with "its veiling of evil in utility, and the irresistible logic of its vested interests" as Schmitt himself avers in ibid., 53.

enemy because every attempt to do so amounts to nothing less than the eclipse of the political itself.⁶³

For Schmitt, the "high points of politics are simultaneously the moments in which the enemy is, in concrete clarity, recognized as the enemy" and another biblical text plays a role in what Schmitt takes to be the amongst the highest of these political moments. Schmitt's own account of this is worth quoting at length:

> With regard to modern times, there are many powerful outbreaks of such enmity: there is the by no means harmless *écrasez l'infame* of the eighteenth century; the fanatical hatred of Napoleon felt by the German barons Stein and Kleist ("Exterminate them [the French], the Last Judgment will not ask you for your reasons"); Lenin's annihilating sentences against bourgeois and western capitalism. All these are surpassed by Cromwell's enmity towards papist Spain. He says in a speech of September 17, 1656: "The first thing, therefore, that I shall speak to is *That* that is the first lesson of Nature: Being and Preservation. . . . The conservation of that, 'namely our National Being,' is first to be viewed with respect to those who seek to undo it, and so make it *not to be*." Let us thus consider our enemies, "the Enemies to the very Being of these Nations": "Why, truly, your great Enemy is the Spaniard. He is a natural enemy. He is naturally so; he is naturally so throughout,—by reason of the enmity that is in him against whatsoever is of God. 'Whatsoever is of God' which is *you*, or which may be in you." Then he repeats: "The Spaniard is your enemy," his "enmity is put into him by God." He is "the natural enemy, the providential enemy," and he who considers him to be an "accidental enemy" is "not well acquainted with Scripture and the things of God," who says: "'I will put enmity between your seed and her seed'" (Gen 3:15). With France one can make peace, not with Spain because it is a papist state, and the pope maintains peace only as long as he wishes.⁶⁴

This is, perhaps, the point at which Schmitt's theological anthropology manifests itself most clearly. Key to understanding Schmitt on this point, however, is his constitutive argument that the friend/enemy distinction is not designed to overcome enmity in general but rather the extreme enmity of civil war in particular. Indeed, he claims that "political unity is the highest unity—not because it is an omnipotent dictator, or because it levels out all other unities, but because it decides, and has the potential to prevent all other opposing groups from dissociating into a state of extreme enmity—that is, into civil war."⁶⁵ His description of civil war as a "self-laceration"

---

63. This point is precisely one on which Schmitt explicitly refers to himself as a jurist instead of a theologian because, for him, "theologians tend to define the enemy as something that must be destroyed." See Carl Schmitt, *Ex Captivitate Salus*, trans. Matthew Hannah (Malden, MA: Polity, 2017) 71.

64. Schmitt, *Concept of the Political*, 67–68.

65. Carl Schmitt, "Ethic of State and Pluralistic State," in *The Challenge of Carl Schmitt*, ed. Chantal

further reinforces this and his claim that "according to Hobbes, the quintessential nature of any state of nature . . . is none other than civil war, which can only be prevented by the overarching might of the state" underscores this yet again.[66] For Schmitt, therefore, the extreme enmity he reads out of Cromwell's citation of Gen 3:15 is not, first and foremost, an enthusiastic militarization of politics but rather an instrument—and, indeed, a gift—that alone is able to quell an antecedent and more primordial form of violence between human beings. The interplay here is reminiscent of the way the exceptional nature of sovereignty functions as a kind of limit concept in which what emerges in a situation of extreme enmity, that is, in the concrete political situation, is an intense struggle to decide what belongs and what is excluded, a struggle in which the enemy is "existentially something different and alien, so that in the extreme case conflicts with him are possible."[67] In this way, as Slavoj Žižek has noted, what seems like a very radical definition of the political turns out to be little more than a displacement of the *inherent* antagonism constitutive of the political on to an *external* relationship between us and them.[68] For our purposes, it is not insignificant that in what Jacob Taubes refers to as his "broken confessions," written while he was imprisoned in 1945, Schmitt comes back to Genesis, albeit one chapter later.[69] Reflecting on his understanding of the enemy Schmitt asks:

> Whom in the world can I acknowledge as my enemy? Clearly only him who can call me into question. By recognizing him as enemy I acknowledge that he can call me into question. And who can really call me into question? Only I myself. Or my brother. The other proves to be my brother, and the brother proves to be my enemy. Adam and Eve had two sons, Cain and Abel. Thus begins the history of humankind. This is what the father of all things looks like. This is the dialectical tension that keeps world history moving, and world history has not yet ended.[70]

In the end, then, what is clear is that a thoroughly negative theological anthropology and a concomitant foundational act of violence must be understood as the fulcrum around which Schmitt's understanding of the political turns.[71] Moreover, it

---

Mouffe (London: Verso, 1999) 203.

66. See Schmitt, *Concept of the Political*, 32; and Schmitt, *Leviathan in the State Theory of Thomas Hobbes*, 21, respectively.

67. Schmitt, *Concept of the Political*, 27.

68. Slavoj Žižek, "Carl Schmitt in the Age of Post-Politics," in *The Challenge of Carl Schmitt*, ed. Chantal Mouffe (London: Verso, 1999) 27.

69. For Tabues's remark see Jacob Taubes, *To Carl Schmitt: Letters and Reflections*, trans. Keith Tribe (New York: Columbia University Press, 2013) 1.

70. Schmitt, *Ex Captivitate Salus*, 71. For the biblical account of Cain's murder of Abel, see Gen 4:1–16.

71. The extent to which Schmitt's theological anthropology more nearly resembles a Catholic

also feeds directly into Schmitt's understanding of history, in which the final of our three examples of scriptural arcana figures prominently.

For Schmitt, the displacement of the inherent violence between human beings onto an enemy is the best we can hope for and this is also the point at which the apocalyptic tone of Schmitt's understanding of the political comes explicitly to the fore. In fact, it is not too much to claim that Schmitt's thinking is underwritten by an apocalyptically inflected aesthetics of violence. Explicitly making the biblical connection, Jacob Taubes describes Schmitt's thought as a "catechontic impulse," that is, as an attempt to "capture the chaos in forms, so that chaos doesn't take over."[72] Schmitt's emphasis on the exceptional need for decision, his reliance on Hobbes and the conservative Catholic philosophers of the counter-revolution, his friend/enemy distinction, and his efforts to combat the terrifying and ever-present possibility of civil war all reflect this underlying impulse. In the course of articulating this apocalyptic impulse the ambiguous figure of the *katechon* or "restrainer," to which Taubes alludes, makes its appearance. Schmitt explains that

> The Christian empire was not eternal. It always had its own end and that of the present eon in view. Nevertheless, it was capable of being a historical power. The decisive historical concept of this continuity was that of the restrainer: *katechon*. "Empire" in this sense meant the historical power to *restrain* the appearance of the Antichrist and the end of the present eon; it was a power that withholds (*qui tenet*), as the Apostle Paul said in his Second Letter to the Thessalonians. . . . I do not believe that any historical concept other than *katechon* would have been possible for the original Christian faith. The belief that the restrainer holds back the end of the world provides the only bridge between the notion of an eschatological paralysis of all human events and a tremendous historical monolith like that of the Christian empire of the Germanic kings.[73]

As Schmitt indicates, he borrows this term from Paul's second letter to the Thessalonians: "And you know what is now restraining him [the lawless one], so that

---

or a Protestant account is unclear. However, he does differentiate between these in his earlier work and suggests in Schmitt, *Roman Catholicism and Political Form*, 8, that "in contrast to the Protestant doctrine of the total depravity of natural man, this Creed [the Tridentine Creed] speaks of human nature as only wounded, weakened, and troubled, thus permitting the use of some gradations and adaptations."

72. Taubes, *Political Theology of Paul*, 69.

73. Carl Schmitt, *The Nomos of the Earth in the International Law of the Jus Publicum Europaeum*, trans. G. L. Ulmen (New York: Telos, 2003) 59–60. For a careful examination of the figure of the *katechon* throughough Schmitt's work see Michele Nicoletti, "Religion and Empire: Carl Schmitt's *Katechon* between International Relations and the Philosophy of History," in *International Law and Religion: Historical and Contemporary Perspectives*, ed. Martti Koskenniemi et al. (Oxford: Oxford University Press, 2017) 363–82.

he may be revealed when his time comes. For the mystery of lawlessness is already at work, but only until the one who now restrains it is removed."[74] The idea of the *katechon* has a long history in Christian political theology as a way to explain the long delay of the return of Christ. For Schmitt, the idea of the *res publica Christiana* that emerged after the conversion of Constantine was that stabilizing force in history that alone could explain "the endurance of the eon and could preserve it against the overwhelming power of evil."[75] The ambiguous nature of the *katechon* is exacerbated by the fact that while Schmitt is confident that there is such a "restrainer" in every eon, this does not mean that they are straightforwardly identifiable. Schmitt's own list of potential *katechons* includes individuals (e.g. Hegel) as well as institutions (e.g. Holy Roman Empire, Roman Catholic Church). Taubes is helpful in setting this figure within the larger context of Schmitt's thought:

> It's one thing to be a theologian, a second thing to be a philosopher, and it's a third thing to be a jurist. That—I've learned in life—is a completely different way of understanding the world. The jurist has to legitimate the world as it is. Schmitt's interest was only in one thing: that the party, that the chaos not rise to the top, *that the state remain*. No matter what the price. This is difficult for theologians and philosophers to follow, but as far as the jurist is concerned, as long as it is possible to find even one juridical form, by whatever hairsplitting ingenuity, this must absolutely be done, for otherwise chaos reigns.[76]

Despite the clear emphasis on the prevention of chaos and destruction, which is, for Schmitt, the prevention of civil war, it is evident that an apocalyptically inflected aesthetics of violence animates not only his understanding of the political, which is fanatically committed to the maintenance of order through the overarching power of the sovereign decision, but also to his vision of history.

Schmitt's Enduring Theopolitical Legacy

What, then, are we to make of the work of this self-proclaimed "theologian of jurisprudence" and the scriptural arcana that is woven into some of his most (in)famous and influential arguments?[77] While any sort of comprehensive answer is well beyond the scope of this essay, what I want to suggest, in conclusion, is that Schmitt's

---

74. 2 Thess 2:6–7. The term *katechon* is a transliteration of the Greek adjectival participle in v. 7, "the one who now restrains." Although the mystery of lawlessness is already at work, this "restrainer" holds back the revealing of Antichrist.

75. Schmitt, *Nomos of the Earth*, 60.

76. Taubes, *Political Theology of Paul*, 103 (my emphasis).

77. Carl Schmitt, *Glossarium: Aufzeichnungen der Jahre 1947–1951* (Berlin: Duncker & Humblot, 1991) 23. Statements like this need to be balanced with the occasions on which Schmitt refers to himself as a "nontheologian" as he does, for example in *Political Theology II*, 148 n2.

enduring theopolitical legacy may well have less to do with the extent to which the scriptural arcana in his work is understood as the mysterious driving force that animates his political theology and more to do with the extent to which his theopolitical vision is not only remarkably prescient but also, and perhaps more significantly, the extent to which his work provokes other tantalizing theopolitical possibilities. This is by no means to eviscerate the role of the scriptural arcana at work in his thinking but rather to suggest that its significance lies as much, if not more, in the subsequent theopolitical receptions and inflections it provokes than in the admittedly limited and mysterious role it plays in Schmitt's own work. By way of an all-too-brief conclusion, then, I will summarize the foregoing account of Schmitt's political theology and, with recourse to the scriptural arcana in Schmitt's work, open the door to one such tantalizing theopolitical alternative that is articulated *with* and *against* Schmitt.

As we have seen, Schmitt's configuration of political theology is primarily *structural* in nature. Recall that for Schmitt, the link between jurisprudence and theology amounts to a structural analogy that illuminates the shape of the political formation of a particular epoch. Thus, Schmitt's political theology is misunderstood when it is read primarily as an attempt to plumb the depths of the Christian tradition in search of a way to legitimate decisionism. The question for Schmitt is *not* how to apply the rationality of the Roman Catholic Church to questions of modern jurisprudence but rather how to think through modern jurisprudence to locate its own metaphysical assumptions, which are often historically imbibed from one of the most developed constellations of western rationalism, namely the Catholic Church. Thus, as Karl Löwith rightly notes, "what Schmitt defends is a politics of sovereign decision, but one in which content is merely a product of the accidental *occasio* of the political situation which happens to prevail at the moment."[78] Schmitt's political theology, then, is primarily concerned with creating the conditions under which a decision, any decision, can be made; what is essential is not "that a question be decided in one way or another but that it be decided without delay and without appeal."[79] Second, Schmitt's configuration of political theology is animated by a thoroughly negative theological anthropology. The innate incapacity to contain the primordial violence between human beings is what motivates Schmitt's link between sovereignty and the decision. This leads directly to the third and final aspect, namely that Schmitt's configuration of political theology acquiesces to the ongoing necessity of violence. As we have seen above, Schmitt's reliance on the ambiguous figure of the *katechon* and its attendant emphasis on the prevention of chaos and destruction explicitly

---

78. Karl Löwith, "The Occasional Decisionism of Carl Schmitt," in *Martin Heidegger and European Nihilism*, ed. Richard Wolin (New York: Columbia University Press, 1995) 144.

79. Schmitt, *Political Theology*, 56.

illuminates the apocalyptic nature of his political theology. However, the hope for Schmitt lies not in the prevention of war as such but rather the prevention of civil war. This hope can only be realized with a structured geographical displacement of the inherent violence between human beings on to a public enemy that is essentially alien and different. It is clear that what fascinates Schmitt most are the borders between norm and exception, "peace" and violence where the real possibility of physical killing lurks behind the political decision. Despite his claims that his political theology is disinterested in either war or pacifism, Schmitt's gaze is most acutely attuned to diagnose and prevent the inevitable eruptions of violence.

Explicitly noting that Jesus's injunction to "love your enemies" is the most formidable challenge to his articulation of the political, Schmitt himself invites contestation.[80] Perhaps the most surprising figure who takes up Schmitt's challenge, particularly given his inextricable association with the Nazi Party, is the Jewish philosopher Jacob Taubes, who astoundingly sat down with Schmitt at his home in Plettenberg in September 1979 to read Paul's letter to the Romans. The extraordinary and fascinating details of this encounter culminate in a confrontation over the meaning of the enemy:

> This is where an almost ninety-year-old man sat with someone who was a little over fifty and spelled out [Romans] 9–11. That's when we came to the sentence: "As regards the gospel they are enemies"—enemies of God! . . . we are not dealing with private feuds, but with salvation-historical enemies of God. "Enemies for your sake; but as regards election they are beloved, for the sake of their forefathers" [Rom 11:28]. And this is the point I challenged Schmitt on, that he doesn't see this dialectic that moves Paul and that the Christian church after 70 has forgotten, that he adopted not a text but a tradition, that is the folk traditions of church antisemitism, onto which he, in 1933–36, in his uninhibited fashion, went on to graft the racist theozoology.[81]

Although Taubes and Schmitt agree that the modern crisis of the political is, at root, a theological crisis and Taubes wonders if Jesus's words in the Sermon on the Mount are simply private as Schmitt argues, he nevertheless insists that Paul's opening lines in his letter to the Romans is nothing less than a "political declaration of war against Rome."[82] In stark contrast to Schmitt, then, Taubes goes on to claim that the "primordial core of Jesus's Christian tradition . . . is the love not of the Lord, but of the neighbor" and that, rather than restraining the enemy as Schmitt proposes, the

---

80. Taubes recounts a phone call he received from Schmitt imploring him to come to Plettenberg in Taubes, *The Political Theology of Paul*, 2.

81. Ibid., 51. Incredibly, Taubes goes on to say of Schmitt that "this is something that he, the most important state law theorist, did indeed receive as a lesson."

82. Ibid., 16.

truly revolutionary (or, in Schmitt's terms, exceptional) act is to recognize the enemy as one's neighbor and to love them as oneself.[83] Of course, this is little more than a sketch of the tantalizing alternative that Taubes presents us with and there are many others that could and should be explored. What I hope this encounter in particular demonstrates is that if a Jew marked as "enemy" by Schmitt can find something in him worth wrestling over, the discipline of theology, too, may well find generative possibilities that remain hidden so long as Schmitt's work is simply dismissed as Nazi propaganda. In the end, then, it may well be possible to read Schmitt's texts while simultaneously holding their author to the consequences of the fate he chose.

---

83. Ibid., 53.

RESPONSE TO GINGERICH HIEBERT ("THE FOUNDATIONS OF ORDER: SCRIPTURE, SOVEREIGNTY, AND EXCLUSION")

Colby Dickinson

Kyle Gingerich Hiebert has done us a great service in presenting a powerful and intriguing reading of Scripture in light of the work of political theorist Carl Schmitt, and, in what follows, I want to raise just a few more salient points that I consider to be, not so much challenges to Gingerich Hiebert's work, but questions from a co-participant in the inquiry he has put before us.

I begin my reflections with a deceptively simple question: if the genre of the apocalyptic can be equated with that of the nihilistic, as Gingerich Hiebert suggests in the introduction to his essay, I wonder if Schmitt can properly be considered an apocalyptic thinker, as his primary instincts were, as Gingerich Hiebert also acknowledges, directed toward restraining chaos and preserving order, as legal jurists are perhaps ultimately bound to do. Such a preservation of social order, as one can imagine, is the defining foundational principle of juridical scholars. Yet it is certainly also true that Schmitt's focus was placed squarely upon that which may be said to bring about the end of a particular established order, what theologically is considered the "end of days." His focus was therefore at once intently upon the *katechon*, or "restrainer," who prevents the chaos from overtaking said order, and the end of that order, which is what enables Gingerich Hiebert to label him as apocalyptic in the first place. The state, from Schmitt's point of view, must be preserved at all costs so that the darkness on the fringes of society is not able to move to the center and overcome the normative order established as the basis of society.

So, despite the fact that Schmitt does contemplate the restraint of a given order's destruction, the apocalyptic could be said to cohere with the nihilistic in the sense that it refers to an established order being completely revalued, upended, and potentially even discarded at some point. Having both principles abide side-by-side indicates to my mind that Schmitt's ultimate interests lie in the recognition that being embedded in an order, *any* order actually, will always prevail in the end, notwithstanding its apparent end. This is the reality of any social or legal construct and one that cannot really ever be avoided in the historical world as we know it. It should come as little surprise then that a legal jurist working toward understanding the nature of political and legal foundations should be concerned with their possible eradication, as well as the forces that allow them to remain in place.

In the context of Schmitt's work, the biblical, scriptural mandate was one that must be maintained as it provides legitimation for an order that has extended itself all the way to present legal codes and statutes. The scriptural (revealed) source of authority was precisely the ultimate foundation for order in a society in that its self-grounding, self-constituting authority was the same tautological reasoning that defined sovereign power. The sovereign is sovereign because they alone can declare themselves to be sovereign, just as Scripture is Scripture because it alone can declare itself to be the revealed word of God. This reasoning, as a tautological self-positing, is what allows a given order to assert its primacy and autonomy in the face of competing claims to power.

The real question, then, though it is one not directly taken up by Gingerich Hiebert in his essay, but only hinted toward, is one concerning the foundations of biblical-canonical order itself. What legitimates a particular canonical formulation as sovereign and autonomous? How is such a source for temporal power linked to political claims to sovereign power? And how might we be able to reformulate our perceptions of the divine vis-à-vis sovereignty, Scripture, exclusion and violence as a result of these connections?

Jan Assmann, for example, has done a great service in pointing scholars toward the nexus between the self-legitimation of the biblical-canonical order and its inevitable creation of a duality between the just and the damned, or the righteous and the idolaters—what he calls the "Mosaic distinction" that lays at the base of ancient Judaism.[1] Such a dualistic formulation of the world, as monotheism in the West inevitably falls prey to, results in a reductionistic violence in order to ground society. Every community, religious or otherwise, enables a certain force of exclusion in order to establish its sense of self as a recognizable identity. The violence of social division is thereby enabled so that a community might understand itself in relation to every element it deems foreign or worthy of exclusion in some sense.[2] These are the grounds of political and social representation as much as they are the grounds for religious representations as well.

---

1. See the trio of studies by Jan Assmann, including *Religion and Cultural Memory: Ten Studies*, trans. Rodney Livingstone (Stanford: Stanford University Press, 2006); *Of God and Gods: Egypt, Israel, and the Rise of Monotheism* (Madison: University of Wisconsin Press, 2008); and *The Price of Monotheism*, trans. Robert Savage (Stanford: Stanford University Press, 2010).

2. These dynamics are expounded upon in greater detail in Peter Sloterdijk, *Spheres*, Vol. 2, *Globes: Macrosphereology*, trans. Wieland Hoban (South Pasadena, CA: Semiotext(e), (2014) 335–403.

Much as the work of cultural theorist and mythographer René Girard has made abundantly clear, such an exclusive violence (what Girard will himself call scapegoating) allows a given society to exclude certain persons or groupings in order to establish its own autonomous sense of self.[3] Identity is granted to community members through an exclusive ordering of society and the heavens (or *cosmos*) that surround it. Through Schmitt's occasional forays into definitions of sovereignty, exceptionality, decisionism and dictatorship, we can see the coordinates of a particular violence unfold in parallel form before our eyes, and in ways that still continue to resonate with contemporary cultural, social, economic, religious, and political violences.[4] The declaration and exclusion of the enemy enables the political community to realize itself and its members as they gather around a particular sovereign entity who is, in turn, defined as the one capable of making the decision between the friend and the enemy. This circular logic is in fact constitutive of the autonomous sphere that delineates the identity of the collective grouping that the sovereign heads. Again, it is also potentially what grounds scriptural texts and the communities that they subsequently found and legitimate.

The Mosaic distinction is what could be said to undergird Schmitt's infamous dichotomy between the friend and the enemy, that which supports his own sense of political order, which cannot simply be effaced, but appears as foundational within a given political society.[5] As with the stories of Moses, certain forms of violence will be deemed acceptable and others unacceptable insofar as they conform or deviate from such a distinction that is yet itself terribly difficult to confirm as absolute in reality. This configuration of order would further explain why the only adequate response to such a facile political division is precisely further to call into question the precise identities of one's so-called friends and one's perceived enemies, as one can easily, and often, become the other. Gil Anidjar, for instance, had pointed out this highly fluid problematic in his book on two such precarious typologies, the Jew and the Arab, much as, I would suggest, Gingerich Hiebert notes in his essay how loving one's enemies can subvert any such simplistic ordering.[6]

If Schmitt's work is merely a "political religion," as the theologian Jürgen Moltmann has put it, then the question will arise as to what degree any religion

---

3. See, among other writings, René Girard, *Violence and the Sacred*, trans. Patrick Gregory (Baltimore, MD: Johns Hopkins University Press, 1977).

4. In particular, see Carl Schmitt, *The Concept of the Political*, trans. George Schwab (Chicago: University of Chicago Press, 1996); *Political Theology: Four Chapters on the Concept of Sovereignty*, trans. George Schwab (Chicago: University of Chicago Press, 2005); and *Dictatorship* (Cambridge: Polity, 2014).

5. This distinction is made in Schmitt, *Concept of the Political*.

6. Gil Anidjar, *The Jew, the Arab: A History of the Enemy* (Stanford: Stanford University Press, 2003).

is so ideologically invested with its scriptures, its moral codes or identifiable laws, as to form the bedrock of any legitimated communal claims to identity. Again, as the work of Girard has made abundantly manifest, any predicated order is founded upon an act of exclusion—even if such an order remains "bloodless," as Jacques Derrida would himself go on to nuance these matters.[7] Every rationality, even the Church's, as Schmitt himself realized, is constructed on an exclusionary basis. Accounting for the potential for violence through such communally established orders then becomes paramount in determining the practical value and function of any scriptural narrative. This insight is what will allow Slavoj Žižek to refer to Girard's thought as helpful and convergent with his own in the context of describing the very displacement of internal antagonisms onto external enemies (or scapegoats) in his book *Less Than Nothing*.[8]

As Schmitt had previously noted, the legal order is founded upon a state of exceptionality to all law that cannot itself be justified or grounded *in* the legal order itself. It is in this sense entirely extra-juridical. Such grounds are moreover where we can locate the emanations of sovereign power, or perhaps of a divine being, but they are not the location of any governing laws themselves. This distinction is what motivated the tensions between sovereignty and governmentality in Michel Foucault's work, as well as its subsequent development in the political philosophy of Giorgio Agamben.[9] Though much scholarship remains to be done regarding the implications of these inquiries in terms of how scriptural claims relate to the everyday governing (moral) norms of religious communities, the days of regarding Scripture as a neutral political actor in our world are seemingly at their end. Every community, no matter its foundational claims, must critically investigate and openly challenge the exclusions that have come to define its self-referential sense of identity.

Would this be the grounds upon which to challenge any claims made by a particular people to be "chosen," "elect" or even special in some particular way, including Jews, Christians, and Muslims alike (all religions founded upon particular revealed and canonical scriptures)? Are such claims not merely an attempt to replicate sovereign power within a particular religious community often besieged by powers that, at least initially, far surpassed those of its own marginalized people? From the earliest

---

7. Jacques Derrida, "Before the Law," in *Acts of Religion*, ed. Gil Anidjar, trans. Mary Quaintance (London: Routledge, 2002).

8. Slavoj Žižek, *Less Than Nothing: Hegel and the Shadow of Dialectical Materialism* (London: Verso, 2013) 975–81.

9. See Michel Foucault, *The Birth of Biopolitics: Lectures at the Collège de France, 1978–1979*, ed. Michel Senellart, trans. Graham Burchell (New York: Picador, 2008); and Giorgio Agamben, *The Kingdom and the Glory: Homo Sacer II, 2*, trans. Lorenzo Chiesa (Stanford: Stanford University Press, 2011).

origins of each monotheism to the internal struggles each has witnessed between its own marginalized persons and their cries for liberation and reform, we perceive again and again the same struggles between an order predicated upon an ultimately unjustifiable sovereign power, and the normative order it legitimates, and those who cry out for justice against its eventual oppressiveness. Christianity's historical, political dominance in the West should only be the most significant indicator that virulent forms of exclusionary violence, including certain forms of anti-Semitism, have been active and legitimated through such processes.

The implications of this critical inquiry have far reaching consequences for traditional and communal theologies, perhaps ultimately even going so far as to demonstrate how all theological claims are inherently comparative—because *competitive* with other autonomous claims to sovereign rights—even if they are caught up in the establishment of what appears to be a completely isolated, sovereign claim of their own (which every revealed truth most genuinely focuses on to the exclusion of all other apparent revealed assertions). Though questioning the basis of particular scriptural claims appears to weaken a given religious community's claims to sovereignty, there is no pretending that such critiques are not finally having their say and offering us alternative ways to configure religious being—whatever such a thing is or is not—in the world today.

Though I find very little to fault in Gingerich Hiebert's suggestive essay, the larger question that remains unaddressed is simply this: what are we to make in the end of a religious Scripture that provides a necessary foundation for sovereign power, and so which functions then as the revealed platform served up *ex nihilo* in order to legitimate the religion that rests upon its grounds? Do such claims have anything to do with the supposed metaphysical existence of a divine being and its relation to humanity, or are such revealed truths posited in order to legitimate a community's often desperate pleas to maintain autonomy amidst an ever chaotic world? I am therefore asking questions about the particularity of revelation itself utilized as a political and ideological platform inescapably intertwined with the rituals and practices of communities committed to the promulgation of their own communal identities through acts of exclusion and the potential violence that accompanies such acts. Unless one can admit that Scripture at least potentially serves this bare minimum communal-ideological purpose, it is hard to envision a critical response to those sovereign powers embedded in religion, or at least in the monotheisms of the West, that takes seriously the ways in which religion has been used in order to establish very real and very this-worldly political institutions. In consideration then of what Gingerich Hiebert calls "other tantalizing theopolitical possibilities," we might be tempted, following the work of Regina Schwartz, to prefer something like a polytheistic religious tradition that is not predicated on exclusivity, or perhaps even to do away with such divisive and potentially exclusive (and so violent in some sense) religions altogether.[10] There is at least nothing prohibiting such alternatives from appearing as preferable options to the dominant forces of sovereign power that have maintained a monopoly on western politics for centuries.

It is of course also possible, however, that things are not so simple and that we are not able so easily to jettison an established normative order, or whatever (revealed) grounds it comes to us standing upon, because, like language, we need such orders so that we might have shared political, cultural, or economic understandings. That is, we might as well admit too that humanity can never truly be free of a normative and exclusive order insofar as we hold onto the realm of representations, language, and common symbolic interactions. Nonetheless, the manner by which a good portion of humanity refers to scriptural arcana as justifiable grounds for an established, normative order (i.e. the political implications of specific theological and doctrinal claims) is what must be further explored, precisely so that one's sense of "chosenness" is not something linked to the creation of external enemies who help to justify a given political identity or ideology, as was the case for Schmitt, but so that the sense of "chosenness" on display is merely the particular story we have chosen to tell, the labor of an absolutely singular form-of-life whose uniqueness we must respect while also doing it the disservice, one must equally admit, of reducing it to an intelligible narrative so that we might understand it. We must also, while understanding it, respect what we do not, and at times cannot, comprehend of it. This is the recognition and preservation of an entirely immanent mystery.

Perhaps also, above all else, we must respect those other forms-of-life that are lived outside of a chosen narration—again signaling something like a respect of the foreignness at the heart of what we do recognize or represent, an otherness *within* the sameness that constitutes one's identity. Such "foreign" elements are not to be further scapegoated, but are to be seen as subjects in their own right, to be respected, allowed to be conversant with, and perhaps even influential upon, the construction and maintenance of every other subjectivity. This reality is what we find in the processes of locating other religious claims (e.g. Egyptian) *within* the biblical, scriptural narrative, as such elements indicate a foreignness within what had initially appeared as a cohesive sameness. This was in fact Freud's lingering insight concerning Moses "the Egyptian" that had once motivated Assmann's own claims regarding the "Mosaic distinction."[11] It is also the basis for any recognition of other autonomous claims to

---

10. Regina M. Schwartz, *The Curse of Cain: The Violent Legacy of Monotheism* (Chicago: University of Chicago Press, 1998).

11. Jan Assmann, *Moses the Egyptian: The Memory of Egypt in Western Monotheism* (Cambridge:

sovereignty that cannot be ignored or made subservient to other competing claims. Indeed, a cosmopolitan world of mutual respect and tolerance, in theo-political terms especially, is what we are currently looking at, and what must be fostered and allowed to bring forth entirely new relationships and understandings.

In addition to contemplating a new world order such as many have already suggested is currently taking place, I am therefore also signaling a general imperative to lessen the inevitable violence that accompanies the establishment of normativity, which humanity might learn someday to tolerate in an entirely bloodless fashion, while also perhaps admitting that we are powerless to do away with (a reductionistic, representational) violence completely, much to the chagrin of something like an absolute (including the realm of the conceptual) pacifist. It is in trying to formulate such thoughts in political terms that we might still benefit a good deal from Schmitt's insights. For his part, he had sought to establish the contours of a sovereign force that conceals itself within language and dictates so much of what we consider to be the domain of a political theology very much still operative within the world. Rather than concede that our world has become less theological over the years, I would rather wager that, if anything, humanity needs to be more engaged in the political-theological claims that still resonate within the construction of every sovereign power and the political communities that are formed as a result of their existence.

I am very grateful for Gingerich Hiebert's essay in that it continues to point us toward the possibilities for political-theological thought in a way that takes seriously both the formation of politics in a theological manner and the possibility of nonviolence in a world that has all-too-often succumbed to the temptations of sovereign violence that would divide the world forever from parts of itself.

Harvard University Press, 1998). See also Sigmund Freud, *Moses and Monotheism*, trans. Katherine Jones (New York: Vintage, 1939).

BLOOD LETTERS FROM A MAO PRISON: A "SELECT SOLDIER OF CHRIST" CONFRONTS REVOLUTIONARY VIOLENCE

Xi Lian

Introduction

What makes the sad topic of human violence a fitting theme for theological reflections is of course the stubborn and persistent reality of violence itself. Such reflections have become all the more important for Christians today because modern ideologies of mass movements—from nationalism to communism—have often succeeded in sacralizing violence as a necessary means to a purportedly noble end. As other essays in this collection show, theologians have abundant arrows in their quiver (if such a metaphor can be tolerated) to counter such heresies.

As a historian, I would like to offer something different—a Christian voice from an unlikely time and place that speaks to us with a prophetic cadence and unsurpassed intensity regarding the heterodoxy of sacralized violence. As a human voice it also speaks with bewilderment and ambivalence at times when the monstrosity of institutionalized and pervasive evil necessitated considerations of a particular form of violence, namely suicide, both as an escape from violence and as a defense of the dignity and sanctity of life. In doing so it leaves us with unanswered questions.

That voice belonged to a young poet and journalist named Lin Zhao, who was martyred just over fifty years ago for her unbending opposition to what she called the "tyranny and slavery" of Chinese communism.[1] It was an opposition rooted in her Protestant faith, which she had acquired in her teens at a mission school in her hometown of Suzhou. A self-styled "select soldier of Christ"[2] and the most important Chinese dissident of the entire Mao era, Lin Zhao waged a doomed and lone

---

1. Lin Zhao, "Zhi *Renmin Ribao* bianjibu xin (zhi san)" (Letters to the Editorial Board of the *People's Daily* [No. 3]), 1965 (Hereafter ZRMRB) 29.

2. Lin Zhao, "Ling'ou xuyu" (Chatters of a Spirit Couple), August 11, 1965, in *Lin Zhao wenji* (Collected Writings of Lin Zhao) (Privately printed volume, Shanghai, 2013). Unless otherwise noted, all of Lin Zhao's writings cited in this essay are from *Lin Zhao wenji*.

battle against the systemic human violence and repression that was Mao's revolution, and she passionately turned to God for guidance in that battle.

Lin Zhao's story is a complex one and is not without ambiguities. However, it points unmistakably to the capacity of the Christian faith to provide transcendent moral guidance amid the savagery and chaos of revolutionary turmoil in China. We will see that her faith became a unique source of moral autonomy in the face of a prevailing revolutionary ideology that sanctified violence. That autonomy led her to decry the violent creed of "class struggle" but also destined her for martyrdom in 1968 at the height of the Cultural Revolution, when she was thirty-six.

A Double Conversion

Born in 1932 into a well-to-do family in the prosperous city of Suzhou, Lin Zhao in her teens attended the Laura Haygood Memorial School for Girls in Suzhou, run by the Southern Methodist mission in China. There she was baptized into the church. Soon afterwards, like many patriotic students disaffected with the autocratic and corrupt rule of the Nationalist government, she became an ardent supporter of the communist revolution that promised a complete cure for the political and social ills of Chinese society. At the age of sixteen, she risked her life to secretly join the Chinese Communist Party (CCP). At her graduation from high school in 1949, she decided against college and enrolled instead at a CCP-run school of journalism, a training center for the party's propagandists. She broke with her family and dedicated herself to the revolution to make sure that future generations would be able to "live under the sun."[3]

Lin Zhao was a frustrated revolutionary. On the eve of the communist victory, she lost her CCP membership after she failed to obey a party directive. In search of political redemption, she threw herself into the land reform movement after the founding of the People's Republic in 1949. She joined one of the rural work teams that, with the help of haphazard peasant associations, carried out the party's program of grain requisition, land redistribution, and bloody campaigns against small landholders. Throughout China, between 1 and 2 million people were killed during land reform.[4]

Lin Zhao was not innocent of the revolutionary violence at the time. As she was overpowered by the logic of the necessary and virtuous violence of the communist movement in China, her Christian conscience was at least muted as she did the

---

3. Lian Xi, *Blood Letters: The Untold Story of Lin Zhao, a Martyr in Mao's China* (New York: Basic Books, 2018) 22–23, 31–32. The rest of this essay contains passages taken from the book, even though they have been rearranged or modified to address the theme of violence.

4. Ibid., 46–47.

party's bidding and helped bring charges against a former landholder, which sent him to the execution ground.[5] "Stored in the depth of my heart is a burning love for the motherland," she wrote to a close friend at the time, "as well as an equal amount of hatred for the enemies."[6] As she later reflected—in her last extant prison letter written a few months before her own execution as an enemy of the revolution—she had been "more or less splashed with blood" during the land reform period, which filled her with "shock and deep grief."[7]

Lin Zhao's dedication did not satisfy the party, for she took the idealism and utopianism of Mao's revolution too seriously and could not help criticizing the abuse of power and hypocrisy of communist cadres. As a result, she was repudiated as an unreformed petty bourgeois. Tormented by guilt over her own bourgeois background and sentiments, she nevertheless also began to develop misgivings about the revolution in which educated urban young patriots like herself exchanged their leather shoes for straw sandals and embraced the hardships of the countryside while CCP cadres of peasant origins changed out of their straw sandals into leather shoes and treated city girls like Lin Zhao as their revolutionary—and sexual—trophies.[8]

In 1954, Lin Zhao was admitted to the Chinese Department of Peking University, where she distinguished herself as a young scholar of ancient literature, a fledgling journalist, and a poet. When students at the university responded in 1957 to Mao's "Hundred Flowers campaign" to criticize and help improve the work of the CCP, Lin Zhao joined the call for democracy out of loyalty to the party and was purged as a Rightist. She was suspended as a university student; months of forced "re-education through labor" followed. Yet it also became a period of political awakening. In a poem written later in her own blood, she remembered that turning point in her life:

> A sudden gale comes toward me from heaven,
>
> and a melody drifts from the bamboo flute, plunging the world in gloom.
>
> The black chrysanthemum opens its pure heart at the approach of night,
>
> and the plum blossom, iron-boned in the frost, goes into bloom.[9]

Lin Zhao's disillusionment and break with communism was accompanied by the rekindling of a fervent Christian faith. Though she had never lost her faith, she had drifted away from the church after she turned to the revolution. In 1960, Lin

---

5. Ibid., 52.
6. Lin Zhao to Ni Jingxiong, March 29, 1951.
7. Lin Zhao to mother, January 14, 1968.
8. Lian Xi, *Blood Letters*, 59–61.
9. Lin Zhao, "Xueshi tiyi bing ba" (Blood Poems on Shirt and Postscripts), Appendix 4 of ZRMRB.

Zhao joined several other student rightists who had been forced into rural exile in launching *A Spark of Fire*, an underground journal that exposed the colossal failures of Mao's "Great Leap Forward"—a radical program of industrialization and agricultural collectivization that claimed at least thirty-six million lives nationwide between 1959 and 1961. She was promptly arrested as a "counterrevolutionary."[10]

Renouncing Revolutionary Violence

At Shanghai's No. 1 Detention House where she was held, Lin Zhao underwent prolonged interrogation and torture. Deprived of writing instruments, she took up blood writing, which would continue through the later years of her imprisonment until her execution in 1968.[11] She drew blood with a makeshift prick—a bamboo pick, a hair clip, or the plastic handle of her toothbrush, sharpened against the concrete floor—and held it in a plastic spoon, in which she dipped a thin bamboo strip or a straw stem she called "pen." The writing was done on paper when it was available, and on shirts and torn-up bed sheets when it was not.[12]

One of Lin Zhao's prison letters to her mother revealed the difficulty of blood writing. She wrote it in her unheated cell in November 1967, as Shanghai's winter was approaching. She had poked the fingers on her left hand so many times that she could no longer draw blood from them. They turned numb when pressed. "The small puddle of blood that I squeezed out for writing is almost all gone now," she explained to her mother. "My blood seems to have thinned lately; coagulation is quite poor. It may be partially due to the weather getting cold. Alas, dear Mama! This is my life! It is also my struggle! It is my battle!"[13]

The fullest expression of Lin Zhao's political beliefs is found in her 1965 letter to the editorial board of the *People's Daily*, the party's mouthpiece. She chose July 14, the anniversary of the storming of the Bastille, as the day to begin writing it. It took her almost five months to complete the letter, which ran to about 140,000 words, 137 pages in all. The letter was done in ink, but she stamped each page repeatedly with a shirt button-sized seal bearing the character "Zhao" and inked with her blood.

---

10. Lian Xi, *Blood Letters*, 108–15.

11. For Lin Zhao, blood writing was more than a matter of necessity when she was denied pen and paper. She was also tapping into a long tradition of blood writing that dates from the early sixth century CE, when Buddhist devotees drew their own blood and used it to copy Buddhist sutras. The ritual came to symbolize utmost piety and sincerity, and also appeared in secular literature as an extreme form of protest. See Yin Wenhan "Zhongguo gudai cixue jingshu zhifeng" (The common practice of drawing blood to copy sutras in ancient China), *Zongjiao xue yanjiu* (Religious Studies) (2016) 1.

12. Lian Xi, *Blood Letters*, 4

13. Lin Zhao to mother, November 14, 1967.

The stated purpose of Lin Zhao's letter was to bring to the party's top propagandists, and through them to the CCP leadership, an indictment against the tyranny of Mao's rule as well as the party's complicity in it. As a Christian she declared herself a "resister" against the party's "unjust, tyrannical rule that is filled with evils and smeared with blood."[14] Underlying that rule was the Marxian theory of "class struggle," which the CCP had upheld since the 1920s as an immutable truth and as intrinsic to human history. After 1949, the CCP had also used it to justify waves of massive state violence—the so called "dictatorship of the proletariat." The doctrine gained new urgency during the 1960s when Mao declared that "class struggle must be talked about every year, every month, and every day."[15] Lin Zhao scoffed at it. "I do not ever believe that, in such a vast living space that God has prepared for us, there is any need for humanity to engage in a life-and-death struggle!" she wrote.[16]

"What we oppose is quite clear," Lin Zhao added, "but what do we want to build in the end? It is not a simple and easy thing to turn the concept of freedom into a blueprint and to build our life accordingly." A central question was the use of violence in opposition to the CCP's rule. "It is true that we do not hesitate to sacrifice our lives and may not even avoid the shedding of blood, but is it possible to build ... life in a pool of blood, through a blood bath?" she asked.[17]

Mao had famously pointed out as early as 1927 that political power came from the barrel of a gun. "Revolution means uprising," Mao reminded his gentler comrades in his March 1927 "Investigative Report on the Peasant Movement in Hunan." "It is the brutal action of one class overthrowing another class," he concluded.[18] For the Chinese communist movement, revolutionary violence had become the sacred creed ever since and remained enshrined well past the establishment of the People's Republic. The party's indoctrination had made it impossible to imagine political change without violence.

To Lin Zhao, that creed was as perverted as the communist rule itself. "Throughout history, there has been too much, not too little, shedding of Chinese blood," she wrote. "Is it possible," she asked, "even in the vast medieval ruins of China, to carry on political struggle in a more or less civilized manner, without resorting to bloodshed? Freedom, as one great American said, is whole and indivisible, and when one

---

14. Lin Zhao, ZRMRB, 28.

15. "Bajie shizhong quanhui" (The Tenth Plenary Meeting of the [Party's] Eighth Congress), *Zhongguo Gongchandang xinwen* (News of the Communist Party of China), http://dangshi.people.com.cn/GB/151935/176588/176596/10556200.html.

16. Lin Zhao, "Kejuan" (Written Homework): "Lianxi yi" (Exercise No. 1) January 1966.

17. Lin Zhao, ZRMRB, 29.

18. Mao Zedong, "Hunan nongmin yundong kaocha baogao" (Investigative Report on the Peasant Movement in Hunan), March 1927, in *Mao Zedong xuanji* (Selected Works of Mao Zedong), vol. 1.

man is enslaved, all are not free."[19] That was a reference to John F. Kennedy's speech "Ich bin ein Berliner," fragments of which were contained in a newspaper editorial denouncing American imperialism, which she had read in prison.[20] She continued:

> In any case, the truth is: as long as there are people who are still enslaved, not only are the enslaved not free, those who enslave others are likewise not free! Therefore, we who feel keenly the pain of tyranny and slavery and no longer want to remain as slaves—are we going to ignore such a painful lesson and debase the goal of our struggle into a desire to become a different kind of slave owners? . . . The nature of freedom dictates that it cannot be built through violence.[21]

Lin Zhao's renunciation of violence as a means toward the end of freedom—as well as her declared opposition to the CCP's violent rule—were both rooted in what she called her "Christian conscience."[22] "As a Christian," she wrote, "one devoted to freedom and fighting under the cross, I believe that killing communists is not the best way to oppose or eliminate communism," adding, "Had I not embraced a bit of Christ's spirit, I would have had absolute reason to pledge myself to bloody revenge against the Chinese Communist Party."[23]

In one of the most impassioned passages of the letter, she told the party's propagandists:

> As a Christian, my life belongs to my God. . . . In order to stick to my path, or rather my line, the line of a servant of God, the political line of Christ, this young person paid a grievous price. . . . I have come to see more clearly and deeply the many terrifying and shocking evils committed by your demonic political party! I grieved and wept for them! . . . Yet even when I touched the darkest, the most terrifying, the bloodiest, and the most savage center of your power—the core of evil—I still glimpsed, I did not completely overlook, the occasional sparks of humanity in you. . . . Then I cried in even greater anguish! I cried for your blood-smeared souls, which are unable to rid themselves of evil and are dragged by its terrifying weight ever deeper into the swamp of death. Most likely you will feel quite indifferent when you read this line, but as I write this, hot tears are rushing into my eyes. Gentlemen, those who enslave others can never be free. What a merciless but certain truth in your case![24]

---

19. Lin Zhao, ZRMRB, 29.
20. Lian Xi, *Blood Letters*, 133.
21. Lin Zhao, ZRMRB, 29.
22. Lin Zhao, ZRMRB, 39–40.
23. Lin Zhao, ZRMRB, 30.
24. Lin Zhao, ZRMRB, 38.

"To Become a Willing Martyr"

The Cultural Revolution broke out a few months after Lin Zhao penned her letter to the *People's Daily*. As "Mao's last revolution," it unleashed popular hysteria and political persecution on a scale unmatched in the entire history of China. It would lead to the downfall of many in the party establishment—including Mao's revolutionary partner-turned-political nemesis, President Liu Shaoqi—who were accused of "counterrevolutionary revisionism."[25] Before it fizzled out with Mao's own death in 1976, the Cultural Revolution would victimize more than twenty million individuals and their families, and claim the lives of some two million people nationwide.[26] Lin Zhao's warnings had failed to prevent the last orgy of violence under Mao.

Meanwhile, confined to an isolated cell in Shanghai's Tilanqiao Prison, where she had been sentenced in 1965 to serve a twenty-year term, Lin Zhao constantly searched for signs of divine approval of her resistance behind bars. As the Cultural Revolution unfolded and the CCP order began to disintegrate both outside and inside the prison, her conditions worsened. Hunger strikes and periodical flare-ups of tuberculosis compounded the mistreatment and turned her increasingly into—in her own words—the "white-haired girl of Tilanqiao."[27] Because of her unending sacrilege against Mao and the CCP, her initial sentence was secretly changed in December 1966 to the death penalty. A report prepared by the Reform through Labor Bureau of Shanghai (which administered Tilanqiao Prison) in support of the death sentence contained the following:

> During her imprisonment, Lin Zhao poked her flesh countless times and used her filthy blood to write hundreds of thousands of words of extremely reactionary, extremely malicious letters, notes, and diaries, madly attacking, abusing, and slandering our party and its Leader. . . . [She] vilified our party as . . . "a totalitarian tyranny that cares only to maintain its power through blood and hatred."[28]

---

25. Roderick MacFarquhar, *Origins of the Cultural Revolution*, vols. 1-3 (New York: Columbia University Press, 1974, 1983, 1999) 252-53; Roderick MacFarquhar and Michael Schoenhals, *Mao's Last Revolution* (Cambridge: Harvard University Press, 2006) 14-17; Yung Chang and Jon Halliday, *Mao: The Unknown Story* (New York: Anchor, 2006) 524.

26. Yang Jisheng, "Daolu, lilun, zhidu—wo dui Wenhua Dageming de sikao" (The Way, Theories, and the System: My Reflections on the Great Cultural Revolution), *Jiyi* (Memories), No. 104 (November 30, 2013) http://www.boxun.com/news/gb/pubvp/2015/08/201508040834.shtml#.Vo1oqrerTIU; Song Yongyi, "Wenge zhong 'fei zhengchang siwang' le duoshao ren?" (How Many People Died "Abnormal Deaths" during the Cultural Revolution?), *Dongxiang* (The Trend) (2011) 9.

27. Lian Xi, *Blood Letters*, 194.

28. Shanghai Shi Gonganju Laogaiju (Reform through Labor Bureau of Shanghai Municipal Public Security Bureau), "Lin Zhao an jiaxing cailiao" (Materials in Support of the Additional Penalty in Lin Zhao's Case), [December?] 1966.

However, amidst the chaotic and ironic turns of Cultural Revolution politics that sent public security officials to their own incarceration, Lin Zhao's case was left in a limbo for more than a year.[29]

Unaware of the death sentence, Lin Zhao stepped up protest against her mistreatment as a political prisoner and produced a steady stream of blood letters to her mother. They documented her "battles" against the makers of Mao's revolution inside Tilanqiao, her thwarted longing to see her mother, and her poignant reflections—as an act of religious penance—on her own youthful naiveté that had led her to communism. She also maintained an unlikely rigor in her religious life. In her prison cell that was stripped of all materials except party propaganda, she called to mind the many hymns and biblical verses that she had learned in the mission school two decades earlier. They became the imaginary bricks with which she built her own chapel in her cell to hold weekly "grand church worship," as she put it—starting promptly at 9:30 am each Sunday.[30]

"My life belongs to God," Lin Zhao wrote. God willing, she would be able to live. "But if God wants me to become a willing martyr, I will only be grateful from the bottom of my heart for the honor He bestows on me!"[31]

The longest blood writing Lin Zhao produced in her final months, entitled "Father's Blood," ran to about 14,500 blood-inked characters. She started writing on November 23, 1967, and finished on December 14. It was her attempt to come to terms with the loss of her father, whose warnings about the communist revolution she had ignored as a teenager. As a former government official under the Nationalists, he had been denounced as an unrepentant, reactionary "diehard" after the communist victory in 1949. One month after Lin Zhao's arrest in 1960, he swallowed rat poison and died a painful death.[32]

Lin Zhao was convinced that her father's death could not be deemed meaningless or futile. If nothing else, he had refused to bend to the evil power of the communist regime, even though he had been vilified as a "historical counterrevolutionary." "Thank God!" Lin Zhao wrote, "for the past eighteen years, there still remained in the foul-smelling Chinese mainland some so-called 'diehards' who refused to bow and 'plead guilty' before the communists." She noted that they had struggled to maintain the "Chinese code of honor" as articulated in the ancient teaching that "a scholar may be killed but would not be insulted."

---

29. Lian Xi, *Blood Letters*, 202–4.
30. See Lin Zhao, "Ling'ou xuyu" (Chatters of a Spirit Couple), July 11, 1965.
31. Lin Zhao, ZRMRB, 118.
32. Lian Xi, *Blood Letters*, 115.

As Lin Zhao put it, the CCP had created masses of downtrodden "heretical people," or *yimin*, a term she coined to refer to all those who had found themselves victims of political purges, and who were "more despised than the untouchables in the Indian caste system."[33] The abuse and persecution were so pervasive that the "heretical people" were left with but one escape—through death, "which has become both protest and release." In her words, those who took their lives left behind "a puddle of blood as silent protest in grief and indignation."[34] (In Shanghai, the outbreak of the Cultural Revolution led to 704 suicides in September 1966 alone.[35]) Lin Zhao had herself also attempted suicide in prison more than once, on one occasion cutting the vein on her left wrist with a piece of broken glass.[36] She continued:

> Blood! Blood! As a Christian I wish to plead with all the Christian churches and the Holy See in Rome: judge the multitude of suicides in mainland China with fairness! . . . Do not view all the suicides of the victims of communist . . . rule as spiritual evil! . . . God's gift of life should have been in itself beautiful! Therefore it is sin to lightly dispose of it! . . . But it is precisely in order to protect the beauty, dignity, freedom, and purity of life that multitudes of victims in China have forsaken their precious lives in resolute protest against the defilement and trampling of life. . . . I imagine that the Heavenly Father will not necessarily pronounce their suicides sinful but will instead pardon the afflicted souls with compassion! Therefore, righteous and holy churches, please hold a memorial service, or a holy Mass for the repose of the soul, for those who died under tyrannical rule in mainland China!

Without such sympathy, she asked, where could the dead "find a trace of human warmth to cover their wronged bones"? It was only by imagining a listening, free humanity that she could find solace. "It is only when I think of you, and picture myself pouring out my heart to you," she wrote, "that my anguished yet numbed heart and soul feel human warmth."[37]

On April 29, 1968, Lin Zhao was shot under orders issued by the Shanghai Military Control Committee of the People's Liberation Army. Her death sentence began with a "Supreme Instruction" from Chairman Mao: "There certainly will be those who refuse to change till they die. They are willing to go see God carrying their granite heads on their shoulders. That will be of little consequence."[38]

33. Lin Zhao, "Fuqin de xue" (Father's Blood), November 23–30, 1967 (Blood writing, revised and copied in ink, December 1–14, 1967).

34. Ibid.

35. MacFarquhar and Schoenhals, *Mao's Last Revolution*, 124.

36. Lian Xi, *Blood Letters*, 141.

37. Lin Zhao, "Fuqin de xue."

38. Zhongguo Renmin Jiefangjun Shanghai shi gongjianfa junshi guanzhi weiyuanhui (The People's Liberation Army Military Control Committee for Shanghai Municipal Public Security,

Before the execution, Lin Zhao was taken to a choreographed "public sentencing meeting" at the 1000-seat prison auditorium, a massive gray structure that stands atop Tilanqiao's former open execution ground. She arrived not from her cell, but from the prison hospital, where she had been taken after coughing up a massive amount of blood in another flare-up of tuberculosis.[39]

Lin Zhao could not have been taken entirely by surprise. More than two years earlier, she had reflected on her political dissent and its probable outcome: "Under the current circumstances, besides treating the prison as her homestead, Lin Zhao only looks to the execution ground as her final place of repose!" she wrote, referring to herself in the third person. Her "long-cherished hope" was to "turn my purest heart and my youthful blood into an exclamation mark in the epic of the struggle of free humanity," she wrote. "By nature people find joy in life; I alone find joy in death!"[40]

After her death, Lin Zhao's mother was ordered to pay a five-cent bullet fee. It was part of a routine revolutionary ritual intended to drive home the point that Lin Zhao's crime against the party and the people was such that her family must pay to have her cleansed from the revolutionary land.[41]

Awaiting Closure: Unanswered Theological Questions

Lin Zhao's political rehabilitation occurred at the beginning of Deng Xiaoping's reform era. In the early 1980s, Shanghai High People's Court posthumously revoked her death sentence and declared her innocent. Her prison writings were returned to the family in 1982.[42] Some of those writings were later posted on the internet and became a Promethean fire to political dissent in China today.[43] The late Nobel Peace laureate Liu Xiaobo called Lin Zhao "the only voice of freedom left for contemporary China."[44] Xu Zhiyong, a prominent, secular human rights lawyer and leader of the

---

Procuratorate, and Court systems), "Zhongguo Renmin Jiefangjun Shanghai shi gongjianfa junshi guanzhi weiyuanhui xingshi panjueshu 1967 niandu Hu zhongxing (1) zi di 16 hao" (Verdict Issued by the People's Liberation Army Military Control Committee for Shanghai Municipal Public Security, Procuratorate, and Court systems, [Serial number] Shanghai Intermediate Court 1967 [1], No. 16).

39. Lian Xi, *Blood Letters*, 234–35.
40. Lin Zhao, "Kejuan": "Lianxi yi."
41. Lian Xi, *Blood Letters*, 237–39.
42. Shanghai Shi Gaoji Renmin Fayuan (Shanghai High People's Court), "Shanghai Shi Gaoji Renmin Fayuan xingshi panjueshu" (Shanghai High People's Court Criminal Case Verdicts), August 22, 1980, and December 30, 1981; Lian Xi, *Blood Letters*, 7.
43. Lian Xi, *Blood Letters*, 7.
44. Liu Xiaobo, "Lin Zhao yong shengming xiejiu de yiyan shi dangdai Zhongguo jincun de ziyou zhi sheng" (Lin Zhao's last words, written with her life, are the only voice of freedom left for contemporary China), April 4, 2004, http://blog.boxun.com/hero/liuxb/146_1.shtml.

New Citizens Movement, called Lin Zhao's struggle behind bars "a spiritual battle. Lin Zhao offered all of herself for a free China. . . . Her body and her blood . . . were laid down as the gravel for the road toward a free China. She was a martyred saint, a prophet and a poet with an ecstatic soul, the Prometheus of a free China."[45]

Lin Zhao's battle for human freedom and dignity and against totalitarian repression and violence was indeed a spiritual one. She claimed that it was because she had "embraced a bit of Christ's spirit" that she chose to forego vengeance, and that all her political convictions were "based on the humanism and the ethics of love rooted in Christian teachings."[46] As a first-generation convert with no theological training, she did not employ theological language or cite biblical passages in support of her political views or her renunciation of violence. Unlike Dietrich Bonhoeffer who in response to the intensification of Nazi violence in the 1930s rebuked the convenient use of "theology to justify our reserved silence about what the state is doing,"[47] Lin Zhao's Christian vision of life and of God's creation led her to rebel instinctively against the logic of revolutionary violence.

On the other hand, the story of Lin Zhao also points to moral dilemmas in a Christian response to evil and violence and leaves us with some lingering questions. We know that Bonhoeffer allowed himself to be drawn into a conspiracy to stage a coup against Hitler.[48] In her case, Lin Zhao found her Christian convictions and revulsion against violence put to the test of a hopeless, non-violent political dissent. In her prison writings she agonized over questions that were both theological and moral: "could Mao Zedong be forgiven if he repented?" she wondered as she prayed for his repentance in her cell. "Is there a place for violence after all in opposing evil?" She wavered at times. Even as she took a firm public stand for non-violent resistance to communist rule, even as she foreswore violence as a means of revenge or to right the wrongs of the past, she admitted in her private writings that she could not rule out violence under certain circumstances. "If shedding one person's blood would prevent the shedding of the blood of tens of thousands of people—yes, I will," she wrote.[49]

---

45. Xu Zhiyong, "Ziyou Zhonghua de xundaozhe: du Lin Zhao 'shisiwan yan shu'" (A Martyr for a Free China—Reading Lin Zhao's "140,000-Character Letter"), March 13, 2013, http://www.epochtimes.com/gb/13/12/19/n4037695.htm.

46. Lin Zhao, "Zhuli 1967 nian shiyi yue ershisan ri xueshu shengming" (Blood-character Declaration on November 23, 1967, the Lord's Calendar).

47. Renate Bethge and Christian Gremmels, eds., *Dietrich Bonhoeffer: A Life in Pictures* (Minneapolis: Fortress, 2006) 79.

48. Eberhard Bethge, *Dietrich Bonhoeffer: A Biography*, rev. ed. (Minneapolis: Fortress, 2000) 671, 674. Bethge notes, however, that Bonhoeffer only played a small role in the conspiracy and did not have any special commission to carry out.

49. Lin Zhao, "Ling'ou xuyu," September 17, 1965; Lian Xi, *Blood Letters*, 138.

Finally, Lin Zhao posed to us a difficult question regarding suicide under conditions when the trampling and ravaging of life becomes insufferable. She did it both explicitly in the blood writing referenced above and indirectly with her repeated attempts in prison to take her own life in order to preserve its dignity. Her plea for understanding and compassion for victim-perpetrators of that particular form of human violence reminds us of the fraught nature of the issue that, in whatever new forms, still confronts us.

Huineng (The Sixth Patriarch) Tearing Up a Sutra by Liang Kai during Song Dynasty (13th century). Mitsui Memorial Museum, Japan. Licensed under a Creative Commons Attribution-ShareAlike 4.0 International License (CC BY-SA 4.0) <https://creativecommons.org/licenses/by-sa/4.0/deed.en>. Original image: https://commons.wikimedia.org/wiki/File:The_Sixth_Patriarch_Tearing_a_Sutra.jpg.

RESPONSE TO XI LIAN ("TEARING UP THE SUTRAS")

Lida V. Nedilsky

Could it be Huineng (638–713), Sixth Patriarch of Chan Buddhism, tearing up a sutra? A lowly figure is depicted in "violent action," in a "fury of rage against conventional, textual sources of enlightenment," pronounces University of California art historian James Cahill.[1] Liang Kai (c.1140–c.1210) painter of this scroll, adapted his style to the nature of his subject. Rough, spontaneous, unorthodox brushwork spoke to the anti-intellectual approach both of artist and of monk.[2] It appealed to a distinct standard of connoisseurship. Collectors in China rejected such brushwork; consequently, a devalued Chinese painting by an Imperial Academy artist was carried by monks to Japan. The scroll has been in the hands of private, Japanese collectors since the fourteenth century,[3] returning to China only in 2011 for exhibition at the Shanghai Museum.

Along with recollections of Buddhist monks demonstrating their literacy and devotion by copying the sutras using their own blood as the ink for calligraphy, this painting sprang to mind while I was reading the life story of Lin Zhao, subject of Lian Xi's book, *Blood Letters*. Like Lin Zhao's words and actions this painting is provocative. *Huineng Tearing up a Sutra*, with its rough, jagged brushstrokes capturing an almost demonic monk committing a sacrilegious act—is it so different from our image of Lin Zhao tearing up Mao's likeness or smearing it with her own blood?

I am neither artist nor art historian; neither historian nor theologian. I am a sociologist. What provokes my thoughts may be something we share in common. But what, in turn, are my thoughts may be quite different. My thoughts probe patterns demonstrated in Professor Lian's account of Lin Zhao. As an accomplished and

---

1. James Cahill, "From Academy to Chan: Liang Kai," Lecture 11D in *A Pure and Remote View: Visualizing Early Chinese Landscape Painting Lecture Series* (Institute of East Asian Studies, University of California, Berkeley, 2011). https://www.youtube.com/watch?v=O2owLWZ7IJU.

2. After leaving the Academy he first took up a life of drinking and painting, and was widely known as Madman Liang, before settling into one of Hangzhou's Chan temples.

3. The note seal at the bottom right-hand corner of the painting is identified as that of shogun Ashikaga Yoshimitsu, 1358–1408. Currently the scroll is part of the collection of Mitsui Takanura, at the Mitsui Memorial Museum, Tokyo.

inspired investigator of China's modern history, Professor Lian reconstructs with archival sources one person's experience.[4]

In doing so, he exposes China's problem of multiplication and division: that any deficit, multiplied by China's immense population, becomes unmanageable or unfathomable; and any benefit, divided by that same population, becomes insignificant. Thus, Lin Zhao's travails, shared by countless others, may seem just another example of life under Mao Zedong, or life under communist dictatorship, or life under totalitarianism. Tens of millions died during Mao's stint as "The Great Helmsman"; what makes Lin Zhao's death special? Likewise, Lin Zhao's open and sustained resistance to authority, awesome in the extent of its deviation, could hardly make a difference. In the year of her death, 1968, she was just one person among nearly 775 million citizens of the People's Republic of China.

I think the place to look for significance is at the jagged lines that frame Lin Zhao. They outline the distinct person at the same time as they mark a connection, a commonality between person and society. The lines are jagged, I suspect, because Lin Zhao was a complicated person, torn in different directions. Her clothes eventually became rags due to the intensity of those tearing forces. I see these tears developing along several seams where two aspects of Lin Zhao's self awkwardly meet:

- woman and intellectual
- Chinese and Christian
- rebel and revolutionary
- freedom fighter and fanatic
- joiner and loner

So, when does Lin Zhao become special? What makes her extraordinary? While convention, in a culture of orthopraxy, has weighed heavily on the category of person in China,[5] Lin Zhao challenged convention and assumed a still heavier weight. Borrowing from various and changing sources of inspiration and instruction—sources available to her as an intellectual, as a reader of Greek mythology and Western political philosophy, international affairs and Chinese state policy—she could express with sophistication what was on her mind.

---

4. Lian taps letters, essays, poems, photographs, and eyewitness testimonies. For a rare cache of photographs documenting the Cultural Revolution see Li Zhensheng, *Red-Color News Soldier: A Chinese Photographer's Odyssey through the Cultural Revolution* (New York: Phaidon, 2003).

5. Where else can you have a campaign for the rectification of names (zhengming)—the resolution of any deviation between the word used to describe something and the action or attitude described, in other words, the word and its intended meaning? Emphasis is placed on the human bringing of action or attitude into line with the word, rather than altering the word in any way. Consider, for example, the Confucian concept of gentleman or junzi.

At the same time, there was a lot on her mind, and much risk involved in revealing her thoughts. And with time and pressure and pain and loneliness, it appears, she could vent with passion what was in her heart. She could put off a lover, marry a ghost, pray to God, write in blood, order a feast, refuse food, scatter her feces, petition the United Nations, sing hymns, get drunk on wine, tear up a picture of Mao, absorb inmates' blows, and curse out party bureaucrats. How do we make sense of these competing, even contradictory impulses? How do we resolve them, not least against our own expectations?

Because of the distinct connoisseurship evidenced in China and in Japan, Professor Cahill suggests, Liang Kai could paint as if he were two different artists. His artistic development, ranging from his time at the Academy in Hangzhou, capital of the Southern Song, to his time as a devoted student of Chan Buddhism, satisfied the standards of two sets of collectors. Among followers of Zen Buddhism in Japan, at least, Liang Kai's *Huineng Tearing up a Sutra* captured the very texture of sudden enlightenment.

For us here today, with different standards of investigation, with different desires for knowledge, how do Lin Zhao and her blood letters function as sources of intellectual inspiration? I myself wonder what questions, doubts, stumbles nagged Lian the historian as he handled the array of materials on Lin Zhao? Now that Professor Lian has painstakingly presented us with the evidence of one woman's life story—evidence that is at times rough, crude, even violent in its action—what should we make of it? Does it provoke our own spontaneous enlightenment? And, finally, can Lian Xi see himself as Liang Kai to Lin Zhao's Huineng?

BEARING WITNESS: FAITH, BLACK WOMEN, AND SEXUAL VIOLENCE

Elizabeth O. Pierre

Introduction: A Critical Public Health Issue[1]

We must reinterpret and bring to life the stories of Dinah, Tamar, and the Levite's concubine because their story is our story; and if we do not give them life, our stories will finish like theirs—in silence.[2]

The increasing rate of sexual violence and the severity of its impact have made it a public health issue.[3] One research study that extended to twenty-two countries discovered that 19.7 percent of women and 7.9 percent of men reported childhood sexual abuse.[4] According to the anti-sexual violence organization, Rape, Abuse & Incest National Network (RAINN), every 98 seconds an American is sexually assaulted.[5] Also within the United States, one in four adolescent girls will experience some form of sexual violence before they reach the age of eighteen.[6]

Most recently, the Centers for Disease Control (CDC) reported that Black and indigenous women have the highest rate of homicide compared to other population groups. Here is what the report states:

---

1. This article is adapted from my dissertation, Elizabeth O. Pierre, "Black Christian Women and Sexual Violence: Caring for the Souls of Survivors" (PhD diss., Garrett-Evangelical Divinity School, 2016; https://search.proquest.com/docview/1808509717/?pq-origsite=primo). My sample group is mentioned throughout the paper. Two women in particular: Rachel and Zipporah (not their real names) will illustrate my key points.

2. Princess O'Nika Auguste, "Ending the Silence about Sexual Assault," *Christian Feminism Today*, 2016, https://eewc.com/ending-silence-sexual-assault/.

3. Centers for Disease Control, "Preventing Sexual Violence," https://www.cdc.gov/features/sexualviolence/index.html.

4. Noemi Pereda, Georgina Guilera, Maria Forns, and Juana Gomez-Benito, "The Prevalence of Child Sexual Abuse in Community and Student Samples: A Meta-Analysis," *Clinical Psychology Review* 29.4 (2009) 328–38, doi:10.1016/j.cpr.2009.02.007.

5. RAINN, "Scope of the Problem: Statistics," https://www.rainn.org/statistics/scope-problem.

6. Elizabeth A. Hodges and Jane Myers, "Counseling Adult Women Survivors of Childhood Sexual Abuse: Benefits of a Wellness Approach," *Journal of Mental Health Counseling* 32 (2010) 139–53.

Non-Hispanic black and American Indian/Alaska Native women experienced the highest rates of homicide (4.4 and 4.3 per 100,000 populations, respectively). Over half of all homicides (55.3%) were IPV [Intimate Partner Violence]-related; 11.2% of victims of IPV-related homicide experienced some form of violence in the month preceding their deaths, and argument and jealousy were common precipitating circumstances.[7]

The exact cause for this phenomenon remains unclear, though recent research hypothesizes that sociohistorical factors, such as slavery and dehumanizing images of Black women, have contributed to their vulnerability.[8] More studies are necessary accurately to assess the nature of this disconcerting proclivity of violence and particularly sexual violence directed toward Black women.

Researchers have also discovered a correlation between the survivor's racial and ethnic background, her experience of sexual violence, disclosure patterns, and recovery.[9] Studies have also shown a higher rate of incest among Black and Latina college students.[10] When comparing the effects of sexual violence upon Latinos and non-Latino Whites, the results show no major differences.[11] However, another study demonstrates that White female survivors show higher levels of anxiety compared to Latina women.[12] Still other research insists that depression, alcohol and drug abuse,

---

7. Emiko Petrosky et al., "Racial and Ethnic Differences in Homicides of Adult Women and the Role of Intimate Partner Violence—United States, 2003-2004," *Centers for Disease Control Weekly* 66 (July 21, 2017) 741-76, https://www.cdc.gov/mmwr/volumes/66/wr/mm6628a1.htm.

8. Hector F. Meyers et al., "Cumulative Burden of Lifetime Adversities: Trauma and Mental Health in Low SES African Americans and Latino/as," *Psychological Trauma: Theory, Research, Practice* 7.3 (2015) 243-51, doi: http://dx.doi.org/10.1037/a00039077; LaDonna Long and Sarah E.Ullman,"The Impact of Multiple Traumatic Victimization on Disclosure and Coping Mechanisms for Black Women," *Feminist Criminology* 8.4 (2013) 295-319, doi:10.1177/1557085113490783; Ellen F. Harrington, Janis Crowther, and Jillian Shippard, "Trauma, Binge Eating and the 'Strong Black Women,'" *Journal of Consulting and Clinical Psychology* 78.4 (2010) 469-79. Carolyn M. West, "Black Women and Interpersonal Violence: New Directions for Research," *Journal of Interpersonal Violence* 19.12 (2004) 1487-93, doi: 10.1177/0886260504269700; Patricia A. Washington, "Disclosure Patterns of Black Female Sexual Assault Survivors," *Violence Against Women* 7.11 (2001) 1254-83, doi:10.1177/10778010122183856.

9. Courtney E. Ahrens et al., "Talking about Interpersonal Violence: Cultural Influences on Latina's Identification and Disclosure of Sexual Assault and Intimate Partner Violence," *Psychological Trauma, Theory, Research, Practice and Policy* 2.4 (2010) 284-95, doi: 10.1037/a0018605; Paul Clear, John P. Vincent, and Gerald Harris, "Ethnic Differences in Symptom Presentation of Sexually Abused Girls," *Journal of Child of Sexual Abuse* 15.3 (2006) 79-98; Maureen C. Kenny and Adrian G. McEachern, "Racial, Ethnic, and Cultural Factors of Childhood Sexual Abuse: A Selected Review of the Literature," *Clinical Psychology Review* 20.7 (2000) 905-22.

10. Linda Kalof, "Ethnic Differences in Female Sexual Victimization." *Sexuality and Culture* 4 (2000) 75-98.

11. Kalof, "Ethnic Differences," 77.

12. Michael D. Newcomb, David T. Munoz, and Jennifer Vargas, "Child Sexual Abuse Consequences in Community Samples of Latino and European American Adolescents," *Child Abuse and Neglect* 33 (2009) 533-44.

phobias, and panic disorders are more frequent within the Latino/a community compared to other ethnic groups.[13] In light of these conflicting results, more research is necessary to determine how the survivor's racial and/or ethnic background affects her experience of sexual violence.[14] However, despite these inconsistencies, what is becoming more evident is that Black women seem to be more vulnerable to sexual violence.[15]

Finally, Black women show greater symptoms of trauma than other racial groups after sexual violence.[16] They are also less likely than other racial groups to disclose that they were abused.[17] There are primarily two reasons that this group is reluctant to disclose. First, Black women generally distrust the justice system and do not believe they will obtain the necessary support.[18] Second, research studies indicate that sexual violence against Black women is not isolated from the history of their systemic oppression, something which both augments their symptoms and deters their recovery.[19]

When the #MeToo movement exploded on the Twitter scene in fall 2017, much of the world did not realize that this movement began more than a decade previously. It was Tarana Burke, an African American woman and survivor of sexual violence, who coined the term and founded the movement in 2006. Ms. Burke formed

---

13. Raquel C. Andrés-Hyman, Melissa A. Cott, and Steven Gold, "Ethnicity and Sexual Orientation as PTSD Mitigators in Child Sexual Abuse Survivors," *Journal of Family Violence* 19.2 (2004) 319–25 (324).

14. Andrés-Hyman, Cott, and Gold, "Ethnicity and Sexual Orientation," 319–25; Kenny and McEachern, "Racial, Ethnic, and Cultural Factors, 905–22.

15. Thema Bryant-Davis et al., "Struggling to Survive: Sexual Assault, Poverty, and Mental Health Outcomes of African American Woman," *American Journal of Orthopsychiatry* 80.1 (2010) 61–70; Kimberly Jacob R. Arriola, Christina P. C. Borba, and Winifred Wilkins Thompson "The Health Status of Black Women: Breaking Through the Glass Ceiling," *Black Women, Gender, and Families* 1.2 (2007) 1–23; Kalof, "Ethnic Differences," 75–98; Gail E. Wyatt and Michael D. Newcomb, "Internal and External Mediators of Women's Sexual Abuse in Childhood," *Journal of Consulting and Clinical Psychology* 58.6 (1990) 758–67; Marie M. Fortune, *Sexual Violence: The Unmentionable Sin* (Cleveland, OH: Pilgrim, 1983).

16. Guiler Boyraz et al., "Posttraumatic Stress Predicting Depression and Social Support among College Students: Moderating Effects of Race and Gender," *Psychological Trauma: Theory, Research Practice, and Policy* 7.3 (2015) 259–68 (259), doi.org/10.1037/a0037967; Danelle Stevens Watkins et al., "Examining Cultural Correlates of Active Coping Among African American Female Trauma Survivors," *Psychological Trauma* 6.4 (2014) 328–36.

17. Long and Ullman, "Impact of Multiple Victimization," 298; Kalof, "Ethnic Differences," 92.

18. Long and Ullman, "Impact of Multiple Victimization," 298.

19. Long and Ullman, "Impact of Multiple Victimization," 296; Caroline V. Wright, Sarah Perez, and Dawn M. Johnson, "The Mediating Role of Empowerment for African American Women Experiencing Intimate Partner Violence," *Psychological Trauma, Theory, and Research Practice and Policy* 2.4 (2010) 266–72 (266), doi: 10.1037/a00117470; Carolyn M. West, "Black Women and Intimate Partner Violence: New Directions for Research," *Journal of Interpersonal Violence* 19.12 (2004) 1487–93 (1490), doi: 10.1177/0886260504269700.

this movement to galvanize other survivors of sexual violence as a means to provide support and empowerment. At the time the movement targeted Black and Brown women in low income communities who were particularly vulnerable to interpersonal violence such as sexual assault and who most likely had minimal access to social services. The movement has since gone both viral and global; engaging women and men from every social class, religion, and racial and ethnic background, which is a significant feat. The #MeToo movement has revealed how prevalent sexual assault actually is, and has also demonstrated that women continue to be vulnerable to this form violence in their homes, at work, walking down streets, at school, or at church. Black and Brown female bodies, however, continue to be more susceptible to this form of violence compared to other population groups.[20]

Black Women and Sexual Violence

She gave this name to the Lord who spoke to her: "You are the God who sees me," for she said, "I have now seen the One who sees me." (Gen 16:13).[21]

The perceptions of Black women generated during slavery continue to plague the experience of Black women and affect their recovery from sexual violence.[22] Such history affects their willingness to seek out help and resources.[23] This is best illustrated by the notion of the Strong Black Woman (SBW).[24] The literature argues that there are both positive and negative implications of the SBW.[25] It can serve as a protective factor when Black women encounter suffering. Some studies indicate that Black women tend to have less depressive and anxious symptoms after a traumatic incident. It may also serve as a "guidepost" to help make meaning of the traumatic event.[26] However, Black women are also in danger of collapsing if they adhere too strictly to being a SBW. This situation may be especially salient for Black trauma survivors whose adherence to this symbol allows for limited and restricted responses to

---

20. Carolyn M. West and Kalimah Johnson, "Sexual Violence in the Lives of African American Women," National Online Resource Center on Violence Against Women (March 2013) https://vawnet.org/material/sexual-violence-lives-african-american-women-risk-response-and-resilience.

21. All biblical quotations are from the New International Version unless otherwise stated.

22. Wright, Perez, and Johnson, "Mediating Role of Empowerment," 266–72.

23. Idelle Fraser et al., "Social Support Services for Help with Abusive Relationships: Perceptions of African American Women," *Journal of Family Violence* 17.4 (2002) 275–363; Washington, "Disclosure Patterns," 1254.

24. Washington, "Disclosure Patterns," 1254–83.

25. Wright, Perez, and Johnson, "Mediating Role of Empowerment," 266–72.

26. Harrington, Crowther, and Shippard, "Trauma, Binge Eating," 470.

suffering.[27] If a survivor maintains that she is a SBW, she must withstand emotional suffering and remain self-contained in order to persevere and to care for her family.[28] Therefore, acknowledging any kind of support or mental health need may be associated with weakness.[29] Although this identity has sometimes been a means of survival for Black women and their families, it has also sometimes been a means of self-destruction.[30] Generations of such perceptions have become so embedded in the fabric of our culture and within the Black community that these images have been difficult completely to eradicate. As much as Black women may oppose such images, it is challenging for them not to be affected by them, since such images become so internalized through cultural socialization.[31] In fact, it is ideal to be invincible, to be the SBW.[32] Therefore, Black women are less likely to disclose sexual violence against them—an essential component to recovery—in order to maintain this image.[33]

It is imperative for pastoral theologians and pastoral caregivers to be mindful of these historical factors when providing care to Black women who are survivors of sexual violence as history has indubitably contributed to contemporary attitudes toward Black women.[34] Furthermore, such images contribute to negative views about Black women's sexuality and may cause survivors to remain silent about the abuse they have experienced.[35] Additionally, these attitudes silence women because they fear being re-victimized by church leaders and/or congregations who may blame them for the assault.[36]

History matters, and the internalization of these images complicate the symptoms and recovery of Black women who are survivors of sexual violence. The literature is vague as to how to provide concrete ways to counter these images, but

27. Ibid., 469–79.

28. Beverly Wallace, "A Womanist Legacy of Trauma, Grief, and Loss," in *Women Out of Order: Risking Change to Create Care in a Multicultural World*, ed. Jeanne Stevenson Moessner and Teresa Snorton (Minneapolis: Augsburg Fortress, 2010) 43–57 (47).

29. Francine Wood, "Take My Yoke Upon You," in *A Troubling in My Soul: Womanist Perspective on Evil and Suffering*, ed. Emilie M. Townes (Maryknoll, NY: Orbis, 1993) 37–47 (40).

30. Tamara Beauboeuf-Lafontant,"'You Have to Show Strength': An Exploration of Gender, Race, and Depression," *Gender and Society* 21.1 (2007) 28–51 (47), doi.org/10.1177/0891243206294108.

31. Harrington, Cowther, and Shippard, "Trauma, Binge Eating," 469–79.

32. Ibid.

33. Ibid.

34. Washington, "Disclosure Patterns," 1254–83; Toinette M. Eugene,"'If You Get There Before I Do . . . ': A Womanist Ethical Response to Sexual Violence," in *Perspectives on Womanist Theology*, ed. Jacqueline Grant (Atlanta: ITC Press, 2006) 92–113; Darlene Clark Hine, "Rape and Inner Lives of Black Women in the Middle West: Preliminary Costs on the Culture of Dissemblance," *Signs* 14 (1989) 912–20.

35. Washington, "Disclosure Patterns," 1269.

36. Sarah E. Ullman, *Talking About Sexual Assault: Society's Response to Survivors* (Washington, DC: American Psychological Association, 2010) 47; Washington, "Disclosure Patterns," 1254–83.

the consensus is that more research is necessary to learn how to deconstruct these images.[37]

Black Women and the Self Selfobjects

> *(Girls and girls of color) will see an image of someone who looks like them hanging on the walls of this great American institution. . . . And I know the kind of impact that will have on their lives because I was one of those girls.*[38]

Heinz Kohut's psychological theory serves as a helpful framework to understand how the trauma of sexual violence psychologically affected my sample group.[39] Kohut claims that there are several components that contribute to one's healthy sense of self.[40] For Kohut the self is the "individual's psychological universe."[41] Kohut also asserts that when the self develops in an environment where there are minimal disturbances and where most needs are met, a cohesive self is developed:

> The new born infant arrives physiologically preadapted for a specific physical environment—the presence of oxygen, of food, of a certain range of temperature outside of which he cannot survive. Similarly, psychological survival requires a specific psychological environment—the presence of responsive-empathic selfobjects.[42]

The definition of selfobject is the "dimension of our experience of another person that relates to the person's functions in shoring up our self."[43] Central to this definition is how the individual *experiences* the selfobject. In other words, an individual may encounter numerous selfobjects in her lifetime, but she will not experience all selfobjects as part of herself. Kohut often refers to parental figures as the primary selfobjects for individuals.[44] Kohut argues that culture, art, music, and religion can also

---

37. Harrington, Crowther, and Shippard, "Trauma, Binge Eating," 469–79; Helen A. Neville et al., "General and Culturally Specific Factors Influencing in Black and White Rape Survivors' Self-Esteem," *Psychology of Women Quarterly* 28 (2004) 83–94.

38. Brittany Britto, "Photo of Girl Staring in Awe at Michelle Obama Portrait Goes Viral, Resonates with Baltimore Artist," *Baltimore Sun*, March 5, 2018, https://www.baltimoresun.com/features/baltimore-insider-blog/bs-fe-little-girl-parker-curry-amy-sherald-michelle-obama-portrait-viral-20180305-htmlstory.html.

39. My sample group consisted of five Black Christian women who were sexually abused as children and/or were raped as adults.

40. Heinz Kohut, *How Does Analysis Cure?* (Chicago: University of Chicago Press, 1977).

41. Ibid., 311.

42. Heinz Kohut and Ernest S. Wolfe, "The Disorders of Self and Their Treatment: An Outline," *The International Journal of Psychoanalysis* 59 (1978) 413–25.

43. Heinz Kohut, *The Restoration of the Self* (Chicago: University of Chicago Press, 1984) 49.

44. Kohut, *How Does Analysis Cure?*, 14–33.

serve as selfobjects for persons.[45] One of the primary ways in which the individual self is sustained is through the healthy interaction between the self and responsive selfobjects.[46] Kohut goes on to explain that there are two types of selfobject that assist with establishing a child's self:

> There are two kinds of selfobjects: those who respond to and confirm the child's innate sense of vigour, greatness and perfection and those to whom the child can look up and with whom he can merge as an image of calmness, infallibility and omnipotence. The first one is referred to as the mirroring selfobject, the second as the idealized parent image.[47]

A critical component of mirroring is an individual's capacity to have empathy. He defines empathy as "the capacity to think and feel oneself into the inner experience of what another person experiences, though usually, and appropriately, to an attenuated degree."[48] Empathy is so essential to self-cohesion that Kohut believes that neglect or insufficient empathy by caregivers was traumatizing and later contributed to "impoverished psychic organization."[49] He goes so far as to assert that the deprivation of empathy contributes to the individual's psychological collapse, "What leads to the human's self-destruction, however, is its exposure to coldness, the indifference of the nonhuman, the non-empathically responding world."[50] Although empathy is crucial during childhood, its impact extends beyond the early developmental stages.[51] It is a way of "rehumanizing" the other throughout the lifespan.[52]

Kohut also stresses that a child's cohesive self is established when the parent allows for herself to be idealized by the child through providing "the uplifting experience of being picked up by our strong and admired mother and having been allowed to merge with her greatness, calmness, and security."[53] Kohut asserts that the failure of parental figures to accept the idealization consequently leads to children's later emotional disturbances.[54] He explains that when parental figures reject the child's idealization, the child internalizes this as a rejection of herself.[55] The child feels

---

45. Kohut, *Restoration of the Self*, 84.
46. Kohut, *How Does Analysis Cure?*, 49–79.
47. Kohut and Wolfe, "Disorders of the Self and Their Treatment," 414.
48. Kohut, *Restoration of the Self*, 82.
49. Ibid., 83.
50. Ibid., 18.
51. Jodi Halpern and Harvey M. Weinstein, "Rehumanizing the Other: Empathy and Reconciliation," *Human Rights Quarterly* 26.3 (2004) 561–83.
52. Ibid., 567.
53. Kohut, *Restoration of the Self*, 50.
54. Kohut and Wolfe, "Disorders of the Self and Their Treatment," 417.
55. Kohut, *Restoration of the Self*, 31.

rejected because she derives her sense of worth from her parents, who are ultimately a reflection of herself.[56] If parents cannot appreciate their own gifts and claim their achievements, how can the child?[57]

Twinship selfobject is another concept that Kohut constructed, which is the need for the self "to experience the presence of essential alikeness."[58] Kohut's description of twinship and its impact on development is quite substantial:

> The mere presence of people in the child's surroundings—their voices and body odors, the emotions they express, the noises they produce as they engage in human activities, the specific aroma of foods they prepare and eat—creates a security in the child, a sense of belonging and participating, that cannot be explained in terms of a mirroring response or a merger with ideals. Instead, these feelings derive from confirmation of the feeling that one is a human being among human beings.[59]

Children cannot thrive in isolation any more than adults. When they are disconnected from those in their families and in their community who are similar to them, emotional disturbances are most likely to ensue. When traumatic experiences occur, such disturbances are exacerbated.

The selfobject needs of mirroring, idealization, and twinship are all necessary for the cohesion of the self.[60] When these are generally met, Kohut asserts that the child will have a more or less healthy sense of self.[61] This does not mean that selfobjects provide these needs perfectly or that the child will avoid emotional pain. It simply means that the core sense of self largely remains intact. However, Kohut contends that it is the *chronic* deprivation of the selfobject needs of mirroring, idealization, and twinship that contributes to pathology.[62] How might sexual violence impact self-cohesion along with the absence of these selfobject needs?

Womanist practical theologian Phillis Sheppard's *Self, Culture, and Others in Womanist Practical Theology* and Stephanie Crumpton's *A Womanist Pastoral Theology Against Intimate Partner Violence* offer critical analyses of Kohut's theory and how it might be relevant for the needs of Black women who are survivors of trauma such as sexual violence.[63] It is their work that will assist further in this discussion

---

56. Ibid.
57. Kohut and Wolfe, "Disorders of the Self and Their Treatment," 417.
58. Kohut, *Restoration of the Self*, 195.
59. Ibid., 200.
60. Ibid., chapter 2.
61. Ibid.
62. Ibid., 198.

63. Phillis Sheppard, *Self, Culture, and Others in Womanist Practical Theology* (New York: Palgrave Macmillan, 2011) 111–27; Stephanie Crumpton, *A Womanist Pastoral Theology Against Intimate and*

of how the tridimensional experience of racism, classism, and sexism, and the loss of the cultural selfobject of the Black church may have exacerbated symptoms of trauma and subsequently impede the recovery of survivors.

Sheppard explains that Kohut failed to consider how one's social and cultural context might impact the experience of selfobject needs such as mirroring. Sheppard argues that for Black women in Western culture, the arts, music, and even our religion do not necessarily contribute to adequate cohesion of the self. On the contrary, the destructive images of Black women portrayed in our culture may actually lead to further fragmentation.[64] How are these images being internalized by Black women who already may have a fragile sense of self because of the legacy of slavery? How does this fragility put them at greater risk for sexual violence and impact their recovery? I believe that one of the key reasons for re-victimization is the indelible mark that trauma leaves on the body, causing the survivor to assume that her body is now defiled. Therefore, what she does to or for it is no longer of consequence. This idea is mirrored and substantiated by the culture through the preponderance of the myths of the Black woman: that she is inferior, dirty, and impure.[65]

Crumpton agrees with Sheppard's critique of Kohut. There are socio-cultural factors that are unique to the Black community that affect Black women intrapsychically.[66] Crumpton argues that negative stereotypes that stem from the history of slavery are so embedded in our culture that they complicate and compound the trauma of sexual violence for Black women. These controlling images have also become part of the fabric of the Black church, the cultural selfobject that is supposed to mirror "back our value in ways that makes us feel uplifted."[67] The very institution that is called to contribute to the cohesion of its congregants instead perpetuates these images. Crumpton writes:

> While these cultural selfobjects certainly show up in the culturally produced stereotypes emerging out of the other groups to depict Black women as loud mouthed (the Sapphire) and the self-sacrificing (the Mammy), some of these cultural selfobjects emerge out of the African American community's own "self" as a result of its intragroup struggles with colorism, sexism, classism. . . . In these instances, the psychological stakes are higher for Black girls and women who encounter language as a cultural selfobject present in conversations that they have with members of their own communities.

Cultural Violence (New York: Palgrave Macmillan, 2014) 1–23, 65–91.

64. Sheppard, *Self, Culture, and Others*, 31.

65. Patricia Hill Collins, *Black Sexual Politics: African Americans, Gender, and the New Racism* (New York: Routledge, 2004).

66. Crumpton, *Womanist Pastoral Theology*, 16.

67. Ibid., 14.

One such example is language in which words like "strong" are used to laud Black women's resilience, without acknowledging the dehumanizing ways in which this descriptor portrays them as invincible in the face of death dealing circumstances.[68]

Sexual violence is a death dealing circumstance. Survivors of sexual violence are less likely to disclose their experience to their church communities if churches project these images. The church is not a safe space if survivors are expected to be "strong" and if their bodies are not deemed as holy as other bodies. Crumpton depicts the challenges Black women face as they seek to navigate their recovery within an institution that maintains and substantiates these myths about Black women.

The selfobjects of many of the participants in my sample group failed them: their parents and their churches. Sheppard argues that this is where the discussion of race, gender, and sexuality is critical.[69] She argues that the self cannot be excised from its "cultural milieu."[70] Black women live in a culture that does not necessarily mirror and promote their self-cohesion; in fact, it may even be damaging.[71] For example, there are legal institutions and churches that defend men instead of protecting the women they hurt.[72] As already discussed, the history of slavery and police brutality all denigrate the female body. The lack of mirroring from the culture continues the fragmentation that has already been caused by the sexual violence. In other words, many of the participants had no real safe place to turn for that mirroring they so desperately needed as Black women.

Despite the Black church's failure as a cultural selfobject, Crumpton explains that Black women will not forsake their beloved community.[73] Therefore, the Black church must use its imagination to provide pastoral care that attends to the complexity of being a woman, Black, Christian, and a survivor of violence.[74] She provides a womanist pastoral care framework that includes the use of Black literature and communal rituals that connect women who share the same trauma.[75]

After a traumatic experience such as sexual violence women feel dehumanized.[76] Therefore, they seek others who are able to offer the empathy that Kohut describes.

68. Ibid., 16.
69. Sheppard, *Self, Culture, and Others*, 61–111.
70. Ibid., 113.
71. Ibid., 137.
72. Crumpton, *Womanist Pastoral Theology*, 89.
73. Ibid., 125.
74. Ibid.
75. Ibid., 128.
76. Judith Herman, *Trauma and Recovery: The Aftermath of Violence from Domestic Abuse to Political Terror* (Cambridge, MA: Basic Books, 1992); Marie M. Fortune, *Sexual Violence: The*

For many Black women, they turn to their church leaders and community for such support and understanding.[77] When empathy is lacking from others—either through minimization; lack of general acknowledgement of the reality of sexual violence within the community, or because of a hermeneutic of disbelief of the survivor's experience—the victim becomes re-traumatized.[78] However, when a community provides an empathic response and validates the survivor's experience a process of healing can take place. It is in the process of remembering and telling her experience that healing for the survivor is more likely to follow.[79]

Can I Get a Witness?

The Jesus I learned about in school would not turn his back on children—not once.[80]

—Catholic clergy sexual abuse survivor

Before Jesus ascended into heaven he told his disciples, "But you will receive power when the Holy Spirit comes upon you; and you will be my witnesses in Jerusalem, and in all Judea and Samaria, and to the ends of the earth" (Acts 1:8). While in college I was a part of a parachurch organization that encouraged my friends and I to be good witnesses to the gospel of Jesus Christ. We shared a miniature booklet that explained the chasm between us and God. And the hope was that our fellow classmates would come to know Jesus Christ after our sharing this booklet with them. At the time I had a very narrow idea of what it meant to be a witness. I thought it solely meant to proselytize. Since graduating from college I have been a pastor and therapist and my notion of what it means to be a witness to Christ is evolving. Yes, certainly being a witness—a martyr—for Christ is the genuine response to his love and to the great sacrifice he has made on my behalf. I must exclaim and proclaim the beauty and goodness of this truth. Yet based on the stories I have heard from congregants, clients, and current students; the meaning of witness and what it means

Unmentionable Sin.

77. Crumpton, *Womanist Pastoral Theology*; Dawnovise N. Fowler and Michele A. Rountree, "Exploring the Meaning and Role of Spirituality for Women Survivors," *Journal of Pastoral Care* 64.2 (2010) 1–13.

78. Ullman, "Talking About Sexual Assault," 59; Fortune, *Sexual Violence: The Unmentionable Sin*, 125–39.

79. Sheppard, *Self, Culture, and Others*, 127–42; Herman, *Trauma and Recovery*, 175–96; Bessel A. van der Kolk, Alexander C. McFarlane and Lars Weisaeith, *Traumatic Stress: The Effects of Overwhelming Experience on Mind, Body, and Society* (New York: Guilford, 1996) 32

80. "Hear Abuse Victims' Messages for the Pope," CNN, https://www.cnn.com/videos/us/2018/08/23/pennsylvania-church-abuse-scandal-victims-pkg-hill-vpx.cnn/video/playlists/church-controversies/.

to be a witness has expanded for me. I agree with Catholic theologians Maria Clara Bingemer and Peter Casarella,[81] who claim that the term witness is perplexing and is often associated only with proselytism though it is so much more comprehensive than this. I also appreciate how they encapsulate the concept of witnessing by employing the meaning of the original term, martyr:

> Witnessing illuminates a path that can be followed. One stands in the company of the poor of Jesus Christ, and their example of sanctity and justice marks out the direction of the journey.... Christians call this path discipleship and enter it wholeheartedly in spite of the known cost.[82]

Bearing witness to Christ does inevitably costs us something. It compels us to go places where we otherwise would not go. It compels us to see things that we would rather not see. Being a disciple, a follower of Christ, compels us to touch things that we are repulsed by. However, we enter these domains because we are called to embody Christ: to be a living witness to his life, death, and resurrection.

My research engages the intersection of trauma, race/ethnicity, and religion. In my doctoral dissertation I examined how theology (primarily atonement theology) played a role in the lives of Black Christian women who are survivors of sexual violence. I focused my research in this manner because there are two primary lacunae in the literature regarding sexual violence. First, though there has been extensive research from various disciplines on sexual violence, there continues to be a dearth of information regarding the correlation between the impact of and recovery from sexual violence and membership of racial and ethnic minorities.[83] Black women seem to be especially susceptible to sexual violence because of poverty,[84] and historical factors such as the physical and sexual exploitation of Black women, which

---

81. Maria Bingemer and Peter Casarella, eds., *Witnessing: Prophecy, Politics and Wisdom* (New York: Orbis, 2014) ix–xiv.

82. Bingemer and Casarella, *Witnessing*, ix.

83. Casey Taft et al., "Intimate Partner Violence Against African American Women: An Examination of the Sociocultural Context," *Aggression and Behavior* 14 (2009) 50–58. http://dx.doi.org/10.1016/j.avb.2008.10.001; Arriola, Borba, and Thompson, "Health Status of Black Women," 1–23; Sarah E. Ullman and Henrietta H. Filipas, "Ethnicity and Child Sexual Abuse Experiences in Female College Students," *Journal of Child Sexual Abuse* 14.3 (2005) 67–89. doi: 10.1300/J070v14n03_04; Paul Clear, John P. Vincent, and Gerald Harris, "Ethnic Differences in the Symptom Presentation of Sexually Abused Girls," *Journal of Child Sexual Abuse* 15.3 (2006) 79–98.

84. Holley Foster, Jeanne Brooks-Gunn, and Anne Martin, "Poverty/Socioeconomic Status and Exposure to Violence in Lives of Children and Adolescents," in *The Cambridge Handbook of Violent Behavior and Aggression*, ed. Daniel J. Flannery, Alexander T. Vazsonyi, and Irwin D. Waldman (New York: Cambridge University Press, 2007) 664–87; Dexter R. Voisin, "The Effects of Family and Community Violence Exposure Among Youth: Recommendations for Practice and Policy," *Journal of Social Work Education* 43 (2007) 51–66, doi: 10.5175/JSWE.2007.200400473.

have been internalized into contemporary culture.[85] With Black women making up a majority of Black congregations and with the influential role that the Black church plays in the community, further research is required to provide guidance to clergy as to how best to support survivors of sexual violence.

Second, there is a paucity of research about the role religion may play for survivors of childhood sexual abuse and rape. Countless studies demonstrate that religion is salubrious for individuals who have traumatic experiences.[86] Surprisingly, many research studies about sexual violence do not include religion or religious affiliations in their methodology even though studies consistently indicate that Black women especially turn to their local church for support instead of mental health services when they have experienced trauma.[87] One study does acknowledge this deficit, "future research should investigate the potential buffering effect of interactions within church structures on self-esteem of rape survivors."[88]

Though my research emphasized the experiences of Black women within Black churches, the lack of support for survivors transcends denominations and racial/cultural lines. Rachel Denhollander, a White Christian woman, who was abused for years by renowned physician, Larry Nassar, says this about her experience:

> Yes. Church is one of the least safe places to acknowledge abuse because the way it is counseled is, more often than not, damaging to the victim. There is an abhorrent lack of knowledge for the damage and devastation that sexual assault brings. It is with deep regret that I say the church is one of the worst places to go for help. That's a hard thing to say, because I am a very conservative evangelical, but that is the truth. There are very, very few who have ever found true help in the church.[89]

---

85. Casey Taft et al., "Intimate Partner Violence Against African American Women: An Examination of the Sociocultural Context," *Aggression and Violent Behavior* 14 (2009) 50–58, doi 10.1016/j.avb.2008.10.001.

86. Jeffrey A. Tamburello, Kyle Irwin, and Martha Gault Sherman, "Religious Coping: The Role of Religion in Attenuating the Effect of Sexual Victimization of College Women and Trust," *Religious Research Association* 56 (2014): 581–95, doi 10. 1007/s13644-014-0165-2; Judith Sigmund, "Spirituality and Trauma: The Role of Clergy in the Treatment of Post-Traumatic Stress Disorder," *Journal of Religion and Health* 42.3 (2003) 221–29, http://www.jstor.org/stable 27511689; Patricia Fouque and Martin Glachan, "The Impact of Christian Counseling on Survivors of Sexual Abuse," *Counseling Psychology Quarterly* 13.2 (2000) 201–20.

87. Nadine J. Kaslow et al., "Suicidal Abused, African American Women's Response to a Culturally Informed Intervention," *Journal of Consulting and Clinical Psychology* 78 (2010) 449–58, doi: 10.1037/a0019692; Martie P. Thompson et al., "Partner Violence and Social Support and Distress Among Inner City African American Women," *American Journal of Community Psychology* 28.1 (2000) 127–43.

88. Helen Neville et al., "General and Culturally Specific Factors Influencing Black and White Rape Survivor's Self-Esteem," *Psychology of Women Quarterly* 28 (2004) 83–94 (92).

89. Morgan Lee, "My Larry Nassar Testimony Went Viral: But There's More to the Gospel Than Forgiveness," *Christianity Today*, January 31, 2018, https://www.christianitytoday.com/ct/2018/january-web-only/rachael-denhollander-larry-nassar-forgiveness-gospel.html.

Tragically, Ms. Denhollander is not the only person to have said this about the church. The women in my sample group essentially shared similar disappointments and hurt. A resounding theme is that the church as a whole does not bear witness to their stories and to their suffering.

Paul, in First Corinthians, explains that no part of the body is exempt from another's suffering: "if one part suffers, every part suffers with it" (1 Cor 12:26). Therefore, regardless of one's racial/ethnic background or gender, this issue should matter to all of us as disciples/witnesses to Christ because we are one body. And one part of our body is suffering—disproportionately. Thus, how is Christ calling the church to bear witness to such atrocities? How is our Lord calling the Body of Christ to respond in light of such suffering?

I have already summarized why Black women are particularly vulnerable to sexual violence. For the remainder of this paper I will define witness within the Black context, and focus on two women from my sample group: Rachel and Zipporah. They provide examples of how the church might bear witness to survivors of sexual violence.

Church Body as Witness

The community of faith can be a valuable resource to victims and offenders if its members are able and willing to open their eyes to the reality of sexual violence.[90]

There are several ways that my sample group is calling the church to be a witness to the trauma of sexual violence. Zipporah wants the church to have liturgies or rituals that acknowledge its prevalence, "I would like to see—a candlelight ceremony. Incorporating in the ceremony where we ring the bell to symbolize the victims in that period of time . . . within this conversation, 90,000 women have been raped."

Theologian Shelly Rambo asserts that the ongoing challenge for churches is to, "continually resist the temptation to cover over—to elide—the suffering in an effort to witness to it."[91] Churches, for various reasons, cannot and do not want to see the trauma that exists within their congregations. Yet is this not what the church is called to do? Is it not to witness to the suffering in its midst? Is it not to embody who Christ is? To act in a manner that reflects the nature of Christ? African American pastoral theologian, Edward Wimberly[92] addresses this when he treats witnessing as a fundamental element of pastoral care particularly within the Black community:

---

90. Marie M. Fortune, *Sexual Violence: The Sin Revisited* (Cleveland: Pilgrim, 2005) 225.

91. Shelly Rambo, *Spirit and Trauma: A Theology of Remaining* (Louisville, KY: Westminster John Knox, 2010) 3.

92. Edward Wimberly, *Pastoral Care in the Black Church* (Nashville: Abingdon, 1979).

The final dimension of the model of pastoral care is the witnessing ministry in the Black church, built upon the prophetic tradition of the Black church, which began with Richard Allen and culminated with Dr. Martin Luther King, Jr. In this context, the goal of the witnessing aspect of pastoral care is to transmit the liberation ministry into action not only within the congregation but also in the community by addressing those forces in society that prevent the growth of persons.[93]

Sexual violence is a force in society that prevents the growth of a person. Without this prophetic witness many Black women will continue to suffer alone and die by the hand of perpetrators or by suicide because of their inability to cope with the trauma. The church simply cannot afford to not engage this issue.

Pastor as Witness

Reaffirm that it's not their fault . . . pastors hold a lot of power.
—Zipporah

There are numerous ways pastors can be witnesses to sexual violence in their churches. First, they can preach about sexual violence. Second, they can be mindful of how they preach atonement themes and remember also to listen for the ways that survivors use atonement themes in their recovery process. Third, they can serve as witnesses by believing the stories that survivors share. In these various ways, their "witnessing presence in trauma will make visible what is rendered invisible."[94]

Wimberly defines witnessing as the "aspect of pastoral care that takes place when the church attempts to change those conditions which prevent persons from choosing healthy crisis coping patterns."[95] One of the fundamental ways that witnessing occurs in the Black church is through preaching. Wimberly argues that:

> Because the black pastor has been the symbolic leader of the church, the preaching function has been very important in the pastoral care of the black people. In worship the pastor used the pulpit to help people find meaning for their existence. The therapeutic context of black worship, and the black preacher as the major symbol of the church combined to form a powerful context for sustaining and guiding ministry of pastoral care.[96]

---

93. Ibid., 92.
94. Rambo, *Spirit and Trauma*, 123.
95. Wimberly, *Pastoral Care in the Black Church*, 79.
96. Ibid., 56–57.

Wimberly also claims that the black pastor "from the pulpit" can expound "the faith of the community that enabled persons to endure the hardships of life."[97] Therefore, it will be from the pulpit that pastors need to preach about sexual violence. What pastors preach on Sunday matters. Pastors are called to be a witness to those who are suffering in their midst. Future research might explore ways to use responsibly those hard passages such as Judg. 19, where a woman is raped and cut up in pieces. In all my years attending Black churches (or any other church for that matter), I have never heard a sermon preached on this text. Then there are the stories of Dinah,[98] and that of Tamar.[99] What would it look like to preach a sermon from their perspective and not from that of the men who killed for their honor? What might Dinah and Tamar have to say to women today about their story? How might we embody their experiences in liturgies and rituals of the Black church in order to give voice to the trauma of sexual violence?

Along with preaching and teaching about sexual violence, Rachel said that she would like pastors to talk more explicitly about sex and sexuality:

> I do feel that it's important to teach people about sex and sexuality.... And by that I mean really both the negative aspect and destructive aspects ... as well as the positive and powerful ...

If the church is uncomfortable addressing issues such as sex and sexuality, it will nearly be impossible to engage sexual violence. The church's difficulty in engaging sex and sexuality has been a challenge for centuries. Sex is usually discussed in the following manner: don't do it until you are married and enjoy it once you are married. Anything that extends beyond these parameters, such as sexual violence, is not addressed. This is problematic for the following reasons:

> The traditional rule which said categorically that sexual activity before marriage was wrong implied that sexual activity in marriage was right; no other criteria need be applied. The primary consideration was *when* sexual activity took place. It gave little consideration to the substance or quality of the sexual interaction after marriage. Using this view, it would be wrong for a man to engage in coercive sexual activity with a woman before they were married, and acceptable for him to engage in exactly the same coercive sexual activity.... The question of the substance and quality of the sexual interaction, the presence of consent, etc., is never raised.[100]

---

97. Ibid., 35.
98. Gen 34.
99. 2 Sam 13.
100. Fortune, *Sexual Violence: The Unmentionable Sin*, 72–73.

When the church holds on to this traditional rule, it assumes that sex is good and acceptable at *all times* within the context of marriage. However, the truth is that marital rape happens. When the quality of relationship is not questioned, it may be hard for pastors to see and hear the reality of abuse when women share that it exists within the marriage relationship.[101] Moreover, when Black churches emphasize the dangers of premarital sex without focusing on the health of any kind of relationship, survivors will most likely be reluctant to share their trauma with their pastors.[102] They fear blame. In other words, if women who engage in premarital sex are raped, they essentially asked for it. These implicit and explicit messages conveyed within the Black church are keeping women silent.[103]

These are some of the issues that encompass what Rachel asks the church to engage. What is healthy sexuality? What does our theology teach us about sexuality? These are discussions in which Black churches must be willing to engage in order to be safe and healing spaces for survivors.

Finally, pastors must be witnesses to injurious images of Black women (Jezebel, Mammy, and Strong Black Women) and how poverty makes Black women more vulnerable to sexual violence.[104] These images are often unconsciously internalized by Black women. Unfortunately, Black churches perpetuate these images through sermons and the manner in which Black women are treated in the community.[105] Again, this is where the church as a cultural selfobject can be detrimental because it does not adequately mirror to Black women their worth.[106] Some pastors may be fully cognizant of their portrayal of women in their worship service. Others may not be aware of the degree to which they have internalized these images and conveyed them in messages to their congregations. Therefore, future research that examines how Black pastors preach about and to women may be an important first step toward the deconstruction of these images. Pastors must pursue a more careful assessment of how racism, classism, and sexism may impede the recovery process. They must listen for the following: does a woman expect to be doubted about her experience because she is Black and/or had premarital sex? What ways does she seek to organize herself around negative aspects of race, gender, and sexuality as means to maintain

---

101. Fortune, *Sexual Violence: The Sin Revisited*, 84–86.

102. Crumpton, *Womanist Pastoral Theology*, 1–25.

103. Ibid.

104. Carolyn McCrary, "Intimate Violence Against Black Women and Internalized Shame: A Womanist Pastoral Counseling Perspective," *The Journal of the Interdenominational Theological Center* 28.1–2 (2001) 3–37, http://digitalcommons.auctr.edu/cgi/viewcontent.cgi?article=1296&context=itcj.

105. Crumpton, *Womanist Pastoral Theology*, 93–123.

106. Ibid., 13–15, 89–90; Sheppard, *Self, Culture, and Others*, 81–127.

cohesion?[107] Attention to these dimensions and how they affect survivors' recovery are critical to providing effective pastoral care.

Another way pastors can serve as a witness to sexual violence is to address the economic injustice that makes Black women more susceptible to violence. Both Wimberly and Carroll Watkins Ali,[108] another African-American pastoral theologian, address the impact of poverty on the Black community. Wimberly claims that critical to the function of witnessing is addressing the economic needs of the Black community:

> The witnessing ministry of the Black church will have to address the economic factor influencing the development of the personality. . . . That is the Black church must work to ensure the basic economic needs of families, to lessen conditions that prevent full participation of all family members in the family, and to lessen environmental influences that hinder the growth of persons within the family.[109]

Wimberly recognizes that economic hardships affect all aspects of Black lives and hinder their growth. Watkins Ali focuses on poor Black women who are especially oppressed by financial challenges.[110] Women who are poor often find themselves in unstable households in communities that are ravaged by violence.[111] These predicaments contribute to their vulnerability to sexual violence.[112] Therefore, pastors must continue to preach about economic injustice and how it affects women and children and their vulnerability to sexual violence. Finally, future research must continue to explore practical ways Black churches can obtain economic justice for poor Black women in their community. By witnessing in this manner, pastors acknowledge the complex layers that contribute to sexual violence.

Pastors can also serve as a witness to how survivors bring voice to their trauma. The trauma of Christ's death and the glory of his resurrection aided the recovery process of each of the respondents. Their identification with Christ in his suffering and resurrection was an important means of making meaning and reintegration. Christ thus fulfills the twinship selfobject function that assists with self-cohesion and meaning-making. In fact, it is Jesus' "witnessing presence" to their trauma that made visible what was rendered invisible in their homes and in their churches.

---

107. Sheppard, *Self, Culture, and Others*, 81–127.

108. Carroll A. Watkins-Ali, *Survival and Liberation: Pastoral Theology in the African American Context* (St. Louis, MO: Chalice, 1999) chapters 1–2.

109. Wimberly, *Pastoral Care in the Black Church*, 92–93.

110. Watkins Ali, *Survival and Liberation*, 3.

111. Ibid., chapters 1–2; Gail E. Wyatt, "Sexual Abuse of Ethnic Minority Children: Identifying Dimensions of Victimization," *Professional Psychology* 21.5 (1990) 318–43.

112. Wyatt, "Sexual Abuse of Ethnic Minority Children," 318–43.

When no one understood them, they looked to Jesus who was just like them. This "alikeness" is what contributes to their recovery. The respondents are not alone in their suffering. They have a companion who experienced similar pain. Moreover, Jesus is ultimately victorious over death. This means that there is hope. Therefore, the trauma of sexual violence does not have the final word. Each respondent testifies to this hope by how they have chosen to live despite their abuse history.

As pastors, it is important to listen to atonement themes that may emerge as survivors share their story. This can help direct the care that is offered. What does Christ's death and resurrection mean for them? In light of Kohut's concept of twinship, how do survivors of sexual violence identify with Christ and the cross? How does the twinship selfobject function contribute to their recovery? More research regarding the psychological implications of atonement theology are necessary adequately to assess how it functions for Black Christian women. My central point is that for the Black women I interviewed, Christ's death and resurrection is not obsolete even though it happened centuries ago. Their connection to Jesus, his suffering, and the hope he offered through resurrection enabled them to survive. Research in this area will undoubtedly enrich how pastors minister to survivors of sexual violence.

Finally, pastors can serve as witnesses by believing women's stories of sexual violence. When I asked Zipporah how pastors could better support sexual violence survivors, here is what she said:

> Reaffirm that it's not their fault . . . pastors hold a lot of power. And to hear that it's not their fault, 'cause if they have not gone to a rape crisis center you may be the first and only person who has told them that it's not their fault. . . . It's important for them to know that it's not their fault. I don't care what you think. And yes, women lie. Just like men do . . . You know. Yes, things happen. Yes, they can be misconstrued. For one that's a lie, there are nine that are not. So let's focus on the nine. Be willing to understand, be willing to do the hard work of why you want to victimize this person. . . . We want to do that hard work because these are people's lives that God has entrusted us with and we must treat the people's needs as holy.

We must treat the needs of survivors of violence as holy. Zipporah emphasized that pastors need to be careful about not re-victimizing women by judging or blaming them. These behaviors are silencing mechanisms that consequently lead to further harm. There may be a myriad of reasons pastors have difficulty believing survivors or blame them. But I think one of the possible reasons is what Rambo describes in the following, "Although suffering is present, it is often not given voice in order to keep a certain understanding of the world."[113] To name and to acknowledge

---

113. Rambo, *Spirit and Trauma*, 42.

survivors of sexual violence and their experiences would mean that Black pastors and the Black church would have to deconstruct what they have understood about sex, sexuality, and sexual violence.[114] It all would have to be *undone*. To truly become a witness to this trauma, pastors can no longer maintain "a certain understanding of the world."[115] They would have *to say* and *to do* something on behalf on so many women who are suffering.

From Wounded Healer to Healed Healer: Sacramental Witnessing

> *I have been able to speak to people in [the] same circumstances . . .*
> *[to] journey with them.*
> —Rachel

The participants have found ways to journey with others who have a history of sexual violence either through their careers or through ministry. As Christ empathized with them, they now empathize with others. Rachel has supported other women in an informal capacity:

> Other women who have been in this circumstance, either their spouses have [been] sexually abusive to their children. . . . I have been able to speak to people in same circumstances . . . journey with them. That's what I mean.

Zipporah stated that her experience has helped her to advocate for others. Zipporah has worked as a rape crisis counselor and is currently in a ministry that also supports other women who have a history of having survived sexual violence. Her ability to engage in this manner is empowering and has given purpose for her own pain. It has assisted with her own recovery:

> I believe in a God that is so overwhelming that we can't describe it, and can see way beyond what we can see. And so it's like though she will be hurting now, I will guide her steps that she will have these empowering moments that will not devastate her and traumatize her but to the point that she'll be able to advocate for so many others.

The ways that the participants have journeyed with others with similar trauma is an example of what womanist theologian, JoAnn Terrell, describes as sacramental witnessing:

> [It is] the aim to foster human freedom and to garner holistic spirituality from whatever resources are revealed. Thus, I do not seek to enjoin one image of

---

114. Crumpton, *Womanist Pastoral Theology*, 93–123; Monica A. Coleman, *Dinah Project: A Handbook for Congregational Response to Sexual Response* (Cleveland: Pilgrim, 2004).

115. Rambo, *Spirit and Trauma*, 42.

God. Rather, God is, as revealed in Christ, loving and challenging, humane and sovereign, culturally engaged yet countercultural, personal, healer and a mystic, a co-sufferer and a liberator. Sacramentally witnessing to the character of God as black person, as a woman, and as a Christian, I maintain, abrogates none of my duties or any human rights.[116]

Sexual violence has left an indelible mark on Rachel and Zipporah. They have not forgotten the history of their trauma but have chosen to not let this narrative define them. They have sanctified it in order to live holistically.[117] They decided to live in a manner that is countercultural and even unexpected: they have made deliberate choices to work and minister in the very environments that remind them of their own suffering. They bear witness to Christ's power of healing and ongoing transformation in their lives.

Both Wimberly and Terrell share the significance of being a witness. Wimberly engages this notion from a pastoral care perspective and Terrell from a womanist Christology. Wimberly claims that a pastoral care model of witnessing is a "prophetic tradition of the Black church . . . to transmit the liberation ministry into action not only within the congregation but also in the community by addressing those forces in society that prevent the growth of persons."[118] Wimberly's definition of witnessing engages a social dimension that transforms entire communities. Terrell, on the other hand, attempts to transform the notion of sacrifice by her definition of witnessing. For her, witnessing is an opportunity for the Black community to embody Christ from a place of empowerment rather than from a place of victimization; it is to be and do what Christ calls us to do despite our traumatic histories. The respondents have embodied the prophetic tradition of witnessing and are living out their commitment in their work and ministry. They are now mirroring to other women what was not mirrored to them. They are now creating a sense of security for others[119] that subsequently contributes to their self-cohesion. As witnesses, they have become the empathic selfobjects who prevent others' self-destruction in an often "nonempathically responding world."[120] I believe they are able to engage in this manner because of their deep faith in Jesus, their co-sufferer and liberator. Their experience of redemption is not as a one-time event but a process that emerges in various aspects of their lives. One of these ways is by advocating for and supporting others.

---

116. Terrell, *Power in the Blood*, 141.
117. Ibid., 140.
118. Wimberly, *Pastoral Care in the Black Church*, 92.
119. Kohut, *Restoration of Self*, 200.
120. Ibid., 18.

Survivors of Violence as Witnesses

Praise be to the God and Father of our Lord Jesus Christ, the Father of compassion and the God of all comfort, who comforts us in all our troubles, so that we can comfort those in any trouble with the comfort we ourselves receive from God. (2 Cor 1:3–5).

I revisit Terrell's notion of sacramental witnessing, "This is what I mean to witness sacramentally to the character of God: loving one's own, not loving others uncritically and most important not being defined by one's victimization but by one's commitments."[121] Rachel, and Zipporah are examples of sacramental witnessing. They each witness to the character of a faithful and loving God. They have attested to this in their stories.

Rachel and Zipporah both find themselves journeying with others with similar stories in their own ways. Despite their horrific experiences of sexual violence, each has made a decision not to be identified by her victimization but by her commitments.[122] Their commitment is primarily to God and the vocation and ministry to which God has called them. In embodying who Christ is, they have become empathic selfobjects to others.

In Ezek. 16 God describes how God first established a relationship with Israel. It is an allegory with vivid and graphic details:

> No one looked on you with pity or had compassion enough to do any of these things for you. Rather, you were thrown out into the open field, for on the day you were born you were despised. Then I passed by and saw you kicking about in your blood, and as you lay there in your blood I said to you, "Live!" (Ezek 16:5–6).

This passage parallels the many experiences of survivors. There are elements of these images in the respondents' own stories. They were left out to die psychologically and at times literally. Thankfully, they are alive and thriving. However, not all survivors of sexual violence have survived to tell their story. Their trauma was too overwhelming and no one or few served as witnesses. But God was the ultimate witness: The Lord saw and engaged. God in all God's holiness and glory engaged fully in the mess of these women stories when others were afraid or blind to their suffering. We are called to do the same. It is not an easy journey but a necessary one because so many lives are at stake. Jacob Denhollander, the husband of Rachel Denhollander

---

121. Terrell, *Power in the Blood*, 140.
122. Ibid., 140.

(survivor of sexual abuse from Larry Nassar), says this about the opportunity the church has at this time to serve as witnesses to the gospel:

> . . . when he looked out over the courtroom, he longed to see churches reaching out to women craving justice and help to cope with the sorrows they've endured: "This is a mission field ripe for the taking if we can speak to these." He longs to see "an army of women healed by the gospel."[123]

For my particular research, this includes witnessing to how the violence has impacted Black and Brown bodies. It is embracing their whole story as those made in the image of God and not less than that. They are the women in society and even in congregations that have been passed by. The harvest is indeed ripe.

---

123. Jamie Dean, "A Time to Speak," *World Magazine*, March 1, 2018, https://world.wng.org/2018/03/a_time_to_speak.

RESPONSE TO PIERRE

Melanie Baffes

In her essay, "Bearing Witness: Faith, Black Women, and Sexual Violence," Elizabeth Pierre raises awareness of a critical public-health issue in the USA today: the increased likelihood that women of color will experience homicide, incest, and sexual violence and, as a result, a greater susceptibility among these women to experiences of depression, alcohol and drug abuse, phobias, panic disorders, and other symptoms of trauma. These factors, coupled with the damaging self-images they have internalized, make Black women especially vulnerable to the devastating effects of sexual violence. Pierre's findings point to the need for further study to understand the impact of, and process of recovery from, sexual violence as it relates to the most vulnerable populations of women. While Black women in particular are less likely to seek support and help after an experience of sexual violence, Pierre offers hope for a path to healing and recovery with her call for the church to bear witness to survivors' experiences. Here, I explore how the biblical text *itself* can bear witness to survivors of sexual violence—particularly Black women who are radically and disproportionately affected by these experiences.

Biblical scholars are well aware that the Bible does not cover up the reality of sexual violence; many would argue that it depicts a "culture of rape" and normalizes sexual violence as an ordinary part of life. Susanne Scholz and Rhiannon Graybill, for example, highlight not only the explicit instances of sexual violence in the text but also the broader ethos of misogyny, the condemnation of female sexuality, the humiliation and punishment of female sexuality, the use of women in power relations between men ("representing women as interchangeable sexual commodities"), the victim blaming, the masculine control of female purity, the conflation of rape and adultery.[1] The text itself even depicts sexual violence as a positive means to an end, as in Ezek 16 where Israel is portrayed as a promiscuous woman and God is an agent of violence by ordering it as divine punishment—or in Gen 16, when Hagar

---

1. Rhiannon Graybill, "Teaching about Sexual Violence in the Hebrew Bible," Oxford Biblical Studies Online, http://global.oup.com/obso/focus/focus_on_sexual_violence/; Susanne Scholz, *Sacred Witness: Rape in the Hebrew Bible* (Minneapolis: Fortress, 2010) 2.

is raped by Abram, bears him a son, and is rewarded by God with a promise to multiply her offspring.[2]

Hebrew Bible scholars underscore the potential for these texts to foster violent attitudes and behaviors, and they raise the question of how to interpret and teach them responsibly in a contemporary culture in which rape is an everyday reality.[3] While it is vitally important to acknowledge the destructive impact these kinds of texts have had and continue to have in reinforcing patriarchy, fostering negative attitudes toward women, condoning sexual violence, and shaping views of sexuality, recent interpretive strategies reveal the potential for these texts to "serve as representations of trauma" and to "facilitate recovery and resilience"[4] for survivors of sexual violence and other types of trauma.

Three of the most troubling stories of sexual violation in the Hebrew Bible are familiar to most readers. In Genesis, we hear the story of Dinah being raped by Shechem, a "prince of the region," who subsequently demands to marry her: "Get me this girl to be my wife" (Gen 34:4). We have no idea what Dinah wants, because she does not speak, but her brothers are outraged about the violation and, pretending to agree to the marriage, demand that Shechem and his men be circumcised. But, while the men are still recovering, Dinah's brothers retaliate by killing every male in the town. We hear no more from Dinah after this. In another story of violence perpetrated by the "son of a king" (2 Sam 13), David's son Amnon tricks his half-sister Tamar into caring for him when he is sick. He then rapes her in spite of her continued protests, insults her, and "casts her out." Tamar's other brother, Absalom, kills Amnon, and Tamar remains a desolate woman in her brother's house (2 Sam 13:20). Finally, the most horrific story of rape in the Hebrew Bible involves the Levite and his concubine (Judg 19–20). The two of them shelter with a man while traveling, but other townsmen demand that the Levite come out so they can rape him. Their host offers instead his own daughter and the Levite's concubine, who is then given to the crowd and repeatedly raped. She is found dead the next morning, so the Levite cuts her body into twelve pieces and sends them to the twelve tribes of Israel, sparking a civil war. These are appalling stories in which the female characters are violated in numerous ways and, because we are not offered many details about the women themselves, we are left to imagine their suffering.

---

2. Beth R. Crisp, "Reading Scripture from a Hermeneutic of Rape," *Theology & Sexuality* 14 (2001) 23–42 (36).

3. Graybill, "Teaching about Sexual Violence."

4. Christopher G. Frechette and Elizabeth Boase, "Defining 'Trauma' as a Useful Lens for Biblical Interpretation," in *Bible Through the Lens of Trauma*, ed. Elizabeth Boase and Christopher G. Frechette (Atlanta: SBL, 2016) 1–23 (10–11).

What do these biblical characters have to do with the women in Pierre's study? Although Dinah, Tamar, and the Levite's concubine do not appear to experience racism and classism—as do many Black women in contemporary society—they are women living in a patriarchal world and are violated at the hands of men with power over them: "princes" and "sons of kings." What they have most in common with the women of Pierre's study is that they are casually dehumanized: "After the rape Amnon adds more humiliation to Tamar's shame by failing to recognize her humanity."[5] Pierre underscores the dehumanizing dimension of sexual violence which, according to Judith Herman, leads to a negation of the individual's autonomy and dignity in which she believes "I am not a person," resulting in "a narrowing of consciousness, a withdrawal from engagement with others, and an impoverished life."[6] This is especially true for women who do not disclose their abuse or seek help for recovery, as evidenced in the increased incidence of trauma symptoms Pierre reports among Black female survivors of sexual violence.

Pierre's findings show that what helps survivors of sexual violence is being able to find empathy through journeying with others who can validate their experience. On one level, Dinah, Tamar, and the Levite's concubine can serve this function—by giving credence to and affirming survivors' stories, mirroring their experiences, giving voice to their trauma, and modeling a way to acknowledge the depth of their pain and grief. Tamar, for example, gives voice to the experience of trauma in her own way by saying "no," by appealing to her rapist, by begging him, and naming his wrong-doing. She also models a response of lament by placing ashes on her head, tearing her robe, and crying aloud in grief: "The lament is the language of suffering; in it suffering is given the dignity of language; It will not stay silent!"[7] The presence of these characters in the biblical text acknowledges the profound anguish of women who experience sexual violence and perhaps gives survivors permission to grieve openly.

But beyond finding affirmation and empathy in the biblical characters, survivors of sexual violence may find these texts witnessing to them in a more significant way—and it involves what happens *after* the women are raped. In the aftermath of the attack on Dinah, her brothers kill the entire male population of the town, and

---

5. Frank M. Yamada, *Configurations of Rape in the Hebrew Bible: A Literary Analysis of Three Rape Narratives*, StBibLit 109 (New York: Lang, 2009) 120, cited in L. Juliana M. Claassens, "Trauma and Recovery: A New Hermeneutical Framework for the Rape of Tamar (2 Samuel 13)," in *Bible Through the Lens of Trauma*, ed. Elizabeth Boase and Christopher G. Frechette (Atlanta: SBL, 2016) 177–92 (181).

6. Judith Lewis Herman, *Trauma and Recovery: The Aftermath of Violence—From Domestic Abuse to Political Terror*, rev. ed. (New York: Basic Books, 1997) 9, 42.

7. Claus Westermann, "The Role of the Lament in the Theology of the Old Testament," *Interpretation* 28 (1974) 31, cited in Frechette and Boase, "Defining 'Trauma,'" 12.

this act is directly tied to the fact that the town's leader raped their sister (Gen 34:2). This can be seen as a clear act of retribution for the violence perpetrated against Dinah. When their father confronts them about this, Simeon and Levi answer by saying "Should our sister be treated like a whore?"—acting as Dinah's advocates and supporters. After Tamar is raped, Absalom becomes her advocate and consoler, and he determines to kill his brother. There is another act of punishment as Absalom plots to kill Amnon and succeeds (2 Sam 13:32). Finally, after the Levite's concubine is raped and dies as a result, the Levite seeks revenge, inciting the Israelites to war by asking, "Has such a thing ever happened?" (Gen 19; Judg 19). A civil war ensues between the tribe of Benjamin and the others, but, in an interesting twist, throughout the battle the Lord is prompting, guiding, and helping the Israelites in their fight—validating the rightness of their actions.

How can reading about violent events help survivors of sexual violence? Writing on trauma and recovery, Herman contends that "traumatic events destroy the survivor's fundamental assumptions about the safety of the world, the positive value of the self, and the meaningful order of creation."[8] We know from trauma studies that serious traumatic events like sexual violence cause profound changes in the survivor's core beliefs and assumptions about the self and the world. They can damage the survivor's assumptions that the self has agency and dignity, that there are people she can trust, that the world is a relatively safe place.[9] Using a hermeneutics of trauma to interpret these biblical texts can help survivors change distorted core beliefs: "altering them requires engaging the traumatic memories so that those memories can be interpreted differently."[10]

One powerful strategy for reinterpreting memories is to construct a trauma narrative to help survivors make meaning of the violent experience. A trauma narrative is the story a survivor tells herself about the event in order to make sense of it, and it has two goals: (1) to recount the full experience of the trauma so that the traumatic story becomes a kind of testimony to the survivor's experience; and (2) to interpret the experience in ways that challenge harmful assumptions resulting from the violence and replaces them with new beliefs—a reframing that helps survivors gain a new sense of order, identity, power, and well-being.[11] Texts like these

---

8. Herman, *Trauma and Recovery*, 51.

9. Christopher G. Frechette, "The Old Testament as Controlled Substance: How Insights from Trauma Studies Reveal Healing Capacities in Potentially Harmful Texts," *Interpretation: A Journal of Bible and Theology* 69.1 (2015) 20–34 (28).

10. Christopher G. Frechette, "Daughter Babylon Raped and Bereaved (Isaiah 47): Symbolic Violence and Meaning-Making in Recovery from Trauma," in *Bible Through the Lens of Trauma*, ed. Elizabeth Boase and Christopher G. Frechette (Atlanta: SBL, 2016) 67–83 (77).

11. Frechette and Boase, "Defining 'Trauma,'" 5–6.

biblical stories, then, can help survivors create a trauma narrative by representing the trauma and re-interpreting it. The violent events in the stories of Dinah, Tamar, and the Levite's concubine—the aftermath of the sexual violence itself—can be seen as symbolic representations corresponding to the actual violence experienced by survivors of sexual violence.

While it may seem counter-intuitive to think that violent texts can lead to healing, Christopher Frechette argues that they can and do serve a healing function in several ways. First, they allow the survivor to *explore the experience through symbols*. Symbols point beyond themselves to something more, allowing traumatic memories to be confronted at a safe distance, and they allow readers to break down one order and replace it with another order.[12] Second, because survivors of violence or trauma often have intense feelings of rage—"they are likely to direct those feelings not only at the perpetrators but also at those whom they perceive to have had the power to help them but did not, especially at God"[13]—these texts provide *a way for a survivor safely to express rage* through a safe, controlled expression of rage directed at the perpetrator symbolically (with no actual harm occurring). When the intensity of the experience is such that mere words do not suffice to enable reframing, violent imagery can serve as a rhetorical strategy for a symbolic (and cathartic) expression of rage.[14] Finally, texts with violent imagery can engage the emotions of the survivor, helping them *reinterpret the traumatic events*. Reading these texts can communicate the message very clearly that the perpetrator and the violent acts were morally wrong, allowing readers to interpret their *own* violation as wrong as they see the violent repercussions enacted.

The reinterpretation step is key to healing, and narratives featuring events similar to that which survivors have experienced have the potential to help them to make sense of the violent event and to restore healthy assumptions about themselves in relation to the world. Because violent events often cause survivors (irrationally) to place the blame on themselves,[15] these texts enable them to transfer the cause of violence from the human realm to the divine realm: "God is in charge, it is not your fault!" This may help the survivor shift the blame from themselves, an important step in healing.[16] Survivors may be able to recover a sense of self, agency, identity, and dignity as they begin to address the fears and loss of control resulting from the experience—and as they remember who they were before the trauma: "Part of the

---

12. Ibid., 12.
13. Frechette, "Daughter Babylon Raped and Bereaved," 77.
14. Ibid., 79–80.
15. Frechette and Boase, "Defining 'Trauma,'" 6.
16. Ibid.

sense-making process of the traumatic event is that the survivor interprets what has happened to her in terms of the values and beliefs that she held before the trauma broke into her life."[17] Not only do these texts have the potential to restore a sense of justice and safety to the world but also, and most importantly, they convey the message that "You have been wronged"—a powerful witnessing function.

We know that the Levite's concubine dies, Tamar lives out her life as a "desolate woman," and we hear no more from Dinah, so there can be no healing for these women. But, for survivors of sexual violence, there is the potential for a powerful witness through the symbolic reinterpretation these texts allow. Biblical scholars using trauma as a lens for reading the text suggest treating "these troubling texts as 'controlled substances,' that is, something that can be injurious when handled improperly but therapeutic when administered carefully."[18] For this reason, we cannot expect survivors to find new meaning on their own; biblical scholars using the lens of trauma affirm that "the safe and supportive presence of others as witnesses and dialogue partners can be crucial for advancing the process of interpreting the experience."[19] As Pierre claims, the power of witnessing is that it can make visible what is rendered invisible. These characters and their stories—coupled with the powerful presence of supportive witnesses and dialogue partners—have the potential to do just that.

---

17. Claassens, "Trauma and Recovery," 184.
18. Frechette, "Old Testament as Controlled Substance," 20.
19. Frechette and Boase, "Defining 'Trauma,'" 7.

KEEPING OUR WORD (2 SAMUEL 9)

D. Darrell Griffin

Beloved, Dr. Calvin O. Butts, the Senior Pastor of the Abyssinian Baptist Church of Harlem, is my mentor. I had the privilege of sitting under his tutelage for several years, and as a result he shaped so much of my early years in ministry. So, it was natural that as I was leaving Abyssinian to become the Pastor of my first church, I would ask him how I could repay him for all that he had done for me. "What can I do to repay you for all of your guidance," I asked, and he replied, "Go evacuate Lodebar." I then responded, "What? Where is Lodebar?" He fired back, "If you search hard enough you will find it." Dr. Butts further went on to say, "Son, if you search hard enough you will find those living in Lodebar. Some are physically trapped in Lodebar, some are mentally trapped in Lodebar, and some are spiritually trapped in Lodebar. You should spend your life evacuating Lodebar." Since that day, I have slowly begun to understand that this was more of a mission than a place.

Many years later, I still remember this conversation like it was yesterday. As the Pastor of Oakdale Covenant Church, located on the southside of Chicago, Illinois, more often than not, I feel like I am leading a congregation that is located in a place called Lodebar. I have witnessed the pain and destruction of violence, and at times it has been unbearable! When I think about the plight of those trapped in the crossfire of violence and poverty, my heart becomes heavy.

If the events of September 11, 2001 became America's state of emergency against terrorism, then the violence in our communities and its impact is a state of emergency for us now! Over 3,000 people were shot in 2017, and we are on track to surpass this number in 2018. This violence is a state of emergency! The communities that I serve feel like we are living in a twenty-first century Lodebar! A physical Lodebar! A mental Lodebar! And yes, even more, a spiritual Lodebar!

Now as I searched to understand this place called Lodebar (2 Sam 9:4–5, 17:27), I discovered that Lodebar was not a place where anyone would want to live. According to the Bible commentaries, Lodebar was a town east of the Jordan River, and was defined as a place of barrenness, and without pasture and greenery. In other words, Lodebar was a place of emptiness, barrenness, and worthlessness. Some translations even call it a place of no communication.

Thus, as a result no one wanted to live in Lodebar, and if you had to go to Lodebar you did not want to stay long! It was a horrible place; a troubled, lonely, and sick place! Beloved, have you ever been to a place called Lodebar? Has somebody or some situation forced you into a place called Lodebar? Keep looking straight ahead because I know some of you present today are in a place called Lodebar right now! There are those of you who are unfortunate victims that have been physically, spiritually, and mentally imprisoned by your past and crippled by your pain, in Lodebar! Thus, my question to you is this: who will rescue those caught in the violent clutches of Lodebar? Who? Who will help those who are unable to help themselves?"

In our text, we find that that Lodebar had a famous resident who personified the difficulties and the struggles of living in Lodebar. This resident represents so many of our men and women and their condition today. No one could better testify to the difficulties and struggle of the hard living in Lodebar like Mephibosheth. His name is a tongue twister, but not nearly as twisted as his life! His name means "shameful thing." What a name to give a child! What a negative prophecy to place over a child's life! A shameful thing is an appalling thing, an embarrassing thing, a disgraceful thing, a dishonorable thing, a shocking thing! I believe that every time the name Mephibosheth was called, they were saying, "Hey, embarrassment! Hey, shameful! Hey, shocking thing, come here!" Imagine what his childhood was like! We say sticks and stones may break my bones, but names will never hurt me, but beloved, names do hurt! Negative names can kill a child's future! Negative names can kill their dreams, and sap all of their self-esteem! How many Mephibosheths are out there who need us to help them to change their name? How many Mephibosheths are out there who need us to help them to change their name from problem to promise! From shameful to successful! And from victim to victor!

Now if the name Mephibosheth was not bad enough, the condition of Mephibosheth was even worse! The Bible says that Mephibosheth was lame in both feet! To have one challenging foot is certainly bad, but to not have the use of both feet presents a problem on another level!

Second Samuel 4:4 gives us an explanation for his lameness and helps us to understand his condition. First of all, we must realize that Mephibosheth was not born lame. He wasn't born with both legs broken. Mephibosheth was not even born in Lodebar. The Bible says that in fleeing the violence from the palace after hearing about the death of his grandfather King Saul and his father Jonathan, his nurse dropped him, breaking both of his ankles, and his ankles never healed. My Lord, some of us can relate to this! Mephibosheth was dropped by someone who was supposed to help him! He was dropped by his nurse.

Some of us here today have also been dropped by people who were supposed to be helping us! And as a result, we have been violently crippled with negative names like dumb, ugly, stupid, or crazy! Family members dropped us! The school system dropped us! And even the church has dropped us because the church was not there! Understaffed, under resourced churches, that dropped us because they just could not help us! They just could not help us!

Many are living in ambiguity, in Lodebar—hanging out, dropping out, and falling out! Forced to hide behind baggy pants or prison bars! Forced to hustle in the streets just to survive! They are walking around with guns, killing each other!

The truth is beloved, Mephibosheth should have been a strong handsome leader like Jonathan, his father, but instead, when we find Mephibosheth we see a twisted, bruised, incapacitated victim whose ankles and limbs were twisted and broken by people who were supposed to help him! Now he is exiled in the violence of Lodebar. He does not want to be there! He did not ask for this! Who will help him? Who will sacrifice for him? Who will go to Lodebar to rescue him, to mentor him, to coach him? Who will answer the call for help?

Beloved, we need to help the Mephibosheths in our community! We need to go to Lodebar, to those places that have been written off, and rescue the men and women who are forced to live in the violence and poverty of Lodebar.

Our text shows that David was willing to help. David was intentional about helping Mephibosheth, and if we are going to help those Mephibosheths of our time who are still living in Lodebar, we must be intentional as well. David was willing to show love and kindness to Mephibosheth. This is important because David was Saul's successor, and under normal circumstances the new king would not show kindness to the former king's family.

In fact, it was a tradition that the new king would wipe out all of the family members of the former king. But this was David at his best, and an example of David living as a man after God's own heart. When we meet David in this particular passage in 2 Samuel 9, he had gained the throne of all of Israel. David successfully returned the Ark of the Covenant of God to Jerusalem, and he reinstituted the centrality of worship of the true and living God. David was on top of the world, and with God's help David experienced victory after victory.

I believe it was at this point in 2 Samuel 9, that David's mind started to go back to the time when he was on the run, and he remembered Jonathan. David remembered the covenant that he made with Jonathan. You see, David was on the run from Saul, and Saul's son Jonathan helped David escape his father's plots. At their last meeting David entered into a covenant with Jonathan that is recorded in 1 Samuel 20. Jonathan tells David in vv.13–15, "May the Lord be with you as he used to be with my father. May you treat me with the faithful love of the Lord as long as I live? But if I die, treat my family with this faithful love, even when the Lord destroys all of your enemies." It is in v. 42, that Jonathan says to David, "Go in peace for we have made a pact in the Lord's name."[1] Then it is recorded in 1 Samuel 31 that Jonathan is killed.

David remembered the covenant he made with Jonathan, and David started thinking about all of the people who helped him get to the top. He thought about all those who made tremendous sacrifices that he might be king. He remembered that Jonathan gave up the throne so that he could be king.

Let me ask you a question! Can you think about that one person or those individuals who helped you gain your success? Can you think of those who brought you to faith? Can you think of those who helped you get your first job or gave you your first break? Because their efforts, their commitment, and their sacrifice caused many of us to survive or succeed! Many of us were so grateful that like David we raised the same question I raised to my mentor, "How can I repay you for all of your help and sacrifice?" And their response was, "You turn around and help someone else."

I believe that David was thinking about those whose shoulders he stood on. I have certainly thought about my own father who was born in the segregated south. He moved to Wisconsin to flee the Jim Crow laws of the South. These laws were designed to keep African Americans locked in a racial caste system. My father and mother barely made it out. Even in the North, because of limited access to education and employment opportunities for people of color, my father's job opportunities were few. These limited opportunities were often jobs that no-one else wanted. They were jobs with low pay and were very dangerous. Yet, my father did these jobs to take care of his wife and five sons. My parents made tremendous sacrifices so that I would not end up in a place called Lodebar and in the condition of its famous resident Mephibosheth. I stand here because of their sacrifice and their courage. I do not just stand on the shoulder of my parents and grandparents, but many people.

David made a commitment to Jonathan, and he was determined to keep it. He understood that part of his integrity was keeping his covenant, keeping his commitment, keeping his word. Therefore, David raised the question if there was anyone left of Saul's family? David wanted to show him kindness in honor of Jonathan. I believe that David was thinking, God has been so good to me, is there anyone that I can help? I have so much, I have been truly blessed, is there anyone that I can help? Jonathan gave up so much for me, sacrificed so much. Who can I help in Jonathan's family?

---

1. Biblical quotations are from the New Living Translation.

Beloved, I would argue that we have been given favor by God to share with others. I believe that God's favor is when we are given access to blessings and opportunities we do not deserve. Some of you are asking me to clarify. What do you mean? Listen, you did not deserve that house, but God gave you favor at the bank! You did not deserve that job! In fact, you do not even know how you got the position, but God gave you favor with the hiring manager! You did not deserve to keep your job when everyone else was laid off, but God said, "Not this one! My favor is on them!"

David had favor with God, and I am here to remind you that God gives us favor and blessings for a reason! I believe that the fact that God saved you, rescued you, delivered you, or healed you is for a reason. It is because God has plans for your life! The reason those drugs did not take you out was because God has plans for you! The reason you could not give up was because God has plans for you! The reason you could not die was because God has plans for you! And the reason you cannot quit now; the reason you cannot throw in the towel; the reason you cannot die—is because God has a plan for you!

Truth be told, Saul should have killed David! David should not have been king! But God saved David for a reason—to help Mephibosheth. And like David, we need to understand that the Lord allowed us to be in certain positions for a reason! God gave us resources to be used for the kingdom! God redeemed us so that we can help to redeem others! God healed us so that we can heal others! God blessed us so that we can bless others! Beloved, God did not save us to sit around and wait for heaven! God placed us here for the Mephibosheths of this world who live in places like Lodebar!

We can learn from David's action that part of living a life of integrity is keeping our word. It is making a commitment that is backed by more than a good intention. If we say that we are going to do something then we must follow through on our promise! If you are a Christian, a man or woman of God, your word should mean something! And it should mean something longer than the day that you utter it!

Beloved, we need to understand that there are people who are depending on us to keep our word. We are their hope. We are their answered prayer. The Mephibosheths of the world need us. They need us to come to Lodebar and rescue them. After many battles and successes, David was still thinking about the commitment he made with Jonathan. David had many ups and downs and hardships, but that did not take away his desire to keep his word. In reality, Mephibosheth should have been the King of Israel. He should have been great, but things happened in Mephibosheth's life that were beyond his control.

Beloved, like Mephibosheth, our issues can leave us in Lodebar, hopeless, and alone. Some of us could have been and should have been, kings and queens, sitting in a palace. But our circumstances have left us crippled in Lodebar. Mephibosheth is the model for every person who should have been in a safe space, but instead ended up out there in a place called Lodebar. The reason we end up in Lodebar instead of in the palace is because something occurred in our life. Something happened so traumatizing that it is keeping us from reaching the hope of our calling. Our handicaps, whatever form they may take, keep us from reaching our potential or fulfilling our dreams.

But what I love about this text is that David made arrangements to bring Mephibosheth to the palace. Although Mephibosheth was called to sit at the king's table, he could not come without assistance. In reality, many of us are invited to sit at the king's table. We have been called to walk in our purpose, but the truth of the matter is that we cannot get to the place of our calling because we are so distracted and crippled by our own brokenness. We hear the voice of God calling us to come out of Lodebar, but we cannot come out on our own.

The Bible says that David had to send his servant Ziba to get Mephibosheth. Our society needs more Zibas of the world. We need more people who will have the courage and strength to go to Lodebar and retrieve the Mephibosheths of the world. When Mephibosheth arrives at the palace, he must be brought in by Ziba. This grown man was literally being carried like a child. This is a very powerful image in my mind. If I look at Mephibosheth's presence, I want to let him walk, but when I see his problems, and where he came from, I realize that he must be carried. There must be someone, some program to carry him, and to help him.

I can see Mephibosheth falling down, clutching David's kingly robe. He was lying on the floor of a palace where he should have been king. Mephibosheth was begging in the place where he was supposed to be king. He was broken and crippled. He was in the right place, but he was not in the right position.

Like Mephibosheth, there are people in the world, people in this place today, that have been violated and abused. Some have been violently raped; others have been secretly molested. Some are consumed by drugs, and others are lost in a sea of mind-numbing alcoholism. These would be kings and queens have become beggars in their own house! They are laying on the floor, unable to rise to fulfill their destiny! David responded to Mephibosheth by saying "I know somebody dropped you!" And I say to you tonight "I know someone dropped you!" The school system dropped you! The health system dropped you! Even the church dropped you! But I, I am here to help you!"

Beloved, you and I have been called to minister to those who are still in Lodebar: to men and women who have been crippled with negative names, like dumb, gang banger, slow. We are called to minister to those who have been dropped and therefore crippled by their families, school systems, and health care systems. We have to let them know that there is more to life then Lodebar! We must let those Mephibosheths know that they deserve more! They deserve to live without the violence! They deserve neighborhoods free of drugs and violence! They deserve to live lives without physical abuse and mistreatment!

We have to tell them, "I know your name is Mephibosheth, but you are not shameful. You are special. The labels are not who you are. Your environment is not an indiction of who you are. You are not a drug addict by nature. You are not violent. You are more than a victim; you are a victor! You are somebody!"

Finally, we have to make sure that Mephibosheth, in spite of his challenges, has a seat at the king's table. The king's table was a big long wooden table—a long wooden table that covered Mephibosheth's problems, covered his difficulties, and covered his crippled condition. When Mephibosheth sat at the king's table, the people could only see him from his waist up.

I am sure that Mephibosheth believed that he was not worthy to sit at the king's table, and that his issues disqualified him from being worthy of a seat at the table. But the truth is, like Mephibosheth none of us are worthy to sit at the king's table. All of us were crippled by sin! Adam sinned and crippled all of us! We were dropped because of sin! But one day, on a hill called Calvary, Jesus died on some wood called the cross so that we can sit at the king's table! All of us are crippled! All of us have issues and problems that would disqualify us from being offered a seat at the king's table. But we are sitting at the table because of the sacrifices that our Father in heaven made for us! We are sitting at the table because Jesus died for us! We are sitting at the table because God loved us and sent His Son Jesus to die for our sins! How do we repay God for what he did? How do we repay God for saving our lives? How do we repay God for looking beyond our issues and giving us a seat at the table, a seat we did not deserve and could never earn? How do we say thank you? We do this by going to Lodebar and finding the Mephibosheths of this world and bringing them to the king's table. Even though millions have come, there is still room at the table for one more. There is room at the table for you.

ANNOTATED BIBLIOGRAPHY ON HUMAN VIOLENCE

Agamben, Giorgio. *Homo Sacer: Sovereign Power and Bare Life*. Translated by Daniel Heller-Roazen. Stanford: Stanford University Press, 1998. In this first volume of a nine-part series, Agamben explores the profound implications of political exclusion as a form of violence latent within the most prominent institutions of western life.

Ahrens, Courtney E., Maria del Carmen Lopez, Libier Isas, and Laura C. Rios-Mandel. "Talking About Interpersonal Violence: Cultural Influences on Latinas' Identification and Disclosure of Sexual Assault and Intimate Partner Violence." *Psychological Trauma: Theory, Research, Practice and Policy* 2.4 (2010) 284–95. This insightful article explains how and why culture fosters reluctance among Latinas to disclose sexual violence. It draws from several studies conducted with Latinas from all walks of life to examine what contributes to this reality.

Arendt, Hannah. *On Violence*. New York: Harcourt, 1969. In these succinct reflections Arendt provides a broad analysis of political forms of violence in order to open up new ways to conceive of reform and revolution alike. Her thoughts on the loss of power as an invitation to violence remain relevant.

Ateek, Naim Stifan. *A Palestinian Christian Cry for Reconciliation*. Maryknoll, NY: Orbis, 2008. Ateek articulates a theology of liberation from the perspective of Palestinian Christianity, interjecting a new voice into the Israeli-Palestinian conflict, while advocating nonviolent resistance and working toward reconciliation between Palestinians and Jews.

Bailie, Gil. *Violence Unveiled: Humanity at the Crossroads*. New York: Crossroad, 1995. Bailie's analysis of the groundbreaking work of cultural theorist René Girard is easily comprehensible and discusses the relevance of Girard's theories in a contemporary, global context.

Baustan, R. S., A. P. Jassen, and C. J. Roetzel, eds. *Violence, Scripture, and Textual Practice in Early Judaism and Christianity*. Leiden; Boston: Brill, 2010. This volume offers a diverse collection of essays on violence in the Scriptures and in early Jewish and Christian literature more generally.

Benjamin, Walter. "Critique of Violence." Pages 277–300 in *Selected Writings*, Vol. 1, *1913–1926*. Edited by Marcus Bullock and Michael W. Jennings. Translated by Edmund Jephcott. Cambridge, MA: Belknap, 1996. In many ways still the most important theoretical introduction to continental philosophical thoughts on violence today, Benjamin's essay offers profound reflections on violence and the possibility of its suspension as a type of "divine violence."

Blount, Brian. *Can I Get a Witness? Reading Revelation through African American Culture*. Louisville: Westminster John Knox, 2005. Revelation is often seen as a violent book, and Blount makes a persuasive case instead that Revelation is calling for faithful, nonviolent resistance. Reading the Apocalypse from an African American perspective and through the lens of African American culture provides Blount with an interpretive key and access

Annotated Bibliography

to the imagery in ways that highlight the context of struggle and strife in an oppressive culture.

Boyarin, Daniel. *Dying for God: Martyrdom and the Making of Christianity and Judaism*. Redwood City, CA: Stanford University Press, 1999. Boyarin challenges preconceptions about the relationship between Judaism and Christianity, arguing that the history of cooperation and interaction between these two rival religions lasted longer than previously assumed. His study focuses on Christian and talmudic texts that highlight the connections and differences between Christians and Jews around the issue of martyrdom and violent persecution.

Brueggemann, Walter. "The Costly Loss of Lament." In *The Psalms and the Life of Faith*, edited by Patrick D. Miller, 98–111. Minneapolis: Fortress, 1995. At the opening of the chapter, Brueggemann points out the significance that psalms of lament had in the faith and liturgy of Israel and the early church. But their significance and use by the church has declined significantly, leading Brueggemann to muse in his closing paragraph, "It makes one wonder about the price of our civility, that this chance in our faith has largely been lost because the lament psalms have dropped out of the functioning canon."

———. *Divine Presence amid Violence: Contextualizing the Book of Joshua*. Eugene, OR: Cascade, 2009. Brueggemann offers a theological interpretation of Josh 11, wrestling with the text's granting of divine sanction for human violence. He argues that interpreted in context God's violence is on behalf of the dominated against those who dominate them.

Butler, Judith. *Precarious Life: The Powers of Mourning and Violence*. London: Verso, 2004. Merging reflections on violence with others on the nature of grieving and human existence, Butler provides deft critical analysis on the ways that society might build a more peaceful political future.

Cavanaugh, William T. *The Myth of Religious Violence: Secular Ideology and the Roots of Modern Conflict*. New York: Oxford University Press, 2009. Cavanaugh makes an important attempt to dismantle the immensely popular and influential thesis that religions are intrinsically prone to violence. By exploring rhetoric, he seeks to unmask the secular state as promoting violence rather than as defending against religious violence and calls for a more nuanced analysis of all forms of violence.

———. *Torture and Eucharist: Theology, Politics, and the Body of Christ*. New York: Wiley-Blackwell, 1998. Cavanaugh's groundbreaking theological analysis of the dynamics of torture and the use of disappearance as a mode for disciplining the body politic yields a constructive presentation of eucharistic theology as a vehicle for engendering resistance to political tyranny and political violence. Focusing on the experience of the Catholic Church in Chile during the Pinochet regime, Cavanaugh argues that the concrete political practice of the Eucharist is the church's response to the atomizing forces of torture that divide the social body and shore up the nation state's ability to discipline its citizens.

Choi, Y. Joon, Jennifer Elkins, and Lindsey Disney. "A Literature Review of Intimate Partner Violence Among Immigrant Populations: Engaging the Faith Community." *Aggression and Violent Behavior* 29 (2016) 1–9. This article discusses particular challenges encountered by immigrant populations (especially around disclosure of interpersonal violence). The authors recognize the role that faith communities play in supporting these populations. The primary sample groups are drawn from Latino, Asian, and Middle East and North African (MENA) communities.

Annotated Bibliography

Coleman, Monica A. *The Dinah Project: A Handbook for Congregational Response to Sexual Violence.* Cleveland, OH: Pilgrim, 2004. A brief book that provides practical ways for churches to address sexual violence. Her target audience is Black congregations but many of the practical tools can be applied in most congregations.

Creach, Jerome. *Violence in Scripture.* Interpretation, Resources for the Use of Scripture in the Church. Louisville: Westminster John Knox, 2013. Aimed at preachers and teachers, this introductory study encourages honest wresting with texts that involve or sanction violence and seeks a theological framework for their interpretation.

Crumpton, Stephanie M. *A Womanist Pastoral Theology Against Intimate and Cultural Violence.* New York: Palgrave MacMillan, 2014. This book is a theological and psychological engagement with the sexual violence experienced by Black women. It provides a rich discussion about the particular obstacles Black women face both as Christians and as persons of color on their journey toward healing.

Derrida, Jacques. "Force of Law: The 'Mystical Foundation of Authority.'" In *Acts of Religion*, edited by Gil Anidjar, 228–98. Translated by Mary Quaintance. London: Routledge, 2002. Providing commentary upon Benjamin's "Critique of Violence," Derrida offers a thoughtful meditation on the nature of "bloodless violence" as a form of an unavoidable cultural inscription.

Dostoyevsky, Fyodor. *The Brothers Karamazov.* Translated by Richard Pevear and Larissa Volokhonsky. New York: Farrar, Straus, and Giroux, 1990. A profound and extraordinarily influential novel that can be read as a complex meditation that encompasses the timeless themes of grace, salvation, evil, and violence.

Ellens, J. H. ed. *Destructive Power of Religion: Violence in Judaism, Christianity, and Islam.* 4 vols. Westport, Conn. & London: Praeger Publishers, 2004. The most comprehensive collection of essays on the three Abrahamic religious traditions from the maximalist perspective of the reader-centered or victim-centered perception of violence.

Ellis, Marc H. *Toward a Jewish Theology of Liberation: The Challenge of the 21st Century.* 3rd ed. Waco, TX: Baylor University Press, 2004. Ellis articulates a Jewish theology of liberation influenced by Latin American liberation theology. He challenges academic perceptions of Jewish identity and politics in light of his critique of the state of Israel's use of repressive violence justified by an appeal to Zionist theology. According to Ellis, the future of Jewish theology begins with a call for justice for the oppressed Palestinian people.

Fortune, Marie M. *Sexual Violence: The Sin Revisited.* Cleveland: Pilgrim, 2005. Fortune takes a very comprehensive theological and psychological look at sexual violence. The first part of the book discusses how the church is complicit in creating a culture that makes it challenging for congregations to address the issue. The second part of the book shares practical ways that churches can care for survivors and confront perpetrators.

Girard, René. *I See Satan Fall Like Lightning.* Translated by James G. Williams. Maryknoll, NY: Orbis, 2001. As but one of many significant reflections on violence and communal formation, this study by Girard guides the reader into a general awareness of his most significant theories regarding imitative (mimetic) desire and the origins of violence in our world.

Gorman, Michael. *Reading Revelation Responsibly: Uncivil Worship and Witness: Following the Lamb into the New Creation.* Eugene, OR: Cascade Books, 2011. Through this book Gorman seeks to correct poor readings of the often-feared book of Revelation. Using a thematic, but still chronological approach Gorman seeks to show that the Book of

Annotated Bibliography

Revelation is a helpful guide to Christian worship rather than a cryptic narrative of future events.

Guelke, Adrian. *Terrorism and Global Disorder: Political Violence in the Contemporary World.* London: I.B. Tauris & Co., 2006. A thorough study of political violence that focuses on terrorism, tracing its development into a global phenomenon while arguing that 9/11 was neither unique nor unexpected, but fits a pattern of escalating violence that began in the 1980s. The author not only looks at terrorism, but also critiques state-sponsored counter-terrorism as another form of potentially illegitimate political violence.

Hamerton-Kelly, R. G. *Sacred Violence: Paul's Hermeneutic of the Cross.* Minneapolis: Fortress, 1992. An interpretation of Paul's theology of Jesus' violent death on the cross according to R. Girard's theory of mimetic desire. In this interpretation, Hamerton-Kelly seeks to show Paul's hermeneutic of the cross as an essential component in his critique of the sacred violence of Judaism and the world as a whole.

Hayes, Michael A., and David Tombs, eds. *Truth and Memory: The Church and Human Rights in El Salvador and Guatemala.* Herefordshire, UK: Gracewing, 2001. This vital collection of essays, most of which reflect a liberation perspective, focuses on the political violence, political repression, and genocide that took place in El Salvador and Guatemala in the second half of the twentieth century. They explore the church's role, and that of Christian ethics, in enabling rebuilding and reconciliation without surrendering the church's commitment to nonviolence.

Hengel, Martin. *The Zealots: Investigations into the Jewish Freedom Movement in the Period from Herod I until 70 A.D.* Translated by David Smith. Edinburgh: T&T Clark, 1989. A landmark study on revolutionary movements in Second Temple Judaism. Although some of Hengel's claims about the "Zealots" as an organized "party" within Judaism are no longer widely held, his observations regarding the biblical and eschatological roots of such movements are of considerable significance.

Herman, Judith. *Trauma and Recovery: The Aftermath of Violence from Domestic Abuse to Political Terror.* Cambridge, MA: Basic Books, 1992. This is a dense and very comprehensive look at sexual violence. Herman takes both a feminist and psychological approach. She illustrates how various systems perpetuate violence against women.

Hobbes, Thomas. *Leviathan.* Edited by Richard Tuck. New York: Cambridge University Press, 1996. One of the classics of modern Western political philosophy that remains crucial for understanding our contemporary theopolitical context. With much explicit biblical engagement, Hobbes argues for the absolute necessity of state sovereignty on the basis of an analysis of human nature.

Horbury, William. *Jewish War Under Trajan and Hadrian.* New York: Cambridge University Press, 2014. An insightful analysis of revolutionary Judaism from 70–135 CE, chronicling the aftermath of the first Jewish-Roman War and offering detailed analysis of the causes and character of the Bar-Kokhba Revolt.

Horsley, Richard A., and John S. Hanson. *Bandits, Prophets, and Messiahs: Popular Movements at the Time of Jesus.* Edinburgh: T&T Clark, 1985. A detailed analysis of the diversity of popular leaders within Second Temple Judaism. It is particularly helpful for understanding the motivations at work amongst different types of individuals, and how these were connected to their specific aims, goals, and hopes.

Jantzen, Grace M. *Foundations of Violence (Death and the Displacement of Beauty).* London: Routledge, 2004. Prompted by the dissonance between beauty and violence, Jantzen argues that a preoccupation with death is characteristic of the West and manifests itself in discourses of violence that are deeply intertwined with issues of race and postcolonialism. This diagnosis is accompanied by an account of beauty that can inspire creative resistance and new life.

Juergensmeyer, Mark, and Margo Kitts, and Michael Jerryson, eds. *The Oxford Handbook of Religions and Violence*. Oxford: Oxford University Press, 2013. This collection of essays on a wide variety of topics examines the intersections between religion and violence in varied historical, cultural, and geographical contexts.

Kalantzis, George. *Caesar and the Lamb: Early Christian Attitudes on War and Military Service*. Eugene, OR: Cascade, 2012. This volume offers well-annotated translations and analysis of pre-Constantinian Christian texts that deal with Christian attitudes toward war and military service.

Kim, Seyoon. *Justification and God's Kingdom*. Tübingen: Mohr Siebeck, 2018. Kim seeks to explain, among other things, how Paul's gospel of justification makes the church of the Lord Jesus Christ, the community of God's justified people, the troops of God's Kingdom who realize its "justice, peace and joy" on earth by living life led and empowered by the Holy Spirit (Rom 14:17).

Klassen, William. *Love of Enemies: The Way to Peace*. OBT 15. Philadelphia: Fortress, 1984. An insightful analysis of the biblical roots of these two topics, which gives way to a powerful vision for how they should impact contemporary Christian thought and action.

van der Kolk, Bessel. *The Body Keeps Score: Brain, Mind, and Body in the Healing of Trauma*. New York: Penguin, 2015. This book explains how trauma impacts one's entire self. Van der Kolk makes psychological and scientific terms accessible to readers by providing stories and pictures to support his argument throughout.

Koo, Kelly H., Hong V. Nguyen, Amanda K. Gilmore, Jessica A. Blayney and Debra L. Kaysen. "Posttraumatic Cognitions, Somatization, and PTSD Severity Among Asian American and White College Women with Sexual Trauma Histories." *Psychological Trauma: Theory, Research, Practice, and Policy* 6.4 (2014) 337–44. This article discusses how race and culture impact issues in mental health such as post-traumatic stress disorder and somatization. It utilizes a study conducted with monoethnic groups of Asian Americans and White Americans and examines the ways in which these groups have responded to trauma.

Lew, Mike. *Victims No Longer: The Classic Guide for Men Recovering from Sexual Abuse*. 2nd ed. New York: Harper Books, 2004. This is an important book because it illustrates the impact of sexual abuse among boys and men. Lew explains the particular challenges that boys and men face as survivors because of their gender. It is thoughtfully written and he includes the stories of survivors throughout the book.

Lian, Xi. *Blood Letters: The Untold Story of Lin Zhao, a Martyr in Mao's China*. New York: Basic Books, 2018. The remarkable story of an important Chinese Christian dissident of the Mao era who in the years prior to her execution expressed her dissent in prison letters written in her own blood.

Matthews, Shelly, and E. Leigh Gibson eds. *Violence in the New Testament*. London: T&T Clark, 2005. A collection of essays about violence and violent incidents in the New Testament that tries to move beyond traditional scholarly approaches focused exclusively on historicity, and beyond those that anachronistically fail to recognize the intra-Jewish and wider Roman contexts of accounts of violence directed toward followers of Jesus.

McCann, J. Clinton, Jr. *A Theological Introduction to the Book of Psalms: The Psalms as Torah*. Nashville: Abingdon, 1993. McCann examines and presents the book of Psalms as

Annotated Bibliography

Torah—a book that provides instructions to believing communities regarding prayer, communion with God, and faithful living. Part of that instruction is the constructive use of lament and imprecation that seek to right the wrongs that arise in society.

Middleton, Paul. *Radical Martyrdom and Cosmic Conflict in Early Christianity.* London; New York: T&T Clark, 2006. This study explores volitional martyrdom in early Christianity, arguing that seeking arrest and death was not regarded as deviant in the way often assumed by historians. Instead, from the late first to the early third centuries it was a widely recognized form of devotion.

Moss, Candida. *The Myth of Persecution: How Early Christians Invented a Story of Martyrdom.* New York: HarperOne, 2013. This engaging yet highly controversial study of early Christian martyrdom offers the thesis that there was no sustained, three-hundred-year history of repression of Christians by the Roman Empire. Rather, the history of martyrdom is an invention of the post-Constantinian church as a means of marginalizing heretics and rationalizing Christian acts of violence against the church's ideological enemies.

Neufeld, Thomas Yoder. *Killing Enmity: Violence and the New Testament.* Grand Rapids: Baker Academic, 2011. A well-balanced and sensible discussion of violent language and violence-related themes in the teachings of Jesus, Paul, and the book of Revelation. It asks the question of whether or not the New Testament justifies or even instigates violence, making a convincing case that, in fact, taken together these texts do exactly the opposite.

Neville, David J. *A Peaceable Hope: Contesting Violent Eschatology in New Testament Narratives.* Studies in Peace and Scripture 11. Grand Rapids: Baker Academic, 2013. Neville explores how the apparently violent descriptions of eschatological culmination in various New Testament texts can be reconciled with Jesus' nonviolent teaching and practice, offering challenging and provocative insights.

O'Connor, Flannery. *The Violent Bear It Away.* New York: Farrar, Straus, and Giroux, 2007. The second of only two novels O'Connor wrote, its central trope of baptism is soaked in blood and invites the reader to wrestle with the scandalous mystery of what the author elsewhere refers to as "the violence of love."

Peterson, Anna L. *Martyrdom and the Politics of Religion: Progressive Catholicism in El Salvador's Civil War.* Albany: State University of New York Press, 1997. Peterson provides a careful study of progressive Catholicism during the 1970s and 1980s in the context of state-sponsored political violence, not only documenting the work of liberationists within the church and the wider society, but also exploring the role of religion in the political realm more broadly.

Portier-Young, Anathea E. *Apocalypse Against Empire: Theologies of Resistance in Early Judaism.* Grand Rapids: Eerdmans, 2011. This study offers stirring insight into the ways that Jewish apocalyptic texts functioned as literature of resistance, offering an oppressed and powerless people the ability to express their hope in the deliverance that would come from God.

Rambo, Shelley. *Spirit and Trauma: A Theology of Remaining.* Louisville: Westminster John Knox, 2010. Rambo takes a theological approach to trauma. She uses the Gospel of John to work through her theme of "remaining." Understanding Holy Saturday as a space of remaining, Rambo seeks to establish a theology that does not exclude trauma as something that is outside of normal human experience.

Rodríguez, Rubén Rosario. *Christian Martyrdom and Political Violence.* Cambridge: Cambridge University Press, 2017. An important comparative study of the use of martyrdom narratives to condone acts of political violence within the three major Abrahamic traditions of Judaism, Christianity, and Islam.

Romero, Oscar. *The Violence of Love.* Translated by James R. Brockman. Farminton, PA: Plough Publishing, 1998. This volume is a collection of extracts from sermons, articles, and letters by the murdered archbishop of San Salvador.

Schmitt, Carl. *The Concept of the Political.* Translated by George Schwab. Chicago: University of Chicago Press, 1996. The understanding of the political, Schmitt articulates, perhaps most contentiously the friend/enemy distinction, continues to animate political discourse and is profoundly relevant for understanding the violence that saturates our contemporary context.

Seibert, Eric. *The Violence of Scripture: Overcoming the Old Testament's Troubling Legacy.* Minneapolis: Fortress, 2012. Seibert thoughtfully explores the Old Testament texts in which God appears to order or sanction human violence.

Sheppard, Phillis Isabella. *Self, Culture, and Others in Womanist Practical Theology.* New York: Palgrave/MacMillan, 2011. Sheppard develops an approach to interpersonal violence that is both psychological and theological. She primarily uses self-psychology and a womanist perspective to engage violence among Black women.

Stassen, Glen. "The Beatitudes as Eschatological Peacemaking Virtues." In *Character Ethics and the New Testament: Moral Dimensions of Scripture*, edited by Robert L. Brawley, 245–57. Louisville: Westminster John Knox, 2007. Stassen helpfully explores the beatitudes in relation to "peacemaking" as an active pursuit, rather than pacifism as passive inaction.

———. *Living the Sermon on the Mount: A Practical Hope for Grace and Deliverance.* San Francisco: Jossey-Bass, 2006. This is a comprehensive exposition of the Sermon on the Mount, but with a focus on justice and peace. It can help readers to understand other similar sayings elsewhere in the Synoptic Gospels, and also Paul's teaching since he echoes many sayings of Jesus in the Sermon (e.g., Rom 12:14–21; 1 Cor 4:12; 1 Thess 5:15).

Strawn, Brent A. "Sanctified and Commercially Successful Curses: On Gangsta Rap and the Canonization of the Imprecatory Psalms." *Theology Today* 69.4 (2013) 414. Strawn compares the imprecatory language of the Psalter with the gangsta rap of Ice Cube. The reception of Ice Cube into mainstream media attests to an audience recognition of something of itself in extreme forms of speech and art, a similar dynamic to that of the imprecatory psalms. However, the imprecatory language of the Psalter "contains" its violent language in a way that gangsta rap does not. Strawn argues that the commercial success of gangsta rap reveals much critique of the cursing psalms to be shallow and disingenuous, if not, in fact, a case of (Freudian) projection.

Swartley, Willard M. *Covenant of Peace: The Missing Peace in New Testament Theology and Ethics.* Studies in Peace and Scripture 9. Grand Rapids: Eerdmans, 2006. Through this work Swartley provides what is perhaps the most comprehensive analysis of the centrality of peace (*shalom/eirēnē*) throughout the New Testament.

———, ed. *The Love of Enemy and Nonretaliation in the New Testament.* Studies in Peace and Scripture 3. Louisville: Westminster John Knox, 1992. A helpful collection of essays discussing the influence of Jesus' teaching on love of enemies and nonretaliation across

Annotated Bibliography

the New Testament. The volume includes an important exchange between William Klassen and Richard Horsley.

Trible, Phyllis. "Take Back the Bible." *Review & Expositor* 97 (2000) 425–31. Using the story of Jacob wrestling at the Jabbok in Gen 32, Trible reminds readers that difficult texts in the Bible need to be "wrestled with" until they give us a "blessing." While she does not discuss the imprecatory psalms, her words are apt reminders to not "give up" on texts that present problems in understanding.

de Vries, Hent. *Religion and Violence: Philosophical Perspectives from Kant to Derrida.* Baltimore, MD: Johns Hopkins University Press, 2002. A survey of various philosophical perspectives on violence in which de Vries illuminates major issues that frequently go unnoticed.

Volf, Miroslav. *Exclusion and Embrace: A Theological Exploration of Identity, Otherness, and Reconciliation.* Nashville: Abingdon, 1996. Volf draws upon his own painful memories of Yugoslavia and its history of ethnic and religious strife to challenge the human tendency to create bipolarities in which the other is viewed as a less than human enemy. He reads the Gospels as requiring an embrace of the enemy, a reality made possible by the crucified Christ.

Yoder, John Howard. *The Politics of Jesus: Vicit Agnus Noster.* 2nd ed. Grand Rapids: Eerdmans, 1994. Yoder offers an analysis of Jesus' concern for the social and political world in which he lived, showing how power and violence are confronted by his teaching. This close reading of Luke restores an understanding of Jesus's refusal of violence as a viable and authentically political vision of discipleship. Revelations of the late author's own violent sexual abuse of women mean that difficult new questions must be brought to bear on this important book.

York, Tripp. *The Purple Crown: The Politics of Martyrdom.* Scottdale, PA: Herald, 2007. York identifies martyrdom as an inherently political act. His draws upon his own Anabaptist tradition as well as the work of Latin American liberation theologians like Jon Sobrino, arguing that a life of faithful witness to the truth revealed in Jesus leads his followers into conflict with the same earthly powers that crucified him. York regards Oscar Romero, the martyred Salvadoran archbishop, as the most authentic example of nonviolent political resistance to tyranny in the modern world.

York, Tripp, and Justin Barringer, eds. *A Faith Not Worth Fighting For: Addressing Commonly Asked Questions about Christian Nonviolence.* Eugene, OR: Cascade, 2012. A collection of essays addressing common objections to pacifism. The work is structured in a way to be both accessible and scholarly.

Zehnder, M., and H. Hagelia eds. *Encountering Violence in the Bible.* Sheffield: Sheffield Phoenix, 2013. A collection of essays on violence and related themes in the various books of the Old and New Testaments. The essays seek to wrestle with the idea of violence as an ethical challenge in the Bible while trying to find ways to interpret the text for today.

Zenger, Erich. *A God of Vengeance? Understanding the Psalms of Divine Wrath.* Translated by Linda M. Maloney. Louisville: Westminster John Knox, 1996. Zenger offers an insightful and balanced treatment of what are arguably the most difficult psalms in the Psalter. He contends that, while many would dismiss them to the periphery of the canon, these psalms have great relevance to people of faith in today's tumultuous world.

Annotated Bibliography

Žižek, Slavoj. *Violence*. New York: Picador, 2008. Žižek's provocative short introduction to the major issues involved in contemporary perceptions of violence guides the reader through a variety of continental philosophical discussions.

NORTH PARK THEOLOGICAL SEMINARY SYMPOSIUM ON THE THEOLOGICAL INTERPRETATION OF SCRIPTURE

SEPTEMBER 27–29, 2018

Human Violence

PRESENTERS

Kyle Gingerich Hiebert
Director, Toronto Mennonite Theological Centre

D. Darrell Griffin
Senior Pastor, Oakdale Evangelical Covenant Church, Chicago

Seyoon Kim
Professor of New Testament, Fuller Theological Seminary

Xi Lian
Professor of World Christianity, Duke Divinity School

Jesse Nickel
Biblical Studies Faculty, Columbia Bible College

Elizabeth Pierre
Assistant Professor of Pastoral Care and of Counseling and Counseling Psychology, North Park Theological Seminary and School of Professional Studies

Rubén Rosario-Rodríguez
Associate Professor of Systematic Theology, Department of Theological Studies, Saint Louis University

Nancy L. deClaissé-Walford
Carolyn Ward Professor of Old Testament and Biblical Languages, McAfee School of Theology, Mercer University

RESPONDENTS

Melanie Baffes
Adjunct Professor, Garrett-Evangelical Theological Seminary

Armida Belmonte Stephens
Theology Teaching Fellow, North Park Theological Seminary

Colby Dickinson
Associate Professor of Theology, Loyola University Chicago

Rebekah Eklund
Associate Professor of Theology, Loyola University Maryland

Lida V. Nedilsky
Professor of Sociology, North Park University

Meredith Faubel Nyberg
Adjunct Professor of Old Testament, North Park Theological Seminary

Julien C.H. Smith
Associate Professor of Humanities and Theology, Valparaiso University

www.ingramcontent.com/pod-product-compliance
Lightning Source LLC
Chambersburg PA
CBHW081353230426
43667CB00017B/2819